EUROPE AND THE GOVERNANCE
OF GLOBAL FINANCE

Europe and the Governance of Global Finance

Edited by

DANIEL MÜGGE

OXFORD

UNIVERSITY PRESS

OXFORD
UNIVERSITY PRESS

Great Clarendon Street, Oxford, OX2 6DP,
United Kingdom

Oxford University Press is a department of the University of Oxford.
It furthers the University's objective of excellence in research, scholarship,
and education by publishing worldwide. Oxford is a registered trade mark of
Oxford University Press in the UK and in certain other countries

© Oxford University Press 2014

The moral rights of the authors have been asserted

First edition published in 2014

Impression: 1

Published in the United States of America by Oxford University Press
198 Madison Avenue, New York, NY 10016, United States of America

British Library Cataloguing in Publication Data
Data available

Library of Congress Control Number: 2013956538

ISBN 978–0–19–968396–3

Printed and bound by
CPI Group (UK) Ltd, Croydon, CR0 4YY

Links to third party websites are provided by Oxford in good faith and
for information only. Oxford disclaims any responsibility for the materials
contained in any third party website referenced in this work

*To Geoffrey Underhill, who first awakened my interest
in the politics of finance*

Preface

As a force in global financial governance, Europe is a strange animal. Its 28 member states are often fundamentally at odds with each other about the direction of future policy. Elementary issues are highly contested: the size of banks' capital buffers, the regulation of hedge funds, bonuses for finance CEOs, and many more. The eurocrisis has exposed serious weaknesses in European financial governance. From the perspective of global financial governance, surely we cannot expect very much from such a divided and weakened continent. At the same time, the 'rise of Europe' in global financial governance fundamentally reshaped the politics of global financial rule-setting. The so-called BRICS remain largely invisible in such rule-setting, for example, in the Basel Committee or the G20. European and American negotiators, in contrast, often see eye to eye these days.

This book provides the first comprehensive mapping and analysis of how the European Union fits into global financial governance. It has its roots in the EU-sponsored FP7 project *Global Reordering: Evolution through European Networks* (GR:EEN). In this project I have been honoured to coordinate the work on financial governance. When asked about the aim of GR:EEN, I usually summarized it as 'understanding Europe's future role on the global stage'. My own mission in GR:EEN therefore has been to explore the future role of the EU in global financial governance. Of course, even speculating about that trajectory is of little use without a solid understanding of how financial regulation both within and outside of Europe have co-evolved in the past. Such a historical perspective highlights the forces and dynamics that shape the global politics of finance and allow us to suggest forward-looking scenarios.

Providing such historically grounded analysis is a key aim of this book. At the same time, its aims go further. However much political weight we accord the EU exactly in global financial governance, it is clear that its rise in global regulatory politics has been the most tangible sign of an end to a global regulatory order that was unambiguously dominated by the USA. The global context obviously remains important for understanding regulatory politics in the EU. At the same time, accounting for global financial governance becomes more and more difficult without explicit attention to the EU as a force within it. This book therefore not only contributes to the specific mission of mapping the terrain of potential future trajectories in global financial governance, it also is meant as a resource for scholars with a historical interest in European or global financial regulation. And, maybe even more importantly, it offers students, researchers, and practitioners with an interest in the contemporary legal and governance landscape an overview of the links between global agreements such as the Basel capital accord, European rules, and regulatory regimes elsewhere in the world, particularly in the United States.

This book draws on the expertise of more than a dozen scholars. At the same time, it strives to offer the coherence and consistency that normally characterize monographs. Together, the chapters cover the whole terrain of financial regulation, not only a sub-set of cases. And all contributors generously committed to contribute original chapters, written especially for this volume, which address the questions set out in the introduction. I hope that reading this book, either as a whole or the specific chapters of interest, is as insightful to you as all the discussions leading up to it have been for the team of contributors.

Daniel Mügge

Amsterdam
March 2014

Acknowledgements

The editor of any book is inevitably at the mercy of the volume's contributors. The quality of the final project entirely depends on the quality of its contributions and the willingness of authors to abide by the guidelines set out for the volume. In both respects, the experience leading to this book could hardly have been more pleasing and rewarding: I remain impressed by the breadth and depth of insight that the authors brought to the table, and by their dedication to the project that is this book. I am deeply grateful for their contribution to this endeavour.

The financing for my own research time and editorial work, as well as that for the workshop leading to this book, the editing, and other support, stem from the EU-sponsored FP7 large-scale integrated research project *Global Reordering: Evolution through European Networks* (GR:EEN, project number 266809). That support, without which this book would not exist, is obviously very much appreciated. Hopefully the goals to which GR:EEN is meant to contribute are indeed furthered by the analyses compiled in this volume.

As a research network, GR:EEN is a complex construction. It could not function nearly as well as it does without the excellent project support from the management team in Warwick, including Shaun Breslin, Nikki Muckle, Laura Downey, and Denise Hewlett. Jonathan Zeitlin, my colleague both at the University of Amsterdam and in GR:EEN, has supported my work on this project with precious advice, and he has been very generous with offering extremely helpful comments to all contributors during our Amsterdam workshop.

Also during the composition and production of the book itself I have been able to benefit from invaluable support. Takeo David Hymans tightened the prose of the chapters with utmost care. Emma Booth and David Musson at Oxford University Press have stood by with support and professional advice throughout the frictionless production process of this volume. And last but not least, a range of assistants at the University of Amsterdam, including Jenny Jouvenaar, Roel van Engelen, Abulhassan Al-Jaberi, and Tim Celik, have provided help at crucial junctures.

Contents

List of Figures

List of Boxes

List of Tables

List of Acronyms

2BCD	Second Banking Coordinating Directive
AIFMD	Alternative Investment Fund Managers Directive
AIFMs	Alternative Investment Fund Managers
AIG	American International Group
AIMA	Alternative Investment Management Association
AMF	Autorité des marchés financiers
AML	Anti-Money Laundering
ARC	Accounting Regulatory Committee
ASIC	Australian Securities and Investments Commission
AuRC	Audit Regulatory Committee
BCBS	Basel Committee on Banking Supervision
BIS	Bank for International Settlements
BRICS	Brazil, Russia, India, China, and South Africa
CAD	Capital Adequacy Directive
CAGs	Consultative Advisory Groups
CAP	Compliance Advisory Panel
CCCTB	Common Consolidated Corporate Tax Base
CCP	Central Counterparty
CDOs	Collateralized Debt Obligations
CDS	Credit Default Swaps
CEA	Comité Européen des Assurances
CEBS	Committee of European Banking Supervisors
CEIOPS	Committee of European Insurance and Occupational Pensions Supervisors
CESR	Committee of European Securities Regulators
CFMA	Commodities Futures Modernization Act
CFTC	Commodities Futures Trading Commission
CRA	Credit Rating Agency
CRD	Capital Requirements Directive
CRR	Capital Requirements Regulation
DFA	Dodd–Frank Wall Street Reform and Consumer Protection Act
DPG	Derivatives Policy Group
DTA	Double Tax Agreement
EBA	European Banking Authority
EC	European Commission
ECB	European Central Bank
EFRAG	European Financial Reporting Advisory Group
EGAOB	European Group of Auditors' Oversight Bodies

EIOPA	European Insurance and Occupational Pensions Authority
EMIR	EU Market Infrastructure Regulation
EP	European Parliament
EPC	European Parliament and Council
ERM	Enterprise Risk Management
ESA	European Supervisory Authorities
ESCB	European System of Central Banks
ESFS	European System of Financial Supervision
ESMA	European Securities and Markets Authority
ESME	European Securities Markets Expert Group
ESRB	European Systemic Risk Board
EU	European Union
FASB	Financial Accounting Standards Board
FATCA	Foreign Account Tax Compliance Act
FATF	Financial Action Task Force
FDIC	Federal Deposit Insurance Corporation
FEE	Fédération des Experts Comptables Européen
FFI	Foreign Financial Intermediary
FIUs	Financial Intelligence Units
FPC	Financial Policy Committee
FSA	Financial Services Authority
FSAP	Financial Services Action Plan
FSB	Financial Stability Board
FSF	Financial Stability Forum
FSOC	Financial Stability Oversight Council
FVA	Fair Value Accounting
G7	Group of 7
G8	Group of 8
G10	Group of 10
G20	Group of 20
G30	Group of 30
GAAP	Generally Accepted Accounting Principles
GDP	Gross Domestic Product
GLASS	Group of Latin American Standard Setters
HCA	Historic Cost Accounting
HFSB	Hedge Fund Standards Board
HFWG	Hedge Fund Working Group
HMT	British Treasury
IAASB	International Auditing and Assurance Standards Board
IAIS	International Association of Insurance Supervisors
IASB	International Accounting Standards Board
IASC	International Accounting Standards Committee
IASs	International Accounting Standards

IESBA	International Ethics Standard Board for Accountants
IFAC	International Federation of Accountants
IFIAR	International Forum of Independent Audit Regulators
IFRSs	International Financial Reporting Standards
IGO	International Governmental Organization
IIF	Institute of International Finance
IMF	International Monetary Fund
IOSCO	International Organization of Securities Commissions
IRB	Internal Ratings-Based
IRS	Inland Revenue Service
ISAs	International Standards on Auditing
ISD	Investment Services Directive
ISDA	International Swaps and Derivatives Association
LIFFE	London International Financial Futures and Options Exchange
LTCM	Long-Term Capital Management
MaRS	Macroprudential Research Network
MFA	Managed Funds Association
MFN	Most Favoured Nation
MiFID	Markets in Financial Instruments Directive
NAIC	National Association of Insurance Commissioners
NCCT	Non-Cooperative Country and Territory
NRSROs	Nationally Recognized Statistical Ratings Organizations
OECD	Organisation for Economic Cooperation and Development
OTC	Over The Counter
PCAOB	Public Company Accounting Oversight Board
PIACs	Public Interest Activities Committees
PIOB	Public Interest Oversight Board
PPRs	Private Placement Regimes
PWG	President's Working Group
QI	Qualified Intermediary
RBI	Reserve Bank of India
RMBS	Residential Mortgage Backed Securities
SARG	Standards Advice Review Group
SEC	Securities and Exchange Commission
SMEs	Small and Medium-Sized Enterprises
SSM	Single Supervisory Mechanism
TIEA	Tax Information Exchange Agreement
UCITS	Undertakings for Collective Investment in Transferable Securities
UK	United Kingdom
US	United States
USA	United States of America

List of Contributors

Andrew Baker, Queen's University Belfast

Jasper Blom, University of Amsterdam

Ian Dewing, University of East Anglia

Eilís Ferran, University of Cambridge

Stefanie Hiss, University of Jena

David Howarth, University of Luxembourg

Daniel Mügge, University of Amsterdam

Sebastian Nagel, University of Jena

Lucia Quaglia, University of York

Peter Russell, University of East Anglia

Bart Stellinga, University of Amsterdam

Eleni Tsingou, Copenhagen Business School

Duncan Wigan, Copenhagen Business School

1

Introduction

DANIEL MÜGGE

Since its beginnings in the 1950s, European integration has been transforming the member states of the European Union (EU) (Bickerton 2012).[1] As the so-called euro-crisis forcefully revealed, one of the most consequential dimensions of European integration has been in finance—the markets themselves as well as the design and enforcement of the rules governing them. Even as national borders continue to shape European financial markets and their governance (Grossman and Leblond 2011), Brussels has become the undisputed hub of financial regulation in Europe.

The concentration of competencies in Brussels and the attendant expansion and modernization of European financial markets have not only left their mark on the social and economic fabric of European societies. The EU has also acquired sufficient market size (Posner 2009) and regulatory capacity (Bach and Newman 2007) to end the unchallenged domination of global financial governance by the USA (Simmons 2001). EU financial regulation and integration had historically evolved in the shadow of global developments and initiatives, for example, the Basel accord on capital requirements. But certainly since the 2000s, Brussels has started to 'talk back'—both to EU member states haggling over EU financial rules and to organizations and governments outside the EU, whose policies it increasingly shapes.

As extra-European initiatives inform the development of European rules and vice versa (Black 2012; Mügge 2011c; Quaglia 2011a), neither can be fully understood without a consideration of the other. But practitioners and scholars have had nowhere to turn to for a systematic charting and analysis of these 'European–global relationships'—their history, their current shape as they cut

---

[1] Historically, the EU was preceded by the European Communities, most importantly the European Economic Community. The EU took over and further developed the legal legacies of these organizations, such that in everyday language 'EU' is often used for its predecessor organizations as well. This book adopts this usage unless the distinction between the Communities and the Union is important for a particular argument.

across different levels of governance, and their implications for future policy, global rule coherence, and European influence. This is the challenge this book accepts as it charts and analyses the past, present, and future of Europe's place in global financial governance. More specifically, the chapters in this volume address three overarching questions:

- How have European and global financial governance influenced each other up to the present day?
- Which factors have conditioned the global influence of European regulatory efforts and the relevance of global initiatives for European rules?
- What does this analysis imply for the future of Europe's place in global financial governance?

Theorizing about governance has its natural home in political science, widely conceived. While much of the relevant scholarship does come from political science, the aim of this book is not to develop theoretical insights for their own sake or to intervene in intra-disciplinary debate. Instead, it offers readers who are interested in European or global financial governance an empirically grounded, systematic, and analytically rich understanding of how the EU fits into global financial governance. In doing so, the volume does not limit itself to a controlled comparison of a handful of financial 'sectors' or policy fields, and it eschews narrower definitions of financial regulation to include issue areas that have become more visible in recent years (for example, credit rating agencies or derivatives regulation) as well as those that cut across financial sectors but have become central to contemporary debate, such as macroprudential regulation, supervisory issues, money laundering, and tax evasion. While the individual chapters focus on specific facets of regulation and the forces that have shaped them over time, this introduction provides a panoramic view of how the EU fits into global financial governance, and how European and global financial governance have co-evolved over time.

THE EU AS AN ACTOR IN GLOBAL FINANCIAL GOVERNANCE: A HISTORICAL OVERVIEW

In the history of resurgent post-war globalization (Frieden 2006), the EU has played a double—and indeed, a double-edged—role. On the one hand, European integration has allowed European countries to unite their forces ('pool their sovereignty' in Hoffman's terms). In a cold war Western camp dominated by the United States, this unity allowed Europe to develop a distinct policy project of its own and emerge as an economic force on the global stage capable of rivalling the USA by standard metrics like GDP, population, and market size.

At least potentially, European integration was seen by participating states as a shield against outside influence and a means to project EU influence onto the rest of the world (Telo 2005; Youngs 2010).

On the other hand, European integration served to anchor EU member states to the US-dominated post-war order and forestalled alternative orientations among Europe's leading economies. This included the commitment to ever freer trade within Europe and under the General Agreement on Tariffs and Trade, as well as a step-wise abolition of capital controls and limits on inward investment, notably from the USA itself. European integration made the EU a global power to reckon with, but also embedded in its member states a fundamental commitment to a liberal economic order. Europe's sway on the global stage can thus be seen as the flip-side of its inability or unwillingness to use it for political and economic projects that drastically depart from the historical context in which it emerged. Indeed, if there is one empirical pattern that emerges in this book, it is that the lion's share of interaction between the EU and 'the rest of the world' has been transatlantic, even if it was channelled through formally international organizations. Apart from minor episodes, neither the BRICS nor Japan have played leading roles in global financial governance over the past decades. These two at first sight conflicting developments also inform the evolution of European financial governance: the EU emerges as a potential rival to US dominance and at the same time finds itself in increasing agreement with the USA over substantive questions of regulation.

Both in the popular press and among scholars, post-crisis debates in financial regulation have focused on differences in regulatory preferences, for example, in the G20 or in the EU–US Financial Markets Regulatory Dialogue. Both American and European authorities have been loath to delegate much rule-making power to third parties (accounting standards, set by the International Accounting Standards Board, are a notable exception here). If anything, we have seen more 'cooperative decentralization' (Helleiner and Pagliari 2011), not global top-down governance or harmonization.

At the same time, any signs of friction should not blind us to the enormous degree of transatlantic consensus. In the late 1990s and early 2000s, the EU actively sought to emulate what it saw as the American model. Reforms since the crisis have not led to a parting of ways between the EU and the USA, but to efforts to not disrupt transatlantic financial business. Arguably, recent financial disintegration within the EU—between member states in the southern European periphery and its core economies—has been more pronounced than any gulf between Wall Street and the primary centres of European finance.

The overall pattern is one in which EU financial governance has strengthened over the past decades, and continues to do so, but in a fashion that has made it, or at least kept it, compatible with a US-led open international financial order. To a significant degree, this is due to the emergence over the years of a transatlantic circle of financial regulators, experts, and professionals who share a common understanding of the regulatory world they inhabit, and who have stayed the course in the face of the largest financial and economic crisis in almost 80 years. This commitment—and its dominance of actual policy—is remarkable when we compare it to the economic, social, and political disruptions and dislocations that the crisis has caused in Europe and the United States overall. It is also remarkable when we think back to how transnational regulatory initiatives first began several decades ago.

First Contacts, 1975–1992

At the global level, cooperation has been most prominent in banking regulation (Porter 1993, 2005; Singer 2007; Davies and Green 2008). Starting in 1975, the governments of the financially most advanced countries entered into agreements on sharing information, and in the late 1980s set common standards for bank capital buffers (Kapstein 1994; Wood 2005; see Ferran, this volume; Blom, this volume). Subsequent revisions of the Basel accord by the Basel Committee on Banking Supervision (BCBS) introduced ever more specific rules which currently form the basis of EU banking regulation (Tarullo 2008; Blom 2011).

Early EU efforts in banking and insurance in the 1970s had limited effects on the provision of financial services. But the single market programme of the mid-1980s ushered in a comprehensive opening of banking, insurance, and securities markets (Underhill 1997a; Story and Walter 1997; also Singer 2007; Donnelly 2010). In banking, the single market programme ran parallel to negotiations for Basel I, which eventually became a template for European legislation—a clear instance of global influence on European rules. For capital buffers on securities trading, the picture was more complicated: while the International Organization of Securities Commissions (IOSCO) attempted to replicate the success of the BCBS, complicated concurrent bargaining in the EU forestalled global agreement (Mügge 2010, this volume). To be sure, the European deal that was eventually struck set in train a trajectory of EU financial market liberalization that would bring EU markets much more in line with US practices, thereby facilitating transatlantic financial integration. But at the time, the lack of internal EU agreement thwarted a global deal on capital requirements for securities transactions.

Finally, in insurance, steps towards meaningful cross-border integration failed to materialize both in the EU and in the global arena (Singer 2007). Insurance markets were to remain distinctly national for years to come, and beyond wholesale (re)insurance, no meaningful drive ever materialized to truly integrate markets across borders. Global initiatives thus remained limited to the drawing up of non-binding best practices and information exchange (using EU practices as a template, see Quaglia, this volume). Intra-European developments in insurance thus unfolded in isolation from significant external constraints or interference.

These initial rounds of negotiation largely focused on terms of mutual market access for banks, insurance companies, and different kinds of securities firms. Even when successful, they stopped short of detailed rule harmonization or the creation of a truly integrated financial space—comparable to early rounds of trade negotiation when 'behind the border' issues often still prevented equal market access for foreign competitors. More detailed mutual adaptation—what in trade terms would be thought of as a 'deep' trade agenda—followed only in the early 2000s, when European enthusiasm for US-style financial markets reached its zenith.

The US as a Model, 1992–2000

The mood in EU financial governance changed perceptibly between the official inauguration of the single European market in 1992 and the end of the millennium. Spearheaded by large financial firms, a coalition emerged in favour of transforming European financial markets to align them more closely to US practices. US firms had been grandfathered into the single European market, meaning that their pre-single market establishment in the City of London gave them pan-European access to the single market in line with rules for European firms. Financial services firms on the continent were thus exposed to American competitors but also to the business opportunities seemingly offered by investment banking in the City (Mügge 2010). Many became vocal advocates of European regulatory reforms that would allow the roll-out of Wall Street and City-inspired business practices across the continent.

More generally, the growing internationalization of financial flows created incentives for the unilateral adaptation of regulation to Anglo-American standards. For example, Germany until roughly the mid-1990s had no well-developed insider trading regime, rendering its stock markets unattractive to foreigners (McCahery 1997). As financial flows continued to internationalize throughout the 1990s and European governments privatized and publicly listed transport, telecommunications, utility, and energy companies, governments faced growing incentives to provide hospitable climates for incoming investment (Lütz 2002).

When the Commission unveiled its first draft of the Financial Services Action Plan (FSAP) in 1998 (adopted in 1999), it was presented as a way for the EU not to fall behind the USA in competitiveness (Bieling 2006). The FSAP contained 43 legislative proposals; to deal with this flurry of legislative activity, the Council and the European Parliament decided to streamline rule-making through the so-called Lamfalussy process (Ferran 2004; de Visscher, Maiscocq, and Varone 2007; Quaglia 2008; Mügge 2010). But in terms of ideas and rules, the 1990s were transatlantic one-way traffic. As more and more European firms sought to list on US stock exchanges, the pressure grew for the EU to unilaterally adopt US (compatible) rules. In the case of accounting standards, the EU threw its weight behind the little-known expert group the International Accounting Standards Committee to forestall the unchallenged dominance of US standards (Dewing and Russell 2004; Stellinga, this volume).

The liberal, capital market-based model of financial regulation was further enshrined in the Compendium of Standards and Codes that the Financial Stability Forum, founded in 1999, compiled in response to the Asian financial crisis (see also Brummer 2011). To be sure, the Compendium was intended more as a guide for emerging markets than as a convergence agenda for authorities in Europe and North America. Even though it featured International Accounting Standards (IAS) as one of its rule-sets, the USA decided in the early 2000s that it was going to stick to home-grown US GAAP. Nevertheless, it encapsulated, at least as an ideal, a putatively coherent set of expertise-based best practice rules for financial market governance (also Büthe and Mattli 2011). While countries continued to opportunistically deviate from these rules (Mosley 2010), the liberal technocratic model of financial governance that they embodied and to which EU member states signed up was an indication of how far regulatory thinking had converged over the course of the 1990s.

The EU as a Maturing Power in Global Financial Governance, 2000–2007

Since the beginning of the millennium, the EU has grown more visible and influential in global financial regulation (Posner 2009). Three factors underpinned this trend: the emergence and growing coherence of a truly European capital market aided by the single currency; the further concentration of regulatory capacity in supranational hands; and the partial delegitimization of US governance and rules through the stock market crash and high-profile scandals of the early 2000s.

One of the key levers jurisdictions have in international standards setting is the size of the market to which they control access (Drezner 2007). The rise of stock markets and cross-border integrated debt markets made Europe a much more attractive market for many non-European, and in particular American, financial firms. Germany and France, but also other European countries, were gripped by an intense, if rather short-lived, stock market mania in the run-up to the year 2000, fuelled by a benign economic climate and large-scale privatizations of government-owned enterprises such as Deutsche Telekom. For some time, observers seriously wondered whether large European economies would 'catch up' with the USA and the UK in terms of, for example, stock market capitalization—implying huge business potential for investment banks

(Walter and Smith 2000). Eventually, French and German patterns of corporate finance proved to be much stickier and the wholesale transformation of continental European finance did not materialize—at least not in the way that was anticipated. Nevertheless, control over an attractive market gave the EU much more leverage in regulatory bargaining with the USA than it had previously enjoyed.

This market size leverage was particularly useful in policy domains in which the centralization of regulatory competencies enabled the EU to speak with one voice. In 2001 the European Parliament and Council decided to delegate decisions over implementing measures in EU capital market legislation to a newly created body, the Committee of European Securities Regulators (CESR). CESR's competencies included advising or deciding on the equivalence of foreign rule-sets with EU rules and thus determining whether foreign firms could receive a waiver for compliance with EU rules. CESR could thus make demands on foreign authorities, including American ones. Although this power was seldom used, the USA did, for example, adapt its reporting rules so that they would be deemed compliant with EU demands for consolidated supervision (Posner 2009; Mügge 2011a; Ferran, this volume).

EU influence was even more tangible in accounting standards, where it decided to back IAS in the mid-1990s. Although the USA withdrew its support for global convergence around IAS in the early 2000s, the EU pushed ahead and in 2002 mandated all publicly listed companies to use IAS within three years (Dewing and Russell 2004; Botzem 2012). The EU, however, has limited leverage over the content of these standards (Leblond 2011), even if in key areas it simply refused to adopt them and drew up its own versions (Mügge and Stellinga 2014). As by far the most important jurisdiction to back IAS (and their successor International Financial Reporting Standards, IFRSs), the EU effectively propelled IAS to become de facto global standards, now even recognized with some caveats by the USA.

Among the less tangible but still widely recognized factors behind the EU's growing voice in global financial governance were the corporate scandals that rocked the USA in the early 2000s—most prominently the disintegration of Enron once its dubious derivatives deals and accounting fraud were discovered (Partnoy 2002a). These scandals showed that US financial rules were not necessarily best practice and that the USA, too, had something to win by adapting its standards. For example, the rule-based system of accounting standards which emphasized adherence to the letter rather than the spirit of the law came under heavy criticism. More broadly, the legitimacy and appropriateness of US financial governance as a whole was questioned around the world. Henceforth, when negotiating cross-border rule-sets with other jurisdictions, the USA could no longer claim to 'self-evidently' have the best regulatory system.

The American response to the corporate scandals in the form of the Sarbanes–Oxley Act of 2002 created new transatlantic regulatory challenges.

Several of its provisions had clear extraterritorial implications, for example, for European firms listed on US stock exchanges. Controversially, these provisions even prevailed when firms delisted and tried to cut their links to American capital markets. As the regulatory cobweb grew thicker (even if not more restrictive in net terms), the USA and the EU were increasingly forced to accommodate each other's rule-sets in the name of an integrated transatlantic financial space for both financial flows and services (see also Posner 2009). The perceived need to make or keep financial standards compatible only grew after the 2001 Al-Qaeda attacks in the USA as, for example, efforts to combat money laundering gained new international prominence (Tsingou 2010, this volume).

Overall, the 2000s witnessed a shift from EU adaptation to US rules to mutual adaptation, often in the form of equivalence regimes (Ferran, this volume). Mutual adaptation caused little overt friction as the EU was not pursuing a financial market model radically different from the American one, and showed little appetite to challenge the continued dominance of US financial institutions in global markets. Although the rise of credit rating agencies and (activist) hedge funds in continental Europe repeatedly led to political controversy (e.g. Mügge 2011a), EU authorities saw little need to establish their own rule-sets to place limits on these institutions (Hiss and Nagel this volume; Howarth and Quaglia this volume). In short, if the EU continued to play second fiddle to the USA in the pre-crisis years (as argued by Leblond 2011, for accounting), this probably said as much about the absence of a clear alternative vision for financial market regulation as it did about the power resources that the USA and the EU could bring to bear on transatlantic and global financial governance.

Responding to the Financial Crisis, 2007–2013

The financial crisis that has beset European and global financial markets since 2007 spawned a wave of regulatory activity, one which consolidated executive capacity at the European level through the creation of financial authorities for banking, capital markets, insurance, and occupational pensions (Moloney 2010, 2011a, 2011b).

The financial crisis triggered a level of international regulatory interaction that far surpassed anything that preceded it. The G20 quickly became the central 'apex forum' (Baker 2010) to deal with regulatory reform, with the EU being granted formal membership alongside four of its member states. The Financial Stability Forum was upgraded into the Financial Stability Board, a clearing house for re-regulatory ideas and initiatives, particularly in areas that had thus far not been addressed by any of the existing organizations.

Given the severity of the crisis and the degree to which it unsettled pre-crisis assumptions, some observers expected the EU to become a leading advocate for a drastic reorientation of financial systems and their regulation. But rather than a parting of ways between regions and countries, or a new global consensus over a new regulatory model, the emergent pattern since the crisis is one of cooperative decentralization (Helleiner and Pagliari 2011). One central lesson of the crisis has been that faulty regulation can carry a hefty price-tag in the form of taxpayer-funded bail-outs and wider economic damage, leading governments around the world to become more sceptical of 'outsourcing' financial regulation to expert bodies. In consequence, they have sought cooperative arrangements that fall short of full harmonization but marry agreement on basic rules with flexibility in national implementation. The flexibility built into the recent revision of the Basel accord (Basel III) can be understood in this light (see Blom, this volume).

Neither the USA nor Europe—the two epicentres of the crisis—seriously targeted the extent of financialization in their economies (Stockhammer 2007). Incremental rule adaptation was meant to address the shortcomings of the extant financial market model, not overturn it. Together with the commitment to relatively flexible rules, this generated remarkably little international friction, as a comparison of recent years with the fraught international economic politics of the 1930s illustrates. While the EU found itself disagreeing with the USA on some issues—for example, executive compensation—the extant regulatory architecture allows different rules to exist side by side (for hedge fund regimes see Howarth and Quaglia, this volume). Differences of opinion did not necessarily translate into transatlantic or international bargaining over harmonized rule-sets but to the accommodation of divergence. Only in a few areas such as derivatives trading was the compatibility of regimes so essential that it necessitated the detailed coordination of regulatory reforms (Mügge, this volume). The most prominent idea to take root since the beginning of the crisis—macroprudential regulation—also underscores the need for flexibility in regulatory regimes (Baker, this volume). Paralleling the Keynesian demand management of the business cycle, macroprudential regulation tries to iron out the extremes of the credit cycle that the likes of Minsky had identified (Borio 2003).

The tailoring of regulation and supervision to local contexts is one of the prominent trends to have emerged from the crisis thus far. Governments have realized that financial regulation and supervision affect other policy domains that continue to be guarded as national or supranational prerogatives: fiscal policy, monetary policy, and social policies, for example, for housing. A strong case can indeed be made that governments need to preserve manoeuvring room to be able to fine-tune regulatory policy. Examples include special resolution regimes for financial institutions that distribute the costs of bank failure among diverse stakeholders, and capital requirements for bank assets that directly or indirectly finance real estate lending. These issues matter especially in the context of the single European currency. The proposed banking union has implications not only for supervision but, through the proposed resolution regimes, for the financial structure of banks and their legal relationships with various classes of creditors. The perceived exigencies of the euro thus delimit the EU's room for manoeuvre.

The crisis has also underlined how the choice for particular regulatory regimes includes value judgments about the distribution of the spoils and risks of any particular financial system (think, for example, of executive compensation or the scope for banks to speculate with depositors' money through derivatives). As societies reach different conclusions on these issues, it is no longer self-evident that technocratic governance provides the best answers (cf. Mügge 2011b). Taken together, these factors imply that the former ideal of a single global rule-set has become obsolete. International regulatory politics in finance is no longer about harmonization but about cross-border rule compatibility and market access.

Seen in this light it is remarkable that one issue that had previously attracted little attention has risen to prominence: offshore financial centres and tax evasion and avoidance (Wigan, this volume). The public debate that intensified in the spring of 2013 focused primarily on non-financial companies such as Google and Starbucks, which were found to make use of complicated corporate structures to minimize their tax contributions. But it also has a direct bearing on financial regulation, as many of the legal constructs that banks use to move risks off their balance sheets and hide them from investors, counterparties, and regulators have relied on secrecy jurisdictions (Palan 2006; Sharman 2010; Tabb 2012).

The EU's role in this global discussion has so far been ambivalent, not least because its own member states have very different interests: many secrecy jurisdictions are dependencies of the British crown while countries such as the Netherlands, Austria, and Luxembourg facilitate the obfuscation of financial flows and risks and function as tax shelters. At the same time, a remarkably strong European consensus has emerged that abusive tax practices should be rolled back and secrecy jurisdictions made more transparent. While it remains an open question whether this counts as meaningful change, the EU has emerged as an advocate of reform in an area of financial governance that has so far been seen as unreformable due to the collective action problems it generates.

CONCEPTUAL ISSUES THAT ANIMATE THIS BOOK

The facets of financial regulation discussed in this book vary in ways that are central to the interaction between European policy and global financial governance: Do they have prudential implications? Do they matter for cross-border market access? Do they concern thousands of firms or only a handful, based in a single jurisdiction? Do they have implications for retail consumers? And do they pose a collective action problem, like global tax policy? We find differences not only between facets of regulation, but also across time. The historical context in which regulatory coordination efforts unfold is decisive for how they play out. How developed is a particular financial sector at any point in time? How sanguine or sceptical are policy-makers about the net benefits for society of ever-expanding financial markets? And however crudely measured, what is the distribution of power between different jurisdictions trying to influence one another's policies?

These considerations argue against the ambition to develop a single theory that would parsimoniously explain the patterns we find in the different chapters of this volume. The chapters discuss *complementary* facets of financial regulation, not individual 'cases', and cover a functional division of labour in real-world financial markets. For example, accounting standards codify how banks have to add up their assets and liabilities; banking rules tell them how much capital they need to keep in hand against the assets thus calculated; auditing standards spell out how third parties (auditors) have to go about checking whether accounts have been drawn up correctly; and supervisors have to keep an eye on the micro- or macroprudential implications of the picture that thus emerges. Standards for accounting, capital adequacy, auditing, and supervision regulate different actors and forms of behaviour, and are analysed in this volume in the chapters by Stellinga, Blom, Dewing and Russell, and Ferran, respectively. It is only natural that much of the variation we find across the chapters is due to the specific nature of the activity or field being regulated.

While we do not want to fit the different chapters into a single theoretical straightjacket, we do strive to offer more than plain historical narrative. In addition to charting how European and global financial governance have influenced each other up to the present day, we ask which factors have strengthened or hampered the extra-European influence of European regulatory efforts as well as the relevance of extra-European initiatives for European rules. Here scholars of European and global financial governance have offered many useful pointers.

The motives of jurisdictions to seek harmonized rules are manifold. The harmonization of standards has been sought in the name of market efficiency and the collective implementation of best practice. At the same time, considerations of competitiveness—protecting the interests of domestic financial firms—have from the outset figured prominently in the dynamics of international coordination (Underhill 1997a; Oatley and Nabors 1998; Mügge and Stellinga 2010; Quaglia 2010b). Even if state–firm relations are more complex than simple lobbying perspectives suggest (Grossman 2004; Young 2012), cooperation has helped regulators to prevent regulatory races to the bottom (Singer

2007). But how successful different parties to international cooperation have been in promoting their own regulatory vision has depended on a diverse set of factors.

Explanations based on economic power have traditionally dominated the field. The size of a jurisdiction's domestic market influences its bargaining power as it can use (privileged) access to its home market as a dangling carrot in negotiations, and restriction of such access as a stick (Drezner 2007). In the past, the USA could easily impose its regulatory preferences on others both due to the size and sophistication of its financial markets and the global dominance of the US dollar (Oatley and Nabors 1998; Simmons 2001). As outlined above, the balance has shifted since the late 1990s due to the rise of capital markets in continental Europe, the introduction of the single currency, the supranational concentration of regulatory capacity in Brussels, and a spate of regulatory scandals in the USA (Posner 2009; Posner and Véron 2010). We observe this dynamic in a range of chapters including those on auditing, banking regulation, supervision, accounting, securities, and insurance. On top of this, the further cross-border integration and consolidation of the financial industry has altered industry coalitions supporting or opposing regulatory harmonization within and beyond the EU (see also Grossman 2004; Mügge 2006; Blom 2011; Young 2012). In the fields of banking and capital market rules as well as accounting standards, these coalitions have exerted pressure for either harmonizing rules or, barring that, making them compatible between jurisdictions.

Within forums debating global rules, it matters whether or not participants can draw on extensive regulatory experience and capacity at home (Bach and Newman 2007). The ability to exert international influence requires strong, clearly articulated preferences as well as the capacity to implement and enforce rules. Enforcement capacity enables regulators to wield influence as they can credibly threaten to enforce rules with 'bite' in their home markets, also for foreign firms. As market segments grew (such as stock trading on the continent) or evolved into truly European markets (such as those for sovereign debt or wholesale lending), EU regulatory capacity 'caught up'. Other financial sectors have long fallen outside of the EU regulatory purview, either because there was no home-grown sector to speak of (credit rating agencies, Hiss and Nagel, this volume) or because it was effectively limited to one country with a light-touch regime (hedge funds in the UK, Howarth and Quaglia, this volume).

While the EU in some respects can be analysed like any other 'big power' in global financial governance, its internal make-up has ramifications both for its global role and for the way in which it accommodates extra-European developments. Differences of opinion among member states can be an asset as they make the EU a less flexible negotiating partner and force others to be more accommodating towards European demands (in line with Putnam 1988). But divisions among EU member states can also keep Europe from formulating clear policy positions and undermine its influence (Mügge 2011c). While such divisions have been particularly visible regarding hedge funds and secrecy jurisdictions for tax avoidance and evasion (Wigan, this volume), it is left to the individual chapters to spell out how differences within Europe have affected EU regulatory relations with the rest of the world.

Since the crisis shook established assumptions about financial markets and their regulation, puzzling about the direction of future reforms has become much more prominent, reflected in the intellectual breadth and diversity of recommendations contained in the array of policy reports published since 2007 (Seabrooke and Tsingou 2014). How such puzzling compares to powering (Hall 1993) is of course not a new question (Haas 1992; Kapstein 1992). The extant scholarship suggests that, other things being equal, the tightness, homogeneity, and isolation from politics of transnational regulatory networks increase the importance of expert deliberation (Bach and Newman 2010; Baker 2010). In such deliberations, intra-European diversity can be a double asset: the multiplicity of standpoints within the EU provides it with a large pool of ideas to consider while the need to find regulatory arrangements that accommodate intra-European diversity can make European solutions promising templates for comparable challenges at the global level (Sabel and Zeitlin 2011). This is particularly true in domains that require on-going cross-border cooperation such as supervision (Posner 2010a). But where convergence on a single set of ideas is necessary, intra-European diversity can hinder the emergence of a coherent template to serve as a focal point for global regulatory efforts.

Timing or 'sequencing' has been important in the co-evolution of global and European rules (Posner 2010b): it has mattered for their global influence whether European rule-crafting efforts historically preceded or followed the emergence of global templates. For example, agreement on global banking rules (Basel I, 1988) preceded European efforts to craft the Second Banking Coordinating Directive (adopted in 1989) to give form to the single European market in banking. Hence European rules were modelled on global ones in key respects. To give another example, the Committee of European Securities Regulators in 2004 recommended not to regulate credit rating agencies (CRAs) (see Hiss and Nagel 2012). This decision was controversial in the wake of the financial crisis, but can only be understood against the prior decision of individual European regulators to support a purely voluntary Code of Conduct for CRAs in IOSCO, the relevant global forum. More recently, the American Dodd–Frank Act has set US rules in stone across a wide range of financial policy domains, effectively leaving it to the EU to ensure the compatibility of rules on both sides of the Atlantic.

WHAT FUTURE FOR EUROPEAN AND GLOBAL FINANCIAL GOVERNANCE?

At the height of the financial crisis, global political leaders stressed the importance of erecting a solid global financial architecture under the auspices of the G20. Since then, efforts to build this integrated global regulatory edifice have lost steam, leading to the emergence of what Helleiner and Pagliari (2011) have called 'cooperative decentralization'. Nevertheless, the cooperation should not be taken lightly. Whatever the transatlantic differences in the past years, at no point has either the EU or the USA seriously considered erecting a regulatory fortress. The on-going political and economic turmoil in the EU may dent further reform enthusiasm or capacity, but it is unlikely that it will either overturn European or global agreements or cause the EU to radically change its regulatory course. But though incremental change has been the dominant mode of reregulation (Moschella and Tsingou 2013), this does not mean that cumulatively these changes cannot cause financial blocks to drift apart. As indicated above, the exigencies of the single currency circumscribe the kinds of supervisory and regulatory arrangements the EU, or at least the Eurozone, can countenance.

Reform fatigue seems to have set in on both sides of the Atlantic. Once pending projects are finalized, we should not expect major new initiatives—unless, of course, extant arrangements were to fail dramatically in the event of a new crisis. But even then, with the exception of banking rules, it is likely that financial regulation will have left the political limelight. To be sure, it has not become less important. But the economic malaise that the subprime crisis precipitated in 2007 has since grown to such proportions that it has required the whole arsenal of economic policy instruments to address it—often with mixed results. If another episode such as that following the Lehman Brothers collapse were to recur anytime soon, policies would most likely have to go beyond regulatory reform and transform the structure of the financial sector and its relationship to public authority more fundamentally.

One of the most remarkable patterns to emerge from this book is the centrality of transatlantic relations in the EU's dealings with 'the rest of the world'. Both conflict and cooperation in international regulatory organizations such as IOSCO can mostly be understood as a function of EU–US relations. Japan, China, India, Russia, and Brazil have all, to date, played only modest roles in the evolution of global financial governance. While this may not come as a surprise for the pre-crisis period, the chapters in this volume show that this pattern has continued to inform regulatory reforms since the crisis, including for example, agenda-setting in the G20. While this can be seen as a sign of continued EU and US strength, a more sceptical reading may see it as a sign of weakness: the EU and the USA are so heavily involved in global financial regulation precisely because it is they who have built their growth regimes of the past decades atop an unsustainable financial sector and expanding debt. Which interpretation prevails will depend on how they emerge from the crisis. In any case, that this point is ambiguous is a reminder that, ultimately, the future of regulatory politics—in Europe and beyond—is inseparable from governments' ability to tackle an economic crisis that will soon have festered for a whole decade.

2

Financial Supervision

EILÍS FERRAN

INTRODUCTION

The EU has unrivalled experience in adapting essentially national systems of regulation and supervision to deal with cross-border financial market activity. The EU has superior knowledge of the preconditions that must be satisfied for supervisors from different countries to trust each other, and of the fallout that can occur when that trust breaks down. It is also ahead of the rest of the world in working out the limits of what can be achieved through collaboration between national systems; it has forged ahead to the next stage in which supervisory responsibilities are closely coordinated and, in limited cases, even conducted by supranational authorities. For certain purposes, then, the EU can be seen as a laboratory of ideas for solving the universally recognized problem of the mismatch between borderless markets and restricted supervisory domains.

But this depth of experience comes from the EU's unique situation, is driven by its single market objective, and depends on the existence of supranational institutions that do not exist elsewhere (Verdier 2011). As the EU moves to install the supervisory reinforcements necessary for a stable, secure, and sustainable single market—and as the particular needs of the Eurozone lead towards the gradual emergence of institutional arrangements to suit a fully fledged monetary and fiscal union—its approach may be becoming progressively less suitable for export elsewhere. Outside the EU, interstate engagement is driven by much more minimalist aims and objectives; if anything, current circumstances evince a trend towards less, rather than more, dismantling of barriers to cross-border activities. There are strains even within the EU as the increasingly strident demands of British political leaders for a 'new settlement' with Europe illustrate.

The EU's unique features and lack of similarity with other regions suggest that other regional integration projects such as the trans-Tasman relationship may now provide governments interested in economic integration but concerned about sovereignty an alternative source of rich data points on regional design (Leslie and Elijah 2012). This trend may, in time, lead to a reduction in the distorting effects of a Eurocentric bias in comparative regionalism (de Lombaerde, Söderbaum, van Langenhove, and Baert 2010). Yet the very fact that the EU has experienced the most severe economic crisis in its short history—in which weaknesses in existing mechanisms and the need for substantial reinforcement were painfully exposed (Eichengreen 2012)—is a compelling reason to continue studying the EU. To develop this line of inquiry, this chapter examines the recent development of five major features of EU financial supervision.

The discussion is split into two parts. The first part examines mutual recognition and equivalence, two key principles and processes intended to facilitate the efficient and effective oversight of cross-border activity. It identifies serious shortcomings in how mutual recognition operated within the EU and considers what equivalence adds. It also draws out the role of these mechanisms in helping the EU exert global influence. While the EU can be described as a laboratory of ideas, the characterization is inadequate to explain the rise of the EU as a global financial regulatory force as its influence does not derive merely from being a source of interesting 'experiments' that others can draw upon. Instead, the EU's strength stems largely from its policy priority to command international influence. The acceleration of EU control over financial market regulation and supervision in the aftermath of the financial and Eurozone crises holds out the possibility of more streamlined and consistent interactions between the EU and the rest of the world in which EU supranational bodies increasingly speak as the single European voice. In particular, equivalency—a process that has strengthened the hand of EU bodies (the European Commission and the European Supervisory Authorities (ESAs) vis-à-vis member states)—could be pivotal to realizing the potential for more effective international engagement.

The next part examines the changing architecture of financial supervision within the EU: the reinforcement of colleges, the supranational coordination of supervision through the establishment of the ESAs, and the conferral of direct supervision powers on supranational bodies. Since supranationalism is ascendant in the EU but a formal international financial regulation body remains a distant prospect, it is here where issues of suitability loom particularly large. There is undoubtedly a need for caution in evaluating how helpful EU experience is in identifying realistic solutions to problems of international governance. But since many of the challenges the EU is facing in building new capacities for the institutional organization of cross-border activity also resonate at the international level, the comparison remains worthwhile.

PRINCIPLES AND PROCESSES FOR CROSS-BORDER SUPERVISION AND THEIR LINK TO THE EXERCISE OF GLOBAL INFLUENCE

Mutual Recognition

'Mutual recognition'—a cornerstone principle of EU law (Armstrong 2002)—is the approach to organizing cross-border financial market supervision most readily associated with the EU. Its use is pervasive: banks, insurance companies, investment firms, market infrastructure providers, listed companies, and conventional and alternative fund managers are all among its beneficiaries. In broad strokes, mutual recognition allows an entity to operate cross-border on the basis of home country authorization and supervision. The operation of mutual recognition in financial markets can be illustrated through the example of credit institutions (i.e. deposit-taking banks), both before and after the financial crisis. Examining a period of boom and bust—during which time EU financial market integration accelerated before suffering a sharp reversal—reveals the major strengths and limitations of mutual recognition.

Under the 2006 Capital Requirements Directive,[1] as amended by CRD II[2] (2009) and CRD III[3] (2010) (together 'CRD'), a bank authorized and supervised by its home member state had a passport to establish branches or provide cross-border services in all member states (Article 23). The CRD passport was facilitated by provisions in the directive that narrowed differences in member states' banking laws and imposed restrictions on the actions host member states could take vis-à-vis incoming institutions. A key feature of the CRD regime was that a host member state could not prevent branching by insisting on the incorporation of a local subsidiary or the imposition of other structural requirements (Article 23). The prudential supervision of a credit institution, including its cross-border activities, was a home state responsibility (Article 40). In cooperation with home state authorities, host member states retained limited and residual responsibilities for the supervision of the liquidity of cross-border branches (Article 41). The responsibility for the consolidated overview of the health of a financial group that included a bank lay with the competent authorities of its home state (Articles 125–126). Home and host state supervisors were required to cooperate, both in going concern situations and in the event of a crisis (Articles 42, 129–131). Amendments in the first wave of the regulatory aftermath to the financial crisis (CRD II) introduced provisions for recognizing branches as 'significant' to host member states (Article 42a). The designation of a branch as significant did not in any fundamental way affect the existing rights and responsibilities of the relevant

---

[1] Directive 2006/48/EC and Directive 2006/49/EC.   [2] Directive 2009/111/EC.
[3] Directive 2010/76/EU.

authorities, but gave host state authorities certain additional rights regarding participation in supervisory colleges. Related amendments added a specific provision for the establishment of colleges of supervisors by consolidating supervisors (Article 131a).

The CRD banking passport was in tune with market trends in the years leading up to the financial crisis. During this period, the European banking sector became increasingly dominated by large cross-border groups. In 2005, 46 groups held about 68 per cent of EU banking assets; in the newer member states, this figure reached 90 per cent (EC 2008c: 12). Since changes in the European landscape in this period were consistent with the global trend towards increasing foreign ownership of bank assets (Barth, Caprio, and Levine 2013), we cannot assume the CRD banking passport played anything more than a facilitative role. But seen through the lens of the integration objective, these statistics provided evidence of success, though they also hinted at the growing risk of cross-border contagion (EC 2007a: 41).

One important feature of the CRD was the degree of harmonization of substantive requirements. In accordance with the minimum harmonization approach often deployed for internal market measures (Dougan 2000), the CRD effected 'only the essential harmonization necessary and sufficient to secure the mutual recognition of authorization and of prudential supervision systems, making possible the granting of a single licence recognized throughout the Community and the application of the principle of home Member State prudential approval' (CRD, Recital 7). Here there was a noticeable difference between the banking passport and the equivalent passport for investment firms under the Markets in Financial Instruments Directive 2004[4] (MiFID), which imposed a much higher degree of regulatory uniformity.

Minimum harmonization leaves member states considerable room for manoeuvre in implementation, with 'a wide margin of discretion in making fundamental choices of economic policy in the specific event of a systemic crisis'.[5] This flexibility can be both good and bad. Where legitimate national specificities exist, there is a sound logic for allowing their different handling. Without elasticity, securing agreement on legislative measures that touch on sensitive issues would be considerably more difficult. It is no coincidence that the CRD passport for banks, which occupy a special place in national economies, was on more differentiated terms than those governing the passport for investment firms.

The crisis showed the CRD's 'pragmatic' (Steil 1999) minimum harmonization approach to be a crucial shortcoming in its system of mutual recognition

[4] Directive 2004/39/EC and Commission Directive 2006/73/EC.
[5] *EFTA Surveillance Authority v Iceland*, 28 January 2013, Case E-16/11, para 227; noted in Babis (2013).

(EC 2011c: 8). The repatriation and ring-fencing of capital and liquidity within home entities by stricken European cross-border banking groups as well as the uncoordinated and short-term steps taken by member states to protect their domestic economies showed that a minimalist approach was unsustainable due to cross-border contagion and the 'beggar-thy-neighbour' consequences of uni-lateral stabilizing action (High-Level Group on Financial Supervision in the EU 2009). To avoid a retreat from single market freedoms, more pan-European standardization of regulation and its accompanying supervisory architecture seemed inevitable (FSA 2009).

On the regulatory side, the 'more Europe' philosophy found a focus in calls for a 'single rulebook' in banking. The new mood has shaped the EU Basel III implementation exercise and has led to a much more comprehensive and rigid package of harmonized requirements—the Capital Requirements Regulation (CRR) and Directive (CRD IV)(together the CRD IV package)—to replace the existing CRD. The CRD IV package is in force from January 2014. To promote uniformity of application in all member states—and in due course, to facilitate the supranational conduct of supervision by the ECB within the European Banking Union (Ferran and Babis 2014)—many of the new requirements are in an EU regulation that does not require transposition into national legislation. For substantive requirements, 'maximum harmonization' has displaced 'mini-mum harmonization' as the guiding approach.

Maximum harmonization has not led to the complete elimination of national options and discretion. Intense negotiations around the CRD IV legal texts within the EU legislative institutions watered down the originally envisaged level of uniformity. A raft of national exemptions means that the reality of the maximum-harmonization 'single' rulebook does not live up to its rhetoric. Certain concessions for national situations were even singled out by the Basel Committee as instances of EU inconsistency with the Basel III framework (BCBS 2012; Buckley, Howarth and Quaglia 2012). Nevertheless, the final package is still much more standardized than the predecessor CRD regime, not only in its substantive regulatory capital requirements but in its supervisory and enforcement regimes. The implementing 'legislative blanket' (Haldane and Madouros 2012) wrapped around international standards to make the position more concrete and practically effective (Ferran and Alexander 2010) has, as is usually the way, added volume.

The trend towards greater uniformity is also evident in the MiFID review (EC 2011a, 2011b). The MiFID II package will comprise both a regulation to address inconsistent implementation and minimize opportunities for harm-ful regulatory arbitrage between member states, and a detailed directive. Uni-form rules should provide more legal certainty, less regulatory complexity, and remove remaining barriers to trade, obstacles to competition, and poten-tial for regulatory arbitrage (Markets in Financial Instruments Regulation, Recital 3).

What can the rest of the world take from the EU's painful learning-from-experience on mutual recognition? In principle, mutual recognition remains a viable way of dealing with cross-border issues at the global level; strong advocates of inter-jurisdictional regulatory recognition can still be found, particularly among global industry participants (e.g. EU–US Coalition on Financial Regulation 2012). Some regional agreements based on mutual recognition remain in good health, for example, those between Australia and both New Zealand and Hong Kong—with which it had close historic links, including those of language and legal systems (Hill 2012; ASIC and FMA 2012). Plans for the integration of a Southeast Asian Nations capital market on the foundations of mutual recognition and harmonization remain alive (Deutsche Bank 2013; Murray and Moxon-Browne 2013), as do some other regional initiatives, for example, in Africa (Onagoruwa 2012).

The stumbling block is the degree of similarity that must exist between systems for mutual recognition to operate safely and effectively. It has long been recognized that low-level similarity between systems is unlikely to be conducive to the development of the cross-border trust on which mutual recognition depends (Nicolaïdis 2007; Nicolaïdis and Schaffer 2005). The recent EU experience reinforces this concern. Whereas it was previously assumed that low-level approximations would suffice as a basis for mutual recognition, experience has fostered better appreciation of the crucial and mutually reinforcing interconnections between the barrier-dismantling aims of a mutual recognition scheme and the appropriate level of harmonization. In a nutshell, the EU has shown that the more successful mutual recognition is in stripping down national barriers, the more serious the potential side-effects that must be countered by cross-border regulatory convergence.

The EU thus provides a powerful case study to support what Helmut Wagner has described as the 'irony' of globalization: 'Deregulation has brought us globalization, and globalization in turn involves global systemic risk and contagion, and thus forces us to (try to) re-install regulation and (partially) harmonize law' (Wagner 2012: 558). Whereas negative side-effects may not be so great when the aim is to achieve a degree of consistency and coordination in international dealings rather than a fully integrated market, disentangling the risks inherent in mutual recognition from those that arise out of the ambitions that underpin its deployment is far from straightforward. Learning from others' experiences includes learning from mistakes as well as from achievements. The health warning now associated with mutual recognition explains why decision-makers may tread quite warily and make a high degree of similarity between systems a non-negotiable precondition to concessionary access.

The attitude of US regulatory authorities towards ambitious market-opening mechanisms relying on mutual recognition has changed in the aftermath of the crisis. In 2008, an apparently historic mutual recognition arrangement between the US Securities and Exchange Commission (SEC), the Australian government, and the Australian Securities and Investments Commission set out a framework for US and Australian stock exchanges and broker-dealers to operate in both jurisdictions without (in certain respects) having to be regulated in both countries (Hill 2012). The arrangement, however, has not been implemented, while SEC interest in similar schemes with other jurisdictions, including Canada and the EU, has apparently evaporated.

Instead, there has been a noticeable retrenchment in US financial regulation, especially in banking. Given the special position of banks and the systemic implications of bank failure, the global financial crisis reminded governments of their exceptional incentives to retain control over banks operating in their territory. This lesson was apparent in a November 2012 speech given by Daniel Tarullo, a member of the Board of Governors of the Federal Reserve System, in which he called for a rebalanced approach to regulating the US operations of large foreign banks and outlined specific adjustments to the US regulatory regime (Tarullo 2012). Tarullo stressed the need for a more standardized regulatory structure, by which he meant a more demanding application of national treatment principles whereby foreign banks would be allowed fewer concessions from US domestic requirements and subjected to more intense scrutiny by US authorities. Governor Tarullo was decidedly unenthusiastic about aiming towards 'extensive harmonization of national regulatory practices related to foreign banking organizations' because 'the nature and extent of foreign banking activities vary substantially across national markets, suggesting that regulatory responses might best vary as well'. Governor Tarullo's remarks foreshadowed formal Federal Reserve Board proposals on foreign banks published in late 2012 (Federal Reserve System 2012)—proposals that controversially mark a step back from efforts to harmonize the regulation of international banking (Davis Polk 2012). Set alongside statements such as the Federal Deposit Insurance Corporation's proposals in early 2013 to amend the definition of insured deposits to exclude deposits in overseas branches of US banks (FDIC 2013), these recent developments clearly indicate just how inward-looking regulators and policymakers in major jurisdictions have become as the domestic politics around financial regulation intensify.

These developments can be seen as part of a wider post-crisis trend in which arguments against uniform global rules have gathered momentum (Wagner 2012). The 'poetic' view that financial regulation needs to be global because financial institutions are global is now confronted by the argument that in 'the disharmonious reality' of the real world, more 'differentiated' responses may often be more appropriate (Brunnermeier et al. 2009: xviii). But there is another challenge as well: global interdependencies demand general consistency and systematic cooperation between countries (G20 2009a). The global consistency imperative—and the market-opening, anti-protectionism sentiments that go with it—cannot be abandoned simply because of the revelation of weaknesses in an instrumental mechanism.

Equivalence

This leads the discussion to the concept of 'equivalence'. 'Equivalence' and 'mutual recognition' are sometimes used interchangeably and conceptually have much in common. Equivalence shares with mutual recognition the notion that where there is an appropriate degree of similarity between different regulatory regimes, wasteful duplication can be avoided by giving concessions to actors potentially subject to multiple regimes. Equivalence implies a high degree of similarity. In this respect it is less ambiguous than mutual recognition, which could, at least in theory, operate between regimes that are poles apart. There is scope for interlocking operation, with equivalence setting the foundational standard of similarity for mutual recognition to function effectively. Though equivalence does not require two-way (mutual) operation, when coupled with 'reciprocity'—as it increasingly is—even this distinction tends to disappear.

The conceptual overlap notwithstanding, the distinction between equivalence and mutual recognition can be seen as a genuine one, if only because they have taken on different associations in EU regulatory discourse. Whereas mutual recognition has been central in the drive to create a pan-EU internal single market and has influenced international financial regulation mostly by attracting admiration and interest from afar, equivalence has been actively deployed within frameworks governing the access of actors from individual third countries to the EU in financial regulatory contexts from accounting and auditing standards and issuer disclosures to rating agencies, hedge funds, and market infrastructures. Equivalence as an access-governing mechanism is used in the insurance Solvency II context; it has also been proposed in the MiFID review (Moloney 2012) where issues relating to access by third country investment firms remain, at the time of writing, unresolved and controversial. Some member states view the introduction of a third country equivalence regime in MiFID as unnecessary and disproportionate, and would prefer to keep national rules.

There are two mutually reinforcing factors that lie at the root of these objections. The first is uncertainty about the meaning of 'equivalence'. Although a number of different interpretations are possible (Schammo 2011; Wei 2007), in principle it is best understood as a holistic test with benchmarks on the comparability of regulatory and supervisory *outcomes*, rather than a rigid line-by-line examination of similarities and differences and a quest for the exact mirroring of practices and philosophies. International standards may be called into use as the benchmark for the equivalency of outcomes. This is the approach adopted in Australia, where the Australian Corporations Act 2001 uses the phrase 'sufficient equivalence' in its third country access provisions. For the Australian Securities and Investments Commission (ASIC 2012), an equivalent regulatory regime is: (1) clear, transparent, and certain; (2) consistent with

IOSCO's Objectives and Principles of Securities Regulation; (3) adequately enforced in the home jurisdiction; and (4) achieves equivalent outcomes to the Australian regulatory regime.

EU authorities describe equivalence in a variety of ways and have so far resisted an overarching definition (Ferran 2012: 102–103). Equivalence in the accounting context has been said to be not synonymous with identical (CESR 2004b). The equivalence-based regime in the Credit Rating Agencies (CRA) Regulation[6] for the use of non-systemically relevant ratings issued in third countries is expressed in a holistic, outcomes-oriented fashion for the comparability of both supervisory regimes and legal frameworks (CESR 2010; ESMA 2012). In the European Market Infrastructure Regulation[7] (EMIR), equivalence is understood as implying substantially similar results and consistency in practical application (Recital 7). Other spheres have adopted more rigid approaches (e.g. ESMA 2013 (prospectuses)). Heavy lobbying has, on occasion, led to the adoption of different wording in legislative texts: for example, the depository regime in the Alternative Investment Fund Managers Directive[8] (AIFMD) refers to third country standards that 'have the same effect' as EU requirements. Nevertheless, the Commission and the European Securities and Markets Authority (ESMA) have not always attached as much significance to the softening effect of alternative formulations as some have hoped.

Suggestions that the real aim of equivalence tests is to restrict rather than facilitate third country access have been widespread in the MiFID review (e.g. European Union Committee 2012; EU–US Coalition 2012). For Commissioner Barnier, equivalence is 'a means for the EU to stay open to the rest of the world' and reciprocity simply meets the concern for 'ensuring fair treatment of our industry abroad' (Barnier 2012). But the concern is that equivalence, especially when coupled with reciprocity, could in practice mean 'unrealistic and impractical tests' (EU–US Coalition 2012) that are impossible to meet, an outcome that 'could lock third country firms out of the EU markets, which, taking into account the risk of regulatory retaliation, would have an extremely damaging effect on European financial markets' (European Union Committee 2012: para 60). The deletion of the equivalence provisions from the Council version of the MiFID II legislative texts, current at the time of writing, is an indication of the level of concern.

Doom-laden predictions about third country actors being locked out of the EU are challenged by some of the evidence. The most developed EU equivalence regime in operation is for financial reporting standards. The Generally Accepted Accounting Principles of the US, Japan, China, Canada, South Korea, and

[6] Regulation (EC) No. 1060/2009, amended by Regulation (EU) No. 513/2011 and Regulation (EU) No. 462/2013.
[7] Regulation (EU) No. 648/2012.   [8] Directive 2011/61/EU.

(initially on a temporary basis) India have been held to satisfy the equivalence test for the purposes of issuer disclosure requirements under the Prospectus Directive and Transparency Obligations Directive.[9] Practical determinations of equivalence/comparable stringency have also been made in the ratings context: ESMA considers the regulatory and supervisory frameworks of a number of countries, including Japan, Australia, Canada, Hong Kong, Singapore, and the US, to be as stringent as the EU regime. The Commission has also adopted formal equivalence decisions for the legal and supervisory frameworks of Japan, the US, Canada, and Australia.

Equivalence-based concessions thus do seem to function in certain contexts as safety-valves for the protectionist pressures that can lie behind the insistence that foreign actors comply in full with local requirements and submit fully to local supervision. As such, they provide reassurance that the dangers of misalignments between limited regulatory domains and the global reach of much financial services business have not been totally side-lined— the inward-looking turn by the financial regulatory regimes of major economies notwithstanding. But as the MiFID situation shows, there is not yet full confidence that the equivalence regime can always be relied upon to operate as intended.

This, then, brings us to the second reason why equivalency is so controversial: member states' unease in ceding control over territorial access. Although the precise 'who does what' details of third country actors' entry to the EU via equivalence-based mechanisms are not yet standardized and the allocation of roles and responsibilities still varies from context to context, we see the broad contours of a process that puts the Commission and the ESAs—so far, mostly the European Securities and Markets Authority (ESMA)—in the driver's seat. One significant departure from this pattern is CRD IV, Article 127, where the assessment of the equivalence of third countries' consolidated supervision is in the hands of national competent authorities. In the more general case, in outline the European Commission determines whether a third country regime is equivalent; the relevant ESA then provides technical advice. In implementation the ESA works closely with national supervisors on access decisions pertaining to specific third country financial institutions, firms or other actors. To illustrate by way of a specific example, in the EMIR framework for third country clearing houses (Article 25), the Commission's equivalence determination enables ESMA to recognize a clearing house established in that country provided certain conditions are satisfied. ESMA must consult with a range of national authorities and central banks to determine whether these conditions have been met.

Can the Commission and the ESAs be trusted with the gatekeeper roles that equivalency grants them? MiFID-related issues concern a still-to-be-finalized

---

[9] Direct 2003/71/EC; Directive 2004/109/EC.

future regime but OTC derivatives regulation—where legal regimes are already in place and discussions with third countries are underway—provides an alternative issue area in which this question can be explored by reference to actual events. Such is the importance of regime consistency in this globalized and highly interconnected market segment that it has been enshrined in law in the form of a statutory mandate under the US Dodd–Frank legislation (Section 752) to 'promote effective and consistent global regulation'. A requirement in EMIR, Recital 6 calls for cooperation with 'third-country authorities in order to explore mutually supportive solutions to ensure consistency . . . [and] avoid any possible overlapping'. But putting these legislative directions into effect has not been easy.

Transatlantic negotiations have been intensive (CFTC and SEC 2012), with controversies over extraterritoriality (CFTC 2012) and warnings of the dire consequences that could flow from a failure to agree (Faull 2012). On the US side, the Commodity Futures Trading Commission (CFTC), which has a track record of recognizing comparable regulatory regimes, indicated its readiness to permit non-US swap dealers and non-US major swap participants to substitute compliance with their home jurisdiction's laws and regulations in lieu of relevant Dodd–Frank Act requirements if the CFTC finds that such requirements are comparable to the analogous US requirements (CFTC 2012). The SEC and regulators of OTC derivatives markets in other major economies have also affirmed their commitment to develop cross-border substituted compliance (SEC 2012). 'Substituted compliance' as used by US regulators (Tafara and Peterson 2007) aims in the same direction as the objectives that the EU is pursuing via equivalency (Faull 2012; Guevarra 2012). Nevertheless, there are fears that the EU equivalence-based approach will be complex and time-consuming (Luettringhaus 2012), and less liberal than that implied by substituted compliance. Speaking at an industry briefing in London in May 2013, Eric Pan, Associate Director at the Office of International Affairs at the SEC, called upon the Commission and ESMA 'to adopt an outcomes-based approach towards equivalency'. With other SEC officials, he warned of severe disruptions to cross-border clearing if accommodations were not found. Yet his statement is best seen as an opening shot in a war of words. A few weeks previously, the European Commission and nine national finance ministries (Brazil, France, Germany, Italy, Japan, Russia, South Africa, Switzerland, the UK) had written to the US authorities expressing concern over the lack of progress in developing workable cross-border rules on derivatives. The letter stressed the need for a shared understanding of the overall outcome being sought; argued that mutual recognition, substituted compliance, exemptions or a combination of these are all valid approaches; and that outcomes-oriented equivalence be determined by reference to compliance with international standards (Barnier et al. 2013).

Much is riding on the Commission and ESMA getting it right, not only for the OTC derivatives market but for the development of equivalency more generally. Equivalence determinations provide EU authorities with opportunities to assess the quality of third country regimes against EU benchmarks (and when coupled with reciprocity, to demand concessions in return). As such, they allow for an assertion of regulatory power and for demonstrations of the hard-nosed self-interest that some see as the driving force behind the conduct of international relations (Helleiner and Pagliari 2011). Equivalency has been explicitly held out as a mechanism for the EU 'to promote its interests and values more assertively and in a spirit of reciprocity and mutual benefit' (EMIR, Recital 60). In an era when financial regulation has become highly politicized and member states and EU authorities continue to disagree over the location of gatekeeper control for third country access to their territories, it is perhaps unsurprising that tensions have escalated. But a high level of intensity is neither sustainable nor desirable. In the longer term, equivalency will be viewed with deep mistrust—both within and outside the EU—if it is too closely associated with crude power politics. It will then not realize its potential.

Financial regulators and other officials from different countries and regions—condemned to cooperate with each other at multiple levels due to the nature of the industry they seek to control—cannot function effectively or efficiently if they are constantly at loggerheads. Self-interest is always an anchor point in international relations, but in a world in which power is becoming increasingly diffused and the ability to impose preferred solutions on others correspondingly constrained, cleverer and more subtle ways of exerting influence need to be pursued. Equivalency has the potential to function as a sophisticated, multifaceted mechanism that involves not only hard bargaining but also cooperative governance, mutual learning, willingness to experiment, and the deepening of cross-border understanding (Sabel and Zeitlin 2008, 2012b). Working out whether another system is equivalent should provide a myriad of opportunities for the deepening of cross-border working relationships, for cross-fertilization of ideas and for coordination. A well-functioning process for securing access to the EU in which EU supranational bodies genuinely play 'a central role in ensuring that Europe speaks with a single voice vis-à-vis regulators outside the European Union' (Ross 2012) should in time deliver efficiency gains that override member states' objections to loss of control (or at least expose their protectionist origins). Visions of a more fragmented world in which achieving multilateral agreement on anything of significance becomes progressively more difficult have led some commentators to predict that bilateral exchanges between countries/ regions will be the most effective mechanism for the advancement of international financial regulation in the years to come. All of this gives greater significance to making a success of equivalency.

STRENGTHENING THE SUPERVISORY ARCHITECTURE
Cross-border Supervisory Colleges

The formalization and concretization of the composition and role of supervisory colleges, and the development of information exchange protocols to underpin their operation, are matters on which the EU has been particularly active (Alford 2010) and where claims of the EU providing a valuable example to the rest of the world are credible (Financial Stability Forum 2008: 41). An important milestone in the development of the European colleges of supervisors was reached in 2011 when—under changes introduced by CRD II to give colleges legal underpinning and to spell out the rights and responsibilities of national supervisors (CRD, Article 131a)—colleges became obliged to reach joint decisions on the level of risk-based capital adequacy for cross-border banking groups, on both consolidated and individual entity levels. Under CRD IV, Article 116, third country authorities may participate in supervisory colleges, subject to an equivalence standard on requirements for confidentiality.

The basic purpose of supervisory colleges is to enhance information exchange and cooperation between supervisors to support effective international supervision; they are meant to foster the mutual trust and appreciation of needs and responsibilities on which supervisory relationships are built (BCBS 2010a). While colleges of supervisors with common interests exist in different contexts, they are perhaps especially associated with the prudential supervision of cross-border financial groups that include subsidiaries incorporated in different jurisdictions; a college then functions as a flexible coordination structure that gathers the authorities involved in the supervision of the group (FSA 2009: 98). The use of colleges is particularly advanced in the insurance sector, where there are already more than 30 global and 90 regional colleges run by supervisors (FSB 2012: 20).

Global weaknesses in existing supervisory colleges were exposed during the financial crisis, leading to interrelated moves to strengthen their functioning at international (BCBS 2010a; FSB 2012) and regional levels (CEBS and CEIOPS 2009; CEBS 2010). College-based approaches are also extending into adjacent issue areas. In the EU, the draft Resolution and Recovery Directive, under negotiation at the time of writing, installs resolution colleges to provide a framework for the group-level resolution authority and to conduct a range of tasks (Article 80, Recovery and Resolution Directive (presidency compromise version, March 2013)). As in the CRD, it envisages the participation of third country authorities as observers, subject to an equivalence standard for confidentiality (Article 80). The development of college-like crisis management groups to coordinate the management of failing institutions is also taking place at the international level (FSB 2011).

Elliot Posner (2014) has identified a close affinity between EU and international models for colleges, which he notes are co-evolving along certain dimensions. He points to evidence, 'some only circumstantial, suggesting that European politicians and representatives pushed for supervisory colleges on the G20 agenda and then shaped their international applications in the image of the EU variants'. This supports the idea that the EU is engaged in the systematic dissemination and exploitation of results from experiments conducted within its own 'laboratory'.

Cross-border Coordination of Supervision

Supervisory colleges and crisis management groups can only ever play a limited role in international financial governance (Alford 2010). Colleges do not function as autonomous decision-making bodies and 'cannot deliver fully integrated global supervision, since legal powers of intervention are national in nature, and since national governments look to national supervisors to protect national interests' (FSA 2009: 99). Accordingly, they must be supported by other mechanisms for the promotion of supervisory cooperation and information exchange, and for the convergence of supervisory good practices.

On these matters, the EU is much more advanced than the international order. International financial governance lacks formal treaty-based global standard-setting bodies; it is left to bodies without legally binding powers, among them the Financial Stability Board and various sectoral committees, to drive forward supervisory as well as regulatory convergence and cooperation. This effort is supported by ad hoc multilateral initiatives to achieve international consistency in particular areas (Ross 2012), complemented by country-to-country bilateral engagements between politicians, public officials, regulators, and supervisors on topics of mutual interest. These bilateral exchanges are in turn often related to and supported by contacts between supervisors on day-to-day operational matters and assistance in enforcement cases. 'Soft' oversight of implementation and compliance with international standards in actual supervisory practices is conducted through a range of mechanisms, including peer review and supervisory self-assessment (FSB 2012; Posner 2014). Nevertheless, weaknesses in international monitoring remain (Brummer 2011: 252–253).

In contrast, EU-wide coordination of national supervisory activity to support the effective and consistent application of regulatory requirements has accelerated in the aftermath of the financial crisis and the exposure of serious weaknesses. The pre-crisis cross-border supervisory framework based on committees of national supervisors in banking, securities, and insurance (known as the Lamfalussy committees) has been upgraded to a more formalized structure of European Supervisory Authorities or ESAs: the European Banking Authority (EBA), the European Insurance and Occupational Pensions Authority (EIOPA), and ESMA. The ESAs are formally constituted bodies with legal personality and have much more extensive formal and informal powers than their predecessor committees. Together with the European Systemic Risk Board (ESRB) and national supervisors, the ESAs form the European System of Financial Supervision (ESFS).

The ESAs do not displace national supervisors as direct overseers of firms and markets (ESMA's special position as direct supervisor of a small subsection of financial market actors aside). Much of the ESAs' work is concerned with promoting convergence and coordinating the work of national supervisors (EBA Regulation, Articles 1, 8, 31).[10] They have a wide range of convergence-promoting functions and powers including: supporting the work of colleges and enhancing their functioning, building information-sharing capacities, developing statistical frameworks and collecting and disseminating data, sharing best practices, developing common methodologies, collecting, analysing and reporting on trends, developing industry training standards, establishing and conducting training for supervisors, and facilitating secondments, through to issuing recommendations, guidance and warnings, developing a supervisory handbook, conducting thematic peer reviews, resolving supervisory disagreements, conducting stress tests, and monitoring financial stability risks and concerns. The ESAs make use of 'soft' oversight mechanisms such as monitoring and peer review (EBA Regulation, Article 30; Moloney 2011b, 2013). Thus far in the description of the ESAs' role, it is possible to find loose parallels in the functions performed by international bodies (e.g. the FSB's Charter, as discussed in Hüpkes 2012). Peer review as conducted within the EU has been described as a 'close analogue' to the international model (Posner 2014).

The ESFS, however, cannot simply be seen as a more advanced version of an approach adopted at the international level. Context is all important. The ESAs operate in the 'shadow of hierarchy' (Héritier 2002) and that shadow has lengthened considerably in response to crisis. Participants in the ESFS are formally bound to cooperate with each other 'with trust and full mutual respect' (EBA Regulation, Article 2) in ways that set the EU system apart from looser forms of cooperation at the international level. The ESAs can reach deep into how supervision is conducted on a day-to-day basis by national supervisors through their powers to write binding technical standards (Articles 10–15) as well as to issue (non-binding) guidance and recommendations (Article 16). Non-binding ESA guidance is reinforced by a 'comply or disclose' type mechanism, an associated compliance table, and other transparency-promoting arrangements (for an example see EBA 2013). Occupying a quite different space from international soft law standards, ESA guidelines provide a clear

---

[10] Regulation (EU) No. 1093/2010. Regulation (EU) No. 1094/2010 (EIOPA), and Regulation (EU) No. 1095/201 (ESMA) contain the same provisions. For convenience the text uses the EBA Regulation as the exemplar.

illustration of the inadequacy of the bifurcated legal taxonomy of 'hard' and 'soft' approaches in capturing the reality of sophisticated situations (Möllers 2010).

Nor are the ESAs confined to 'soft' powers. In contrast to processes for monitoring compliance with non-binding international standards (and their predecessor committee), the ESAs have powers to impose binding supervisory decisions in certain situations (Articles 17–20), including the authority to settle cross-border disagreements between national supervisors inside or outside a supervisory college. The ESAs' law enforcement powers include actions at different levels, progressively ratcheted up from recommendations to decisions to the possibility of formal enforcement proceedings before the Court (Article 17).

The European System of Financial Supervision is also distinctive in that the ESAs have specific powers to intervene in markets, for example, under the Short Selling Regulation, which confers power on ESMA to prohibit short selling under certain circumstances.[11] The ESAs participate actively in coordinating the work of supervisory colleges and are not merely called upon to settle disputes (Article 21). They are empowered to engage in international relations (Article 33). Provisions in sector-specific legislation—including those relating to alternative investments, market infrastructure, rating agencies, and recovery and resolution—whereby member states are expected to work within a common framework when agreeing to bilateral arrangements with third country authorities, further extend the international reach of the ESAs.

The cumulative impact of these numerous powers and responsibilities is powerful, as Niamh Moloney has shown for ESMA. Even though it has been operational only since 2011, it is already possible to see a clear 'intensification effect' as ESMA extends its grip (Moloney 2013).

Since it is the world's most advanced system for the organization of cross-border supervision, the ESFS naturally merits attention in a search for a better international order. Analytically, there is still value in examining peer reviews, surveillance, 'naming and shaming', and other strategies deployed within the ESA frameworks as mutual learning processes that advance an essentially polyarchic system of governance (Sabel and Zeitlin 2008, 2012b). Useful lessons can still be extracted from the ESA's operational work, much of which may be 'mundane but practically significant' (Moloney 2013). But at a deeper level of inquiry, it is becoming increasingly hard to envision the ESFS as an inspiring ideational model for the rest of the world as issues of suitability loom large. A few years ago, Eric Pan suggested that 'It is especially helpful to look at the . . . European-wide supervisory system as a model of international cooperation' (Pan 2009). But from today's perspective, the ESFS looks an unlikely blueprint for the international organization of cross-border supervision. Supervisory institutional models in general do not travel well due to their

---

[11] Regulation (EU) No. 236/2012.

high dependency on local circumstances; the ESFS provides an illustration of this observation writ large.

The ESFS represents a pragmatic and incremental solution to a very particular set of problems within the EU internal market. The financial crisis exposed serious weaknesses in a more avowedly 'soft' system of supervision based on a committee-based network of supervisors and also rendered the case for more ambitious institutional change more politically palatable. However, the crisis did not provide carte blanche for supervisory institutional reform (Ferran 2012). The ESFS is thus the product of a potent mix of impulses in which frictions between the manifest need for stronger supranational structures to provide protection against the vulnerabilities of a single market, and member states' reluctance to relax their grip on key areas (including their fiscal sovereignty and in the area of external relations) loomed large. The result is a fiendishly complicated institutional set-up, full of nuances not easily accessible to those not steeped in the intricacies of EU institutional relations, politics, and law. Outsiders considering looking towards the EU for inspiration on the design of cross-border supervision may be further deterred by the strong sense of the ESFS being a system in evolution, whose ultimate direction of travel is hard to discern (Schammo 2012). Whether the EU is a forerunner or outlier in the organization of cross-border financial market supervision is a question still worth asking (Sabel and Zeitlin 2008). But as the singularity of the EU's approach becomes ever more pronounced, the answer is becoming clearer.

Supranational Supervision

There are numerous radical proposals in the scholarly literature for some form of global financial authority able to coerce countries to conform to international standards and even potentially direct powers of enforcement against market actors (e.g. Avgouleas 2012). In his major study of soft law and the global financial system, Brummer reviews some of the key suggestions and concludes that the likelihood of a world financial organization of this sort is 'small to non-existent' (Brummer 2011: 269). He points out that even when powers in the EU were centralized in regional bodies, power remained shared between local and supranational authorities. This assessment suggests that the EU is hardly encouraging for models of better global financial governance that depend on building institutional capabilities at the international level. If countries bound together in a sophisticated regional grouping supported by a mature supranational institutional infrastructure are reluctant to embrace the denationalization of responsibility for supervision, what hope is there for the strengthening of the international institutional order?

The position in Europe is changing rapidly, however, and the published literature is hard pressed to keep abreast of the significance of major developments. The

European Banking Union provides unequivocal evidence that dramatic institutional breakthroughs are sometimes possible. However, the background circumstances to its first step—the single supervisory mechanism (SSM) in which the European Central Bank (ECB) is to be given exclusive competence for a list of supervisory tasks relating to the prudential supervision of credit institutions—were so extreme and so driven by the need to shore up monetary union that it is most unlikely that proponents of models for the vesting of supervisory power at the international level would look to it as a useful precedent. On the contrary, it might be said that the most striking aspect of the deliberations around the European Banking Union was the persistence of deep-rooted and diverse national priorities and sensitivities that made countries reluctant to compromise, even in the face of a massive systemic shock. The intensity of Eurozone member states' concerns about ceding supervisory responsibility for their banks to the ECB has resulted in the ECB's role becoming more 'differentiated' than was originally envisaged by the Commission. Member states' objections to the pooling of liabilities have led to the postponement of plans for a single resolution mechanism—despite powerful arguments that a single supervisory mechanism will struggle for credibility and effectiveness without a single resolution mechanism (Sapir et al. 2012). Member states' insistence on retaining control over deposit protection arrangements has resulted in plans for a single deposit protection scheme being effectively dropped for the immediate future.

Those looking to Europe for guidance on supervisory functions that, over time, could become realistic candidates for denationalization might do better to direct their attention to the breakthrough decisions that made ESMA responsible for the direct supervision of, first, credit rating agencies and, second, trade repositories. Rating agencies were among the first targets of EU post-crisis reforms; at the outset, the supervisory architecture was based on a complicated supervisory college and coordination by the Committee of European Securities Regulators, ESMA's predecessor. The founding instrument acknowledged that this was not 'the long-term solution for the oversight of credit rating agencies' and that a college 'may not substitute all the advantages of more consolidated supervision' (Recital 51). The establishment of ESMA provided an alternative option that was quickly exploited.[12] This direct conferral of supervisory power was not meant to set a precedent. But experience—in the form of provisions in EMIR for ESMA to assume direct responsibility for the registration and surveillance of trade repositories—suggests that once a door is opened, developments become possible (Articles 55–77). The capacity of institutions to take on lives of their own is well known (Pierson 1996). In ESMA's case, the process was accelerated.

Set against a background of reluctance to equip supranational supervisors with real power, ESMA's relatively painless rise to a direct supervisory role

---

[12] Regulation (EU) No. 513/2011.

looks remarkable. Two interrelated factors help to explain why the initial break-through on rating agencies did not stir up intense national sensitivities. The first is the nature of the industry: the ratings business is dominated by the three major US agencies; there were no major domestic 'champions' over which EU member state governments had strong reasons to maintain protective control. Second, the major impediment to governments relaxing their grip on financial market actors—the risk of those actors failing in ways that could burden the public purse—was not present: rating agencies are not viewed as significant sources of systemic risk. Similar considerations apply for trade repositories. The significance of the potential threat to the public purse is underscored by comparison with the position on central counterparties. An incidental conse-quence of the G20-led post-crisis efforts to introduce mandatory clearing for derivatives is that central counterparties have become systemically more important. That this has implications for the allocation of supervisory respon-sibilities is clear. The recitals in EMIR explain 'Where a CCP risks insolvency, fiscal responsibility may lie predominantly with the Member State in which that CCP is established . . . It follows that authorization and supervision of that CCP should be exercised by the relevant competent authority of that Member State' (Recital 52).

The ESMA/rating agencies and trade repositories example points to the kinds of market actors or activities for which the vesting of oversight powers at the international level may be plausible. The arguments for streamlined supervision—a single point of contact, greater consistency in the application of rules, and significant efficiency gains—are present in every case. They won out in the rating agencies context because the wider surrounding conditions were right. Practical experience confirms that while we can expect great political reluctance to surrender control over institutions for which national taxpayers could be ultimately responsible (Hüpkes 2012), this is not the case when such considerations do not obtain. Much now depends on how well ESMA does as a frontline supervisor. If ESMA succeeds, it could lead to a greater accretion of central supervisory power within Europe. It could also reshape international regulation by reinforcing arguments for the viability of some aspects of super-vision being conducted at the international level.

3

Banking

JASPER BLOM

This chapter analyses the policy domain of bank capital adequacy standards, a crucial domain within the wider framework of financial governance in the European Union. Due to the bank-based nature of many member states' financial markets, the European banking market in terms of assets and liabilities is the world's largest (Howarth and Quaglia 2013). European companies rely heavily on bank financing. The crisis in the banking sector and the resulting regulatory reforms therefore have direct implications for the growth prospects of European economies, even more so than in other advanced economies.[1]

At the global level, the Basel capital accords of the Basel Committee on Banking Supervision (BCBS) set the standards for bank capital adequacy. While supervisors from several European countries with large financial sectors are members of the BCBS, there is no formal EU membership—the European Central Bank (ECB) and Commission are observers. The Basel accords have been transposed into the EU context through several directives, most recently through the Capital Requirements Directive IV (CRD IV). Notably, the EU applies the Basel capital accords to *all* banks, even though they were originally envisaged to apply only to large internationalized banks. This wide-ranging implementation contrasts with, for example, the USA.

The current case reveals the global 'embeddedness' of European financial regulation as well as the EU dynamics that inform the implementation of global-level standards. The chapter traces the emergence of supranational bank capital adequacy standards from the European Community's First Banking Coordination Directive in 1977 to the 2010 Basel III Capital Accord and its European implementation in the form of CRD IV.

---

[1] See, for example, the influential IIF (2010) study on the cumulative impact of post-crisis financial reform. Even though this particular study is biased and flawed, the relative impact on different regions is in line with other findings.

There is extensive international political economy literature on the negotiation of the Basel capital accords.[2] One body of work focuses on state-based explanations where the preferences of public supervisors either follow from a functionalist interpretation of the consequences of global financial integration (Kapstein 1994) or derive from the structure of the domestic banking sector (Oatley and Nabors 1998; Wood 2005; Howarth and Quaglia 2013). Other authors have focused on the 'global' nature of the negotiations in the BCBS. Tsingou (2008) points to the emergence of 'club-like' policymaking forums which crafted consensus on Basel II. Claessens, Underhill, and Zhang (2008) as well as Lall (2011) point to the importance of financial sector lobbying to explain the outcomes of BCBS policymaking. Young (2012) criticizes the claim of private sector capture of policymaking and emphasizes the discretion available to public policymakers in the BCBS.

The aim of this chapter is not to settle this debate between 'nationalist' and 'globalist' explanations. Rather, it will contribute to the literature and the aims of this volume by analysing how the global and European levels have influenced each other in a multi-level governance setting.[3] By including the European level in the analysis, we see how the EU functions as an intermediating variable influencing the preferences of private and especially public actors. Public actors at the European level, with an eye to establishing the common market, have reinforced preferences in the BCBS for a level playing field. Vice versa, European policymakers have used the Basel capital accords to further European financial market integration (compare Bieling and Jäger 2009). This can be seen in the application of the Basel capital accords to all banks (not just the large internationally active ones) and the strengthened provisions on consolidated supervision in the CRD IV (Christopoulos and Quaglia 2009: 196); and demonstrates the discretion available to European public policymakers.

The analysis in this chapter builds on the theoretical framework developed in Blom (2011) which addresses both private and public actors' preferences in the context of exclusionary policymaking forums and changing market structures. Interaction in exclusionary policymaking forums leads to skewed argument pools. As a result, public policymakers have developed shared assumptions, including the superiority of market mechanisms and the desirability of levelling the playing field ('increased competition leads to more efficient financial services provision'). The problem of bank capital adequacy has therefore been addressed through a market-oriented lens.[4] The 'theoretical' axioms held by public policymakers on how markets should function, however, can also lead to preferences that counterbalance or complement the more narrowly self-interested preferences of private actors (e.g. the inclusion of operational risk in

---

[2] See also the literature review in Blom (2011: 109–112).

[3] For a multi-level analysis of Basel II focusing on its implementation in Central and Eastern European member states, see Spendzharova (2010).

[4] See also Baker (2006, 2010) on the development of this consensus in the G7.

Basel II, as discussed below). This is especially relevant at the European level, where the development of the common market has been a key consideration for many public policymakers when discussing the Basel accords and its related directives. This theoretical framework captures what Young calls the 'discretion' of public policymakers and explains how and why public policymakers may not always be prey to private sector lobbying ('regulatory capture').

The chapter begins in the next section with the first international-level talks on banking regulation in the 1970s. This sets the stage for the negotiations for the first Basel Capital Accord in section 2. The third section deals with the renegotiation of Basel I into the second Basel capital accord. After the most recent global financial crisis derailed the implementation of Basel II, yet another accord was negotiated addressing issues highlighted by the crisis. These nego- tiations will be the subject of the fourth section. The final section concludes and will elaborate on the evolution of EU involvement in the negotiations.

BANKING REGULATION IN THE 1970s

The demise of the Bretton Woods regime in the early 1970s provided banks with new global opportunities and strengthened the trend towards global integration and liberalization which had begun with the rise of the Euromarkets. But the currency volatility resulting from the abandonment of the gold–dollar peg also implied risks for banks. These risks materialized with the 1974 Bankhaus Her- statt collapse, which underscored that crises in an era of internationalized bank- ing could quickly spread through the global system. Banks and supervisors alike realized the importance of bank counterparts being adequately supervised and capitalized. In response, banking supervisors of the G10 established the Basel Committee on Banking Supervision (BCBS) in 1974. Reflecting the urgency of the issue, the BCBS in 1975 reached an agreement on the division of home–host supervisory responsibilities (the so-called Concordat), an important first step in the globalization of bank supervisory standards.

Supervisors in the European Community were not only concerned about the division of supervisory responsibilities between home and host countries. Simultaneous negotiations on bank capital adequacy standards had been taking place in the European Community in the 1970s in the context of the programme to integrate European markets (the '1992 agenda'). These negotia- tions culminated in the European Council's adoption of the First Banking Coordination Directive in 1977.[5] The directive addressed home–host country issues within the Community, and included preliminary steps towards the

---

[5] First Council Directive 77/780/EEC of 12 December 1977 on the coordination of laws, regu- lations, and administrative provisions relating to the taking up and pursuit of the business of credit institutions.

harmonization of supervisory standards. The directive required supervisory authorities to 'establish ratios between the various assets and/or liabilities of credit institutions with a view to monitoring their solvency and liquidity and the other measures which may serve to ensure that savings are protected'. But these ratios were only 'for the purpose of observation', to be used alongside domestic measures (Directive 77/780/EEC, Article 6.1). The directive not only aimed to ensure the soundness of banks, but also aimed to create equal conditions of competition for banks in the Community. In other words, supervisors were led by a preference for safety and soundness *and* working towards a common market (see also Kapstein 1994: chapter 6).

While the coordination of banking regulation in the Community was informed by the goal of market integration, the harmonization of bank capital adequacy standards remained tentative: different banking systems (e.g. the universal banks of continental Europe versus the commercial banks of the UK) prevented fruitful harmonization (Underhill 1997b). Given the difficulty of setting common capital adequacy standards in the EU—where public officials at least shared the underlying goal of market integration—it is hardly surprising that the BCBS did not get far either. In the 1970s and early 1980s, conceptual work on bank capital adequacy ratios resulted in a definition of capital consisting of six tiers and a risk-weighting of assets consisting of seven risk buckets (in addition to a gearing ratio) (Norton 1995: 184–185). But from 1982, emerging market debt crises (the 'Latin American debt crisis') changed the dynamics of negotiation by revealing the dangers of steadily eroding levels of bank capital.

NEGOTIATIONS FOR BASEL I AND THE CAD

The Latin American debt crisis revealed the capital buffers of many leading banks in international sovereign lending to be completely inadequate. Estimates of Western banks' direct exposure to the 17 most indebted emerging markets in 1982 ranged from 31 per cent of capital and reserves in Germany to 85 per cent in the UK to 130 per cent in the USA. American money centre banks, in particular, were virtually bankrupt in the face of defaults by emerging market borrowers; the exposure of the nine largest US banks was a whopping 194 per cent of capital and reserves (Cline 1995: tables 2.10–2.14). Clearly, the Latin American debt crisis risked a systemic banking crisis. Supervisors noted that this was not due to the circumvention of domestic-level supervision, but was simply because capital adequacy rules did not suffice (Wood 2005: 68). The political mood in the USA turned decidedly against the internationally active banks. In return for the IMF bail-out funds required by the emerging markets, Congress demanded stringent capital adequacy standards. This resulted in the imposition of a capital ratio based on risk-weighted assets, a technique pioneered in the UK.

Internationally, supervisors chose different means to deal with the emerging market debt crisis. Japanese banks, which posed a growing competitive challenge to US banks on the global market, received favourable tax treatment of losses as a way to redress their impact on bank solvency (Kapstein 1994: 103). This led to concerns in the USA that its stringent capital regulations were having a negative impact on the competitiveness of US banks, and strong private sector lobbying to push for the internationalization of American standards. The burden of stringent regulation was to be borne by all, particularly the Japanese competitors (Oatley and Nabors 1998). This was the opening shot for the negotiations that led to the first Basel capital accord.[6]

The limited success of earlier attempts at harmonization, both in the EU and in the BCBS, made most BCBS members reluctant to enter negotiations with the USA. But for the Bank of England, it was an opportunity to counterbalance the EU's efforts at harmonization (Kapstein 1992). In other words, the preferences of UK public supervisors were in part determined—in this case negatively—by the European integration agenda. In addition, the UK and US banking sectors were similar in structure; US regulations were already based on UK practice. Encouraged by their private sectors, the USA and UK quietly engaged in negotiations over the course of 1986. In January 1987 they reached an agreement, providing an incentive for other BCBS members to overcome their initial reluctance. Building on the foundation of the US–UK agreement, the BCBS negotiated a deal that resulted in the July 1988 Basel capital accord. The original US–UK accord proved flexible enough to address competing demands among European BCBS members. For example, France pushed for the inclusion of loan-loss reserves in capital, opposed by Germany which wanted a strict definition of capital. The two-tier capital structure in the accord could accommodate this difference by maintaining a strict definition for tier one capital, and including loan-loss reserves in tier two capital (Reinicke 1995: 173; Tarullo 2008: 57).

EU agencies were hardly involved in the negotiations for Basel I. The USA was in the lead, the BCBS mostly followed, and the European Community was only involved in implementation. But harmonized standards for banks fit well in the Delors 'Europe 1992' agenda (Kapstein 1994: 142–143). Reflecting the close ties and cooperation between the main European banking supervisors— the result of their interaction in the BCBS—agreements on how to deal with differences in supervisory approaches were reached quite easily.[7] In 1989, the

---

[6] See Reinicke (1995) for an extensive discussion of American politics in the field of banking regulation.

[7] Off-the-record interview with public actor, 1992.

Own Funds Directive (covering bank capital) and Solvency Ratio Directive (covering bank solvency) implemented Basel I in the European Community.

Although actors promoting European financial integration used Basel I to advance their cause, the goal of a common market also led the European-level policy community to go beyond the BCBS accord. An important role here was played by the continental tradition of universal banks involved in both commercial and investment banking. These banks were not only exposed to credit risk (which Basel I addresses) but also to market risk. Addressing both types of risk in a single supervisory framework would spur European market integration in investment services, an agenda strongly supported by European financial services firms.[8] This resulted in the agreement for the Capital Adequacy Directive (CAD) of 1992 to include elements of market risk.[9]

The de-segmented financial markets of continental European countries were at the forefront of a global trend. It is therefore unsurprising that the BCBS followed the EU's lead in developing a market risk amendment to Basel I (see Underhill 1995). In the BCBS consultative process that followed, market participants, especially those from the USA, were highly critical of the proposed approach to market risk. The original BCBS proposal was modelled on the European 'standardized' approach, which treated market risk in a manner similar to the treatment of credit risk under Basel I. US banks, however, backed the use of internal Value-at-Risk (VaR) models to determine market risk. The BCBS took two years to respond to private sector comments—by incorporating them. The lobby of the large, international banks had been successful. Although the BCBS set limits to the use of internal models, it was a first step towards a new approach to bank capital adequacy standards (Tarullo 2008: 61–64). We now turn to this new approach, codified in the Basel II capital accord.

NEGOTIATIONS ON BASEL II AND CRD III

Basel I and its implementation through European directives altered the structure of global and European banking markets (see Blom 2011: 119–125). It provided incentives for further internationalization and for market innovations such as the use of capital market instruments and off-balance sheet activities. This led to the proliferation of complex financial instruments, sometimes developed with the single aim of exploiting regulatory inefficiencies. Especially for the globally active and increasingly large banks with diversified portfolios, the economic capital required by their 'sophisticated' risk management models

[8] Off-the-record interview with public actor, 1998.
[9] Wood (2005: 95). The CAD formally passed into European law in March 1993 as Directive 93/6/EEC.

diverged (on the lower side) from the regulatory capital required by Basel I. Following their success in the market risk amendment, these banks lobbied for the use of internal models to determine total capital requirements. On the other hand, supervisors increasingly realized that regulatory capital arbitrage led to capital ratios that might underestimate the actual risk on bank balance sheets (see e.g. Jackson et al. 1999). This made supervisors receptive to bank appeals that a complete renegotiation of Basel I was necessary.

Global-level institutions such as the G30, consisting of representatives of both the most prominent public actors and the largest international banks, drove the consensus for a new supervisory approach (Tsingou 2012). In addition, the Institute of International Finance (IIF) in 1998 published its influential report 'Recommendations for revising the regulatory capital rules for credit risk', which proposed allowing banks to use their own models. These ideas were injected into the BCBS when the New York Federal Reserve Bank's William MacDonough became its chair in June 1998; in the following month, it was announced that a new capital adequacy framework would be negotiated (Tarullo 2008: 91). Given the global consensus among private actors and supervisors, negotiations were conducted in the BCBS from the start, with its secretariat managing a consultative process in which different drafts were open for comments.

The Commission and ECB (established in 1999) are observers in the BCBS, which means they can participate in task forces and working groups but have no formal voice in negotiations (De Meester 2008: 144). Parallel to, but following the lead of the BCBS negotiations, the Commission conducted a review of the CAD, hoping to influence the Basel process through European-level market consultations (De Meester 2008: 115). Many of the responses to the BCBS by European stakeholders were simultaneously submitted to the Commission.

Elsewhere, I have shown that the vast majority of comments on the consultative papers came from private financial actors (about 70 per cent) and supervisors (another 15 per cent).[10] The regional spread of responses was also revealing. The EU's use of the Basel accords to further market integration by applying it to all financial institutions was reflected in the share of comments originating from Europe. Different types of banks, including cooperative and regional (public) banks, had an interest in the BCBS negotiations. The importance of bank funding for the European real economy heightened the interest of associations representing small and medium-sized enterprises (SMEs)— although, as noted, input from real economy actors was limited. Consequently, almost half of the responses to the BCBS consultative papers originated in Europe, even though the accord is implemented globally.

---

[10] Blom (2011: 133, table 4.5). Supervisor comments were regularly drafted in explicit consultation with the domestic financial sector.

The responses to the consultative papers point to three major issues: (1) the implications of using ratings and internal models for a diverse banking market; (2) the inclusion of operational risk; and (3) lending to SMEs. While these issues were mainly negotiated at the BCBS level, they have particular salience in the European context due to the wide application of the Basel capital accords and the specific structure of the European banking market. These three issues in the negotiations are discussed below.

Internal Models and Ratings

The large internationally active banks lobbied hard on the use of internal ratings and models to determine capital adequacy. It led to anxiety and opposition among smaller, domestic-oriented banks such as the German and Austrian public banks (Bieling and Jäger 2009) which feared the competitive consequences of large banks using internal models which they did not have the capacity to use themselves. Building a bank capital adequacy standard on the basis of internal models was more complicated—and supervisors were more hesitant—than the G30 consensus suggested. In its first consultative paper (CP1) of June 1999, the BCBS made only a very tentative step towards market-based risk assessment by proposing the use of external ratings to refine the risk categories of Basel I. Further study on the use of internal ratings was proposed. Representatives of global banks reacted with disappointment and fierce lobbying, pointing out that internal ratings were superior to external ratings in assessing risk.

The lobbying by large internationally active banks paid off in the second consultative paper (CP2), released in January 2001. It proposed not one but two approaches to the use of internal ratings: the Foundational and Advanced Internal Ratings-Based (IRB) approaches. The BCBS acknowledged private sector influence in the introduction: 'The Committee has developed an approach to regulatory capital that more accurately reflects a bank's individual risk profile. Work with industry associations and data collected through surveys have been essential to the development of a risk sensitive IRB approach' (BCBS 2001: para 93). In responding to CP2, the British Bankers' Association and London Investment Banking Association were 'pleased that the Committee has so obviously listened to the industry lobby and believe that the proposals, in sum, represent a substantial step towards a more risk based Accord'.[11]

Among European banks, these feelings were shared only by the large internationally active banks. The European Savings Bank Group expressed concerns that small banks would incur higher regulatory capital. Cooperative bank representatives noted that the accord was ill-suited to them. The Finnish Bankers'

---

[11] BBA and LIBA (2001).

Association summarized it neatly: 'the proposals seem to be prepared to a large extent with large international capital markets in mind, and do not, as a whole, take sufficient account of financing for households and small and medium-sized enterprises in particular'.[12]

The concerns of small banks notwithstanding, the ECB remained supportive of the work done by the BCBS and reiterated its broad endorsement of the proposed framework[13]—likely because it perceived the accord as an opportunity to further integrate European financial markets.[14] Given the aim of furthering the common market, it is not surprising that the ECB noted, 'the objectives of competitive equality and a level playing field call for extensive convergence in supervisory approaches' (2001: 13). The concerns expressed by segments of the European banking sector were brushed aside by claiming that the inclusion of the Foundational IRB ensured many European banks would be able to adopt IRB (although the ECB did express concern about the impact of the operational risk charge on smaller banks).[15]

The concerns of parts of the banking community notwithstanding, policy-makers at the BCBS continued on the path of IRB. Following the ECB, they argued that the menu of options (Standardized, Foundational, and Advanced IRB approaches) would suffice to cater to the needs of different types of banks. After extensive negotiations on the exact calibration of the three approaches, they were included in Pillar 1 of the Basel II capital accord.

Operational Risk

The second substantive issue arising from the consultative process was the inclusion of operational risk. Here the implications of ideological consensus among policymakers were most visible. Based on the underlying assumption that the new accord would provide a comprehensive, market-based measure of risk, public supervisors pushed for the inclusion of operational risk.[16] But the rigorous reasoning of supervisors was resisted by most private actors, who argued that they could deal with operational risk in the course of their normal

[12] Finnish Bankers' Association (2001). See the various responses to CP2 on the BCBS website.

[13] ECB May 2001, August 2003 (responses to CP2 and CP3).

[14] On the convergence of supervisory practices, the ECB explicitly states that the work of the BCBS will have a positive impact on corresponding work in the EU (ECB 2003: 5).

[15] 'The introduction of a simpler (foundation) methodology in the internal ratings-based (IRB) approach means in practice that many EU banks may be able to adopt it. Therefore, concerns that the EU banking system could be placed at a disadvantage with regard to the standardized approach, owing to the low number of rated non-financial counterparties in the EU, have now diminished' (ECB 2001: 1–2).

[16] Alternatively, one interview source hinted that the inclusion of operational risk in the accord was a backhander to European supervisors suspicious that IRB would lead to too low levels of capital.

business and that no specific regulatory capital charge was necessary. The issue seemed to pit public supervisors working from a 'theoretical' perspective against private banks keeping an eye on the bottom line.

Particularly in the European context, asset managers and insurance companies were concerned about the application of operational risk requirements. The European Asset Management Association responded to CP2:

> We are deeply concerned about the provisions of the proposed new Basel Capital Accord insofar as they relate to the asset management industry, in particular the provisions relating to a capital requirement for operational risk. . . . We believe that the proposal that internationally active banks should be required to hold a high level of regulatory capital to cover operational risk in their asset management subsidiaries is based on a misconception about the nature of the asset management business and its relationship to systemic risk. (European Asset Management Association 2001)

Similar concerns were voiced by the European Federation of Investment Funds and Companies, and various national associations and individual companies in investment management. As mentioned above, the ECB had also warned about the impact of the operational risk charge on small and medium-sized banks.

In the face of broad private sector opposition, the BCBS watered down its proposal for an operational risk charge, offering the possibility to use either a straightforward indicator, a standardized approach which offered banks more flexibility, or even an internal measurement of operational risk. As will be seen below, in CRD III the operational risk charge was further adjusted to the realities of Basel II application in the European Union (i.e. accommodating the asset manager's concerns).

SME Lending

The third major issue concerned lending to SMEs. The early proposals for Basel II hinted at possible negative effects on bank lending to SMEs, which was particularly salient in the EU. This was in large part due to the fact that most European SMEs were not rated, meaning they would incur the highest risk weighting; lending to them would be relatively expensive for banks. This became an especially hot topic in Germany, where national elections were underway. Several German SME associations (and even the ministers for the economy of two *Länder*) provided comments in the consultative process. On the national level, Chancellor Schröder intervened by stating that higher borrowing costs for the *Mittelstand* were unacceptable (*Financial Times*, 1 November 2001). The German opposition to external ratings was supported by other continental European countries and Japan, albeit less vocally. In December 2001, the BCBS announced further work on the draft accord to ensure that credit to SMEs was treated appropriately. As a compromise, it was decided not to give unrated SMEs the highest risk-weighting. The BCBS defended this compromise by arguing it would reduce the pro-cyclicality of the accord.

In sum, the negotiations for Basel II addressed a number of issues with particular salience for the European Union. These issues were brought to the table in the BCBS through direct lobbying of European banking associations and the interventions of EU member states. In the end, the IRB approaches were implemented, although adjustments were made to accommodate specific European concerns. The G10 governors approved the Basel II framework in June 2004. The next step was EU implementation.

The CRD Implementation of Basel II

Since the implementation of Basel I, the development and implementation of financial regulation in the EU had been transformed by the Lamfalussy report (see e.g. Quaglia 2008; Mügge 2010). After this rearrangement of policymaking on financial services regulation in the EU, the European Parliament (EP) emerged with increased co-decision powers. The European Central Bank was also a new player which had not existed when Basel I was implemented. Details of the directives were now hammered out in so-called Lamfalussy committees composed of national-level experts. This new set-up for European policymaking made the EP a magnet for lobbying on specific exceptions to the Basel rules.

EU member states had already agreed at the beginning of negotiations for Basel II that the accord would be implemented by amending the existing Banking and Capital Adequacy Directives into the Capital Requirements Directive (Christopoulos and Quaglia 2009: 184). From the consultative process it was clear that both the ECB and the Commission supported Basel II. The Commission issued a draft of the third Capital Adequacy Directive, passing the Basel II framework into European financial services law only one month after the publication of the accord.

The banking sector was closely involved in the negotiations at the European level, leading the European Banking Federation to commend the Commission for the unprecedented level of consultation (*Financial Times*, 15 July 2004). It simply provided another chance for private sector lobbying.[17] While a package of almost 600 amendments was tabled during discussions between the Commission, Council, and Parliament, these left the main philosophy and thrust of Basel II intact (Dierick et al. 2005). Many amendments aimed to address national idiosyncrasies, while the internationally active private sector lobbied to reduce national discretions—and thus to defeat such amendments.

A particularly contentious issue was the treatment of mortgage loans for real estate. This had already led to a rift in the BCBS between most continental

---

[17] Interview with private actor, Germany, 2008.

European countries and the more Anglo-Saxon oriented countries. Germany demanded a low risk weighting for commercial mortgages and the *Pfandbriefe* of mortgage banks, and was supported by France and Spain. Other BCBS members, notably the US, UK, and Italy, feared this would give German mortgage banks a competitive advantage. Since the BCBS could not overcome the divisions, the issue was addressed through the CRD; in the end, the EU gave real estate special treatment under the standardized approach. Given the importance of covered bonds in many European capital markets, these were also subject to a different risk weighting than foreseen in Basel II. ECB staff noted with regret: 'Since the most common form [of covered bond] (the German *Pfandbrief*) is well-known outside European capital markets, even a specific treatment under Basel II might have been desirable' (Dierick et al. 2005). European-level implementation could thus serve to iron out difficulties in BCBS negotiations.

Two other issues in the EU-level negotiations on the CRD showed how the goal of a common market influenced public actors' preferences. The first concerned supervisory disclosure, one of the ways through which the private sector hoped to reduce national discretions in the implementation of the CRD. The British Bankers' Association and European Banking Federation both lobbied for disclosure to increase peer pressure for convergence in the implementation of Basel II.[18] As mentioned above, the ECB supported this idea to further the aim of a common market for financial services. In the end, and in the spirit of market integration, the CRD subjected EU supervisors to a set of minimum requirements on the publication of rules and regulations, and sometimes limits their range of options in implementing Basel II.

The second issue was consolidated supervision (see Christopoulos and Quaglia 2009: 186–187), which had not been addressed in Basel II. In the view of the ECB and other European public actors, consolidated supervision would facilitate financial integration and lower compliance costs. This view was supported by internationally active banks, especially those from the UK and Germany, and converged with public actors' common market preferences. This confluence of preferences resulted in an enhanced role for the 'consolidating supervisor' in the CRD.

The CRD thus diverged from Basel II on several issues (see Dierick et al. 2005 for an overview), which in part can be traced to the underlying preference of public actors to level the competitive playing field in an integrated EU financial services market. The European Parliament and Council approved the CRD in the autumn of 2005. Both Basel II and the CRD included concepts that were not clearly defined, thus offering national authorities considerable leeway. It was up to the Committee of European Banking Supervisors to continue work on the convergence of concepts and the elimination of national deviations from the

---

[18] Interview with private actor, UK, 2008.

framework. In general, we may conclude that the main political struggle had taken place at the global level of the BCBS, whose standard was used to promote harmonization and market integration at the European level. But before Basel II could be fully implemented, the crisis knocked it off the rails. This led to the development of a third Basel accord, to which we now turn.

BANK CAPITAL ADEQUACY REGULATION AFTER THE CRISIS: BASEL III AND CRD IV

The global financial storm gathering pace in 2007 revealed the insufficiency of extant bank capital adequacy levels. The internal models of banks as well as external rating agencies spectacularly failed to assess the risks associated with complex securitized products, while the credit crunch following the collapse of Lehman Brothers underscored the importance of liquidity in the banking market.[19] Although the crisis originated in the US subprime mortgages market, it spread quickly across markets and continents. EU banks were not immune: many experienced liquidity or even solvency problems and required state support. It was clear to supervisors and banks alike that the global bank capital adequacy regime had to be strengthened.

The financial crisis had two important consequences for global policymaking.[20] First, the G20 emerged as the dominant policymaking forum. This was also reflected in the technical forums dealing with specific policy domains in global finance, which meant that membership of the BCBS was extended to all G20 members in June 2009. As significant steps towards Basel III had been taken by the time of this change, inclusion of the G20 members had little impact on the new accord's substance—though it will likely impact the future work of the BCBS. The second important change in the policymaking process was the temporary weakening of the global banking lobby. The political contestation around financial regulation increased with the need for state support.

The negotiation of 'enhancements' to Basel II began in the autumn of 2007. Both the chair of the BCBS (the Dutch governor Wellink) and former Federal Reserve president Alan Greenspan mounted a defence of the Basel II approach, including the importance of a level global competitive playing field. They were supported by the IIF, which cautioned against knee-jerk reactions from supervisors in the form of blanket capital increases but conceded that specific elements of Basel II warranted modification (such as liquidity risks) (*Financial*

---

[19] An interviewee involved in the BCBS noted that liquidity standards were identified as an issue for future work at the time of conclusion of Basel II (off-the-record interview, 2008).
[20] See Underhill and Blom (2012) for an analysis of the wider changes in the global financial architecture.

Times, 22 October 2007). However, with the crisis spreading and deepening in early 2008, Germany joined the calls of the Bank of Canada and the UK FSA for higher capital requirements and a more stringent application of Basel II. The German minister of finance even stated that if more stringent standards could not be achieved at the BCBS or European levels, Germany would implement them alone.

International momentum for more stringent capital requirements grew further when Bear Stearns collapsed. The USA joined the fray, calling for adjustments to off-balance sheet exposures and liquidity risks. The collapse of Lehman Brothers and the narrowly avoided global financial meltdown in September 2008 was the final straw. As the newly appointed FSA chair Lord Turner put it: a clean slate for capital adequacy standards was needed (*Financial Times*, 17 October 2008). The BCBS published a consultative paper outlining its 'enhancements' to Basel II in January 2009. These included liquidity risk provisions, the better modelling of securitizations, a stricter definition of capital, cyclically adjusted capital buffers, higher capital requirements for systemically relevant banks, and a gearing ratio. Shortly thereafter, it was acknowledged that this ambitious wish list would result in a 'Basel III capital accord.'[21]

As in the Basel II negotiations, there were issues of particular salience to European stakeholders. Three issues will be discussed below: (1) the timing and cumulative impact of regulations; (2) liquidity requirements; and (3) the inclusion of a leverage ratio.

Timing and Cumulative Impact of Regulations

When the BCBS published its first more extensive reforms in April 2008, the IIF signalled that changes would need to be prudent and proportional to actual risks.[22] The private sector warned of the negative macroeconomic impact of stringent capital requirements, especially in combination with the wider regulatory reforms then underway. This line of defence was central to private sector lobbying and was repeated in almost all private sector responses to the various consultative papers.[23] The international banking lobby used the weak economic environment to plead for a delayed phase-in of stringent Basel III requirements. They pointed to politicians' demands that banks contribute to funding the economic recovery, and claimed they would be unable to do so with the 'excessive' Basel III requirements (*Financial Times*, 12 April 2010).

This argument resonated with Eurozone supervisors, where the financial crisis had transformed into a sovereign debt crisis hampering economic recovery.

---

[21] Goldbach and Kerwer (2012) provide an overview of the changes under Basel III.
[22] Dallara (2008).
[23] See the BIS website for the consultative papers and the responses.

European supervisors (joined by their Japanese counterparts) were especially hesitant to phase out hybrid forms of capital which formed an important part of the capital of European banks (e.g. the German public banks). In the period running up to the September 2010 BCBS governors' meeting to finalize the accord, German banks made a last-ditch effort to further water down Basel III. Both the Bundersverband Deutscher Banken and the Bundesverband Offent-licher Banken Deutschlands (the private and public sector bank associations) warned of the negative effects of the proposed Basel III on the German econ-omy as banks would have to rebuild capital if hybrid capital was disallowed (*Financial Times*, 7 September 2010). Reflecting their dependence on bank funding, the French and German business federations echoed the warnings of the banking lobby (*Financial Times*, 15 June 2010).

The opposition was successful in paring down the most controversial aspects of Basel III. Given the uncertain economic conditions, supervisors were hesi-tant to push stringent regulations. Although the new accord includes an effec-tive tier one capital requirement of 7 per cent of risk-weighted assets, its phase-in is planned to last until 2018.

Liquidity Requirements

The crisis revealed liquidity to be a key channel of contagion, while banks were not required to hold buffers against liquidity risk. Such buffers were undeniably necessary, and negotiations to update provisions for liquidity risks in the BCBS had begun in the autumn of 2007. This resulted in a consultative document issued in June 2008. Compared to earlier consultations in the Basel II negotia-tions, this document yielded relatively few comments (30 in total), again mostly from private financial actors (about 80 per cent). With almost ironic timing, the BCBS issued the final '17 principles for sound liquidity risk management and supervision' in September 2008.

Liquidity risk became a prominent issue with the more extensive renegotia-tion of Basel II. The 'enhancements' to Basel II published in January 2009 included an explicit provision for liquidity risk and a detailed proposal for an 'International Framework for liquidity risk measurement, standards and mon-itoring' was put up for consultation in December 2009. Although there was little opposition to the principle of a liquidity requirement, private financial actors lobbied against a 'one-size-fits-all' approach. Furthermore, there were many proposals to include specific securities in the category of 'liquid assets'. For example, a number of continental European countries led by Denmark pushed for the inclusion of covered mortgage bonds under liquid assets.

In response to the push-back from private sector actors and supervisors from continental Europe, Basel III uses a broader definition of liquid assets than originally proposed to accommodate specific features of continental

European markets. The liquidity ratios will be phased in no earlier than 2015, and will be subject to an observation and review period to address any unintended consequences.

Leverage Ratio

One of the new elements in Basel III is the so-called leverage ratio (or gearing ratio). This measure, long in place in the USA, sets a capital requirement against the balance sheet total (without risk-weighting). This was contentious in Europe, where banks were unfamiliar with the practice. In the consultative process, American banks (especially the smaller ones) often welcomed the inclusion of a leverage ratio in Basel III.[24] But the response from European banks was completely different. In its response to the BCBS consultative papers of December 2009, BNP Paribas stated: 'except for its extreme (excessive...) simplicity, this indicator has no clear objective and justification; furthermore, it has proven failures or flawed definitions wherever it has been applied, in particular in the USA'.

In response to criticisms from especially the European financial sector, the leverage ratio will only be 'tested' until 2017. In other words, the precarious economic situation in Europe led public supervisors to give in to the demands of their private sector. This was certainly also related to the weak balance sheet of German and French banks, which would simply not be able to meet stringent capital requirements (Howarth and Quaglia 2013).

In sum, Basel III is presented as the first of the building blocks of a 'broad strategy' for a 'new approach' to the post-crisis financial system (BCBS 2010b). After Basel I and II had encouraged off-balance sheet activities and international integration, Basel III tried to mitigate some of the resulting risks. But with the BCBS remaining the main policymaking institution (although augmented by G20 supervisors halfway through the process), the general philosophy of Basel II—market-based capital requirements—was kept intact in Basel III. Market discipline and price signals remain central to the practice of banking supervision (see also Underhill and Blom 2012). This is hardly surprising when one considers that the BCBS had spent years building consensus on the superiority of market-based approaches in a process of groupthink and skewed argument pools. Moreover, in light of the weak balance sheets of many banks and the on-going economic crisis in the Eurozone, the BCBS toned down many of its

[24] For example, the response of Bank of America: 'We support a globally consistent backstop leverage ratio as a component in Pillar 1 in the interest of the stability of the sector and a level playing field across jurisdictions. As a backstop measure to control leverage, the ratio should be designed to ensure it does not undermine the risk-based capital framework' (BofA, 16 April 2010).

earlier stringent proposals and/or delayed their implementation. This process continued in the implementation of Basel III in the EU.

Basel III Implementation Through CRD IV

While Basel III was concluded remarkably quickly compared to Basel II, the accord's implementation at the European level offered renewed opportunities for contestation. Though the Commission was unsuccessful in coordinating the positions of European members in the BCBS negotiations, it was in the driver's seat for European-level implementation (Quaglia 2012a: 177).

The strained economic environment led some (notably German) supervisors, who traditionally favoured stringent standards, to plead for laxity. The plight of continental European banks and economies thus led to the less stringent implementation of some of the Basel compromises in CRD IV. As with the implementation of Basel II, this was in part the consequence of the application of CRD IV to all banks. For example, the more stringent definition of capital in Basel III was widened to include forms of capital used by cooperative banks (Quaglia 2012a: 179).

But even in the face of financial crisis, European public actors did not forget the goal of market integration. An important part of Basel III will be transposed through a 'regulation'—meaning it will apply directly in member states. This will limit the scope for the national idiosyncrasies that emerged under CRD III. Another Commission proposal hinted at setting Basel III norms as an absolute rather than a minimum standard (as the BCBS sees it). Such 'maximum harmonization' would certainly level the playing field in the EU. It would also mean that countries with large banking sectors can no longer set additional capital requirements (e.g. the traditional 'gold plating' of the UK). In other words, risks for small countries with large banking sectors would increase, which would be a curious outcome. Maximum harmonization was supported by some banks but was defeated in the European Parliament.

CONCLUSION

This chapter has analysed the policymaking process on bank capital adequacy standards in the Basel Committee on Banking Supervision and its interaction with European banking regulation. It showed how European-level policymaking functions as an intermediating variable influencing the preferences of especially public actors in BCBS negotiations. Consensus on the desirability of a 'level playing field' and an 'integrated common market' translated into the application of the Basel capital accords to all European banks, even though segments of the private financial sector opposed this measure. In other words, public actors had discretionary room for manoeuvre, but stayed within the confines of a normative consensus in favour of market-based governance mechanisms—formed in an exclusionary policy community in which internationalized banks had significant influence.

Public policymakers' 'theoretical' understandings of how markets should function can lead to preferences that counterbalance or complement more narrowly self-interested private actor preferences (e.g. the inclusion of operational risk in Basel II). This effect was especially important at the European level, where furthering the common market was an important consideration for many public policymakers when discussing the Basel capital accords and their related EU directives. This is, for example, reflected in the (fortunately defeated) Commission proposal to set the Basel capital requirements as a maximum standard in the EU, instead of the minimum standard intended by the BCBS. Although bank capital adequacy standards at the global and European levels are not a one-on-one reflection of the 'capture' of public regulators, it is a matter of serious doubt whether public interests have received sufficient consideration. As the world has once again experienced the devastating effects financial instability can bring, this is a worrying conclusion—the more so in light of the continuing softening of Basel III proposals in their implementation under pressure from private sector lobbying.

4

Securities and Derivatives Markets

DANIEL MÜGGE[1]

INTRODUCTION

This chapter traces how securities regulation in Europe and the rest of the world, including at the global level, have co-evolved over the past decades. Compared to banking, global agreements in the securities sector have been less consequential for national and European regulation (Singer 2007). As securities markets on the European continent matured over the 1990s, first national authorities and then the EU itself unilaterally oriented their regulatory reforms to standing US practices (for example, in the field of insider trading). Since the early 2000s, rule adaptation across the Atlantic has become more of a mutual affair but the United States has continued to lead. Although the financial crisis added new urgency to cross-border regulatory reforms, the 'global' context that really mattered to rule evolution in the EU remained reforms in the USA. Given the enormous controversies surrounding, for example, credit derivatives, it is remarkable how easily consensus between Brussels and Washington was reached on the way forward for derivatives markets.

This contrast with the banking sector is easily explained: as host to the most prominent securities markets, the USA has had little incentive to internationalize its own securities markets rules. In banking, competitive and prudential considerations argued in favour of an agreement between at least the leading financial centres (Oatley and Nabors 1998). But for securities markets, it mattered relatively little to the USA what kinds and level of prudential rules other jurisdictions adopted, such that it could leave it to other countries to adapt their rules unilaterally should they so desire. This dynamic only changed once the EU became a sufficiently relevant market, speaking with a single (Brussels) voice. The USA then started to make concessions in order to sustain unimpeded market access for US firms in Europe.

[1] I am grateful to Tim Celik and Matthias Thieman for very valuable research assistance.

Securities are commonly divided into stocks (equity), bonds (debt/credit), and derivatives. While bond markets constitute a large part of international capital movements, their regulation has proven relatively uncontroversial and has attracted scant cross-border regulatory attention.[2] Hence this chapter concentrates on the two remaining pillars of securities markets: equities and derivatives. Up until the financial crisis that began in 2007, most regulatory efforts focused on share trading, with the implications of new rules for on-exchange derivative trading almost a corollary. But since the crisis, stock trading has practically been a non-issue in public debate, whereas derivatives—and a strong and coherent global rule-set to govern them—have been one of the key issues on the international reform agenda.

The structure of this chapter mirrors this two-step process. Its first part traces how the strengthening of the EU in securities regulation, first within EU member states and then at the supranational level, affected global (non-)agreement on rules, and how the continued prominence of the USA in global capital markets informed the diffusion of US (inspired) regulation to the European continent. In a nutshell, EU capital market liberalization and reforms since the 1990s have been inspired by the American experience; policy often emulated that of the USA. Conflicts or stand-offs, such as those in the Basel Committee (see Blom, this volume) or over accounting standards (see Stellinga, this volume), were rare. Fundamental disagreements rarely obstructed regulatory cooperation. Derivatives played a minor role, not least because the USA was, up until the crisis, firmly committed to not expanding the regulation of derivatives, in particular those negotiated 'over the counter' (OTC derivatives).

The second part of this chapter chronicles and analyses what has happened since the crisis, when derivatives suddenly topped the agenda. Given the gravity of the crisis and the depth of the problems evidenced in these markets, the lack of discord between the EU and USA in their approach to re-regulating derivatives markets is surprising. Complex derivatives in particular had traditionally played a much more modest role on the European continent than on Wall Street or in the City of London (Partnoy 2002a; Das 2006). Derivatives were now portrayed as one of the villains of the crisis and an area requiring fundamental overhaul. Even before the 2009 summit in Pittsburgh, which outlined the official G20 approach, the two jurisdictions—in the absence of a strong global body to coordinate efforts such as the Basel Committee in banking—had de facto agreed on the angle of future reforms.

Nevertheless, some friction was difficult to avoid. The crisis starkly illustrated that deficient regulatory and supervisory arrangements have fiscal

---

[2] Bonds are mostly traded directly between professional investors, not on stock exchange-like platforms. As issuers generally have an interest in attracting as wide a pool of potential investors as possible, they have an intrinsic motivation to facilitate cross-border business. The only recognizable instance of a link between European regulation and global initiatives is the Prospectus Directive (2003/71/EC), modelled on IOSCO templates (Casey and Lannoo 2005).

consequences. Public authorities therefore demanded control over financial operations that could lead to costs for their taxpayers or more diffuse damage to their economies. For cross-border transactions, and certainly those that involve parties outside the EU, this entailed an extraterritorial application of securities rules that may prove difficult to square with earlier, more permissive arrangements that focused on the mutual recognition of regulatory regimes. Even if there was remarkable agreement on the direction of financial reform in this domain, the fiscal strings that are now visibly attached to financial regulation imply a stronger territorial grounding of regulation than had prevailed prior to the crisis. Given the prominence of derivatives in contemporary financial markets, the final section of this chapter will also concentrate largely on derivatives.

A EUROPEAN DEAL THWARTS GLOBAL AGREEMENT

International initiatives in the field of securities regulation go back to the 1970s (Porter 1993). The cross-border trading of equities was then still relatively limited and the bourses of the USA and the UK enjoyed clear pre-eminence worldwide. In continental Europe and East Asia (with the exception of Hong Kong and later Japan), equities markets were hardly developed, and where they existed, they were dominated by national corporate insiders, often non-financial corporations. Given the underdevelopment of stock markets in many jurisdictions around the world, two common drivers of global harmonization attempts—the fear of systemic disruption through cross-border spillovers and the hope of ironing out regulatory differences to ease cross-border market access—hardly mattered. The earliest relevant agreements, housed in the Inter-American Association of Securities Commissions and Similar Organizations (founded in 1974), were first bilateral and later multilateral Memoranda of Understanding on information exchange between securities commissions (i.e. stock market regulators), largely to aid the USA in attempts to detect and prosecute securities fraud.

As membership grew, the association was rechristened in 1983 as the International Organization of Securities Commissions (IOSCO). IOSCO long had the reputation of a talk-shop, not least because its 'hard' accomplishments compared unfavourably with its banking twin, the Basel Committee on Banking Supervision, which produced the Basel concordat in 1975 and the first Basel capital accord in 1988 (see Blom, this volume). Until the second half of the 1980s, cross-border influence in securities market regulation remained relatively limited (see Singer 2007: 67ff).

Within the European Community, there were likewise few attempts to coordinate the regulation of securities markets until the mid-1980s, when it embarked on the single market programme (Underhill 1997a; Steil 1993). Financial markets, including the market for investment services (as it was then conceived), were clearly on the to-do lists of member states in the run-up to the single market, meant to be operational by 1992. But whereas a basic agreement for banking had been hammered out by 1989 (the Second Banking Coordinating Directive, 2BCD), an agreement for securities proved more difficult (Brown 1997; Mügge 2010). The 2BCD basically transposed the first Basel agreement into a directive, which was then adopted by member states. For securities, the absence of a global template complicated intra-European agreement. The basic problem was similar to that in banking: the competitive playing field had to be levelled before allowing foreign firms into domestic markets. In concrete terms, this meant that capital charges against assets had to be levelled, too.

The 2BCD, concluded in 1989 after less than two years of negotiations, had serious implications for competition in investment services.[3] It applied the mutual recognition approach—which had become central to the construction of the single market (Egan 2001)—to credit institutions. From the envisaged implementation date, 1993, a banking licence issued by an EU member state would function as an EU-wide 'single passport', allowing financial institutions to carry out functions they performed at home throughout the EU. The resulting directive gave German and French universal banks the right to engage in just about anything except insurance on a pan-European scale (Underhill 1997a). London investment banks had received no such licence through the 2BCD and now felt the urgent need to 'level the playing field' against the universal banks, which could use their banking assets as buffers against volatile and risky operations in securities markets.

While EU member states were busy negotiating provisions for the single market, no less than four other international forums were drafting functional rules: IOSCO; the so-called Barnes Committee of the Basel Committee on Banking Supervision; the so-called Hexagonal talks between the UK, the US, and Japan; and a European securities regulators' group convening independently of the EU single market talks (Waters and Kellaway 1990; Lee 1992). Although EU negotiations were embedded in global developments, the sense of urgency in the two arenas differed greatly. In the European context, negotiating common capital adequacy rules (eventually codified in the Capital Adequacy Directive, CAD) was a sine qua non for issuing pan-European 'passports' to securities firms (through the eventual Investment Services Directive, ISD), including to firms from the USA which would be 'grandfathered' into the new system.[4] Such a passport, in turn, was a top priority for firms operating from the UK once the continental universal banks had gained unrestricted access to the City through the 2BCD without any reciprocal provisions.

---

[3] Council Directive 89/646/EEC.
[4] The CAD is Council Directive 93/6/EEC; the ISD is Council Directive 93/22/EEC.

This link between common minimum standards and mutual market access was absent at the global level (in IOSCO and the Barnes Committee). In terms of market access, negotiating capital adequacy rules is a zero-sum game: some players gain while others lose. With the additional transaction costs it would entail (for negotiating, implementing, and monitoring), and without mechanisms for coercion, agreement appeared unlikely. In the case of capital adequacy standards for banking (Basel), there was still the 'public, common good' of allegedly greater systemic stability (Kapstein 1992). A competitively neutral regime that had something for everybody through higher system stability thus created a theoretical win-set (also Singer 2007). Even then, it took arm-twisting by the US and the UK to force others into agreement (Oatley and Nabors 1998).

According to the wisdom of the day, such a 'systemic stability' incentive was considerably smaller in securities markets; the day that the Lehman Brothers collapse in 2008 was to prove otherwise still remained in the distant future. While policymakers recognized that securities firms caught in falling markets with illiquid positions could falter, any impact—compared to bank failures—was thought manageable. The 1987 stock market crash had led to the failure of some securities firms, most prominently Tuffier & Associés and Drexel Burnham Lambert. But wider effects had been limited (Bush 1990; Graham 1990). Though following the Basel example in securities was bound to be an uphill struggle, in 1989 IOSCO's most powerful body—the Technical Committee, which brings together securities regulators from the core global markets—tabled a report on 'Capital Adequacy Standards for Securities Firms' at IOSCO's annual conference (Filipovic 1997). A deal fell through, however, because participants could not agree to what extent subordinated debt should count as part of capital reserves (Filipovic 1997: 183). The issue proved so contentious that the conference ended in failure; in the three years that followed, IOSCO made little headway.

IOSCO negotiations were reinvigorated in 1992 but stalled once again as the potential EU deal gained clearer contours. In particular, the SEC grew sceptical as the momentum at the European level excluded it—and the interests it represented—from the discussions. When Great Britain acceded to the EU presidency in July 1992, she was determined to end the standstill and open continental securities markets for City-based firms. UK negotiators managed to rally support for a common position on the CAD among all Ecofin members by November. Now that the EU countries had locked themselves in through joint agreement, the SEC effectively withdrew support for the IOSCO–BCBS initiative (Singer 2007; Corrigan 1992). The lock-in had decreased the EU's win-set to such an extent that compromise in global negotiations was now impossible. Indeed, less than half a year later—tellingly coinciding with the official adoption of the CAD in Brussels—IOSCO's attempts to reach a capital adequacy compromise were formally abandoned (Bacon 1993; Waters 1993). With the CAD in place, the second leg of the EU securities regime—the ISD—could also be agreed.

In this first episode of simultaneous European and global rule-making, we find a clear trade-off between the two. The perceived need to unlock European securities markets in the context of the single market programme prevented a global deal on capital adequacy for securities trading. In contrast to the experience in many other fields (Simmons 2001), the USA was unable to impose its preferences on other parties because intra-European negotiations had made a deal imperative for the UK. Reminiscent of some of the dynamics described in this book's other chapters on more recent developments, EU regional integration and the political dynamics it generated prevented global agreement in line with US preferences. European integration was a drag on global rules, rather than one of its pillars.

The Global Integration of Securities Markets Moves European Rules Closer to American Ones

Although a global agreement on capital standards for securities trading was thus prevented, the growth of securities markets in continental Europe and their growing cross-border integration meant that regulation in Europe was increasingly adapted to the example set by the USA. The key issue was the level of market regulation necessary for US authorities to recognize a market as properly regulated and hence allow it to offer trading services to US clients. In the early 1990s, this link proved a crucial avenue for insider trading regulation to penetrate the continent. In particular, German recalcitrance to move on this issue (which had lasted for years) was broken when banks began fearing the reputational damage Frankfurt could suffer from continued embarrassing discussions with US authorities (McCahery 1997). For example, when the Deutsche Terminbörse, the German derivatives exchange, wanted to set up trading screens outside Germany, many foreign authorities expressed doubts about the quality of German regulation (Lütz 2002). As elsewhere in Europe, there was a strong business case to adopt 'state of the art' securities regulation— meaning US-style standards—to attract international business.

The attractiveness of Wall Street for issuers also meant that many of them 'voluntarily' started applying US rules to their own operations. To avoid a regulatory double burden, they pushed securities regulators in their home jurisdictions to adapt their rules to avoid mismatches or simply declare them 'equivalent' to US rules. By the early 2000s, more than 170 European firms, mostly from the UK, the Netherlands, and France, were registered with the SEC for listings, creating pressure for regulatory convergence (Lanois 2007). While US securities law always had extraterritorial reach, serious frictions began to emerge when the USA adopted the Sarbanes–Oxley Act in the wake of the Enron and Worldcom scandals, which also applied to the foreign issuers of securities in the USA. As its key elements do not concern trading but auditing and corporate governance, its substantive impact will not be treated here (Lanois 2007; see also Dewing and Russell, this volume). But it made the New York Stock Exchange and the NASDAQ less attractive compared to, for example, the London Stock Exchange, which has since become the first choice for Russian or Chinese issuers wishing to list on a 'Western' bourse. Sarb–Ox limited the regulatory magnetism of the USA, which until the early 2000s had seemed the natural centre of gravity (Simmons 2001; Posner 2009).

The growing relative weight of the EU in global finance did not generate a strong international regime comparable to the Basel accord. But it did mean that what had previously been one-way traffic—with the US imposing (relatively at will) its own rules on other jurisdictions—became more a game of mutual adaptation. The EU in this period emerged as a more interesting marketplace as the business potential of continental securities markets became clear (at least as seen through pre-crisis eyes). In 2004, the EU replaced the ISD with the Markets in Financial Instruments Directive (MiFID), with two key effects. It harmonized many more rules than the mutual recognition-based ISD, such that the post-MiFID European Union constituted much more of a regulatory block than had previously been the case (Posner 2009). The MiFID also entailed much more comprehensive coverage of securities markets, creating an integrated European regime from which there were few exceptions (Casey and Lannoo 2009). The MiFID further coincided with the establishment of the Committee of European Securities Regulators (CESR) (Mügge 2010), which duly entered negotiations with the US derivatives regulator—the Commodities Futures Trading Commission (CFCT)—about facilitating transatlantic market access (CFCT 2005).

In the field of securities trading, negotiations concerned not only the most prominent conflict: the use of International Accounting Standards (see Stellinga, this volume). In the early 2000s, the USA also made concessions to EU demands on the conditions under which EU securities exchanges could mount trading screens in the US, thus giving US traders direct access to European markets (Posner 2009: 671f), and on the ease with which European companies could delist from US stock exchanges to escape onerous Sarb–Ox rules. Frequently, these rule adaptions facilitated transatlantic market access without fundamentally changing regulation in the domestic jurisdiction. For example, the EU Financial Conglomerates Directive required non-European financial firms operating in the EU to be supervised on a consolidated basis—a requirement that many US investment banks would not have passed at the time (Posner 2009: 672f).[5] The SEC therefore introduced a voluntary regime for pro forma consolidated supervision that did not, however, entail substantive compliance with what EU authorities had intended (Mügge 2011c). Whether meaningful or not, recognition of the 'equivalence' of rules in other jurisdictions (see Ferran, this volume) became in the years

---

[5] Council Directive 2002/87/EC.

before the financial crisis the instrument of choice to facilitate cross-border market access without resorting to fully fledged rule harmonization.

A Global Regime for Derivatives

Derivatives did not play a particularly important role in cross-border arrangements and debate until the second half of the 1990s. In the USA, the large-scale trading of financial derivatives began on the commodity exchanges of Chicago in the 1970s, buttressed by an intellectual climate conducive to financial innovation (MacKenzie 2006) and exchange rate volatility following the disintegration of the Bretton Woods fixed exchange rate regime.

Exchange-traded derivatives appeared in Europe in the 1980s: at the London International Financial Futures and Options Exchange (LIFFE) in 1982, the Paris MATIF in 1986, OFFEX in Switzerland in 1988, and the Deutsche Terminbörse in 1990. While LIFFE's remit was broader, the continental exchanges focused on derivatives with a clear domestic link: the tradable debt of domestic issuers (including different levels of government), equities, interest rates, and local currency. LIFFE's attempted inroads into the trading of Bund futures, for example, were short-lived (Mügge 2010: 90f). Competition between exchanges remained limited, obviating the need to agree on global rules to manage it. The standardization of contracts—essential to limit transaction costs in OTC derivatives dealings—had been incrementally furthered by the International Swaps and Derivatives Association (ISDA) since the mid-1980s and was enshrined in the ISDA Master Agreement, the de facto industry standard for derivatives (Partnoy 2002b).

Though most major financial centres had their own derivatives exchange by 1990, the drive to develop international standards remained limited. As the derivatives business boomed over the next decade, the USA moved away from rather than towards tight regulation. To the extent that the USA had long functioned as the global standards setter, its firm anti-regulation stance encouraged a permissive environment in Europe; it let it be known that any European push towards more regulation would stand no chance of swaying the world's most important financial market. US firms moreover played leading roles in the derivatives business in Europe and the City of London in particular; neither from the inside nor the outside was there much private sector pressure.

The financial scandals in which derivatives had been implicated since the late 1980s (Partnoy 2002a) were insufficient to sway opinion in the US Treasury and US Fed. Opponents of tight regulation could point to a G30 report containing a series of transnationally applicable but locally non-binding principles (Tsingou 2003). The private sector Derivatives Policy Group (DPG), charged with developing rules for the sector, fended off public intervention (Faerman, McCaffrey, and van Slyke 2001). The DPG also provided a template for dealing—through similar private initiative—with hedge funds and counterparty risk in the wake of the LTCM collapse in 1998 (Faerman et al. 2001: 384). Despite much public discussion, Alan Greenspan, SEC chairman Arthur Levitt, and Robert Rubin, at the time Clinton's secretary of the treasury, fiercely opposed the more intrusive regulation of derivatives markets.

To cement this policy stance, Congress passed the Commodities Futures Modernization Act (CFMA) in 2000, removing oversight for OTC derivatives from the Commodity Futures Trading Commission (CFTC) for good. The UK, equally interested in benefiting from the seemingly unstoppable rise of OTC derivatives, passed a similar law in the same year. The Financial Markets and Services Act exempted most OTC derivatives trading from oversight (Latysheva 2011: 481); though it included limits on which institutions could trade in complex products, it imposed no serious restrictions on the growth of derivatives markets between eligible parties. Between the passage of these laws in the US and the UK and the onset of the crisis, the wholesale regulation of OTC derivatives never again became an issue. In 2001 the ECB Governing Council tabled a proposal for regulating central counterparties in OTC derivatives trading; the idea was picked up again by the Council for Payment and Settlement Systems in 2007. But each time, no regulatory action followed (Latysheva 2011).

THE CRISIS AND ITS EFFECTS

Helleiner and Pagliari (2010) have traced the first phase of regulatory responses in the field of derivatives to the demise of first Bear Stearns (March 2008), then Lehman Brothers (September 2008), and finally the government bail-out of American International Group (AIG), a key dealer of the credit default swaps (CDS) widely identified as culprits in the crisis. Given the pre-crisis hostility of especially US and UK financial institutions and public authorities to the public regulation of OTC derivatives, it is remarkable how smoothly the US and the EU converged on a largely compatible set of rules. As will be discussed below, several areas of mismatch remain, and in light of the extraterritorial effects of regulation on both sides of the Atlantic, it is unclear whether ironing them out completely is possible. Nevertheless, from the perspective of avoiding serious fragmentation in global financial markets, the crafting of two rule-sets that, in the end, are unlikely to generate major frictions between the two jurisdictions must count as a major achievement.

Getting to the Pittsburgh G20 Agreement

In the aftermath of the Lehman Brothers collapse, two features of unregulated OTC and credit derivatives markets immediately caught the eye of many observers: (1) markets were opaque, both to public authorities and market participants; and (2) the high volume of bilateral contracts drastically increased the potential for unanticipated domino effects. These observations have sub-sequently framed international reform efforts. Other criticisms—such as questions about the social usefulness of derivatives or the degree to which they constituted an unchecked expansion of credit that fuelled massive asset bubbles—spawned no follow-up in international regulatory efforts, a point to which we will return below.

As Helleiner and Pagliari (2010: 82) document, following the Lehman collapse the Financial Stability Forum advocated the use of central counter-parties (CCPs) in the trading of CDS. This was endorsed at the G20 summit in Washington in November 2008; the communiqué urged market participants to use multilateral trading platforms and to enhance market transparency. At this stage, proposals were limited to CDS rather than credit derivatives or OTC derivatives more broadly. And in the absence of firm agreements, G20 efforts were largely pleas to market participants rather than commitments to implement binding rules.

The G20 communiqué nevertheless foreshadowed the approach eventually implemented on both sides of the Atlantic, only then in binding form and more comprehensive in coverage. In February 2009, the De Larosière Report, com-missioned by the EU to study the way forward in financial regulation and gov-ernance, recommended that OTC derivatives be simplified and standardized and that at least one clearing house for CDS in Europe be introduced, the use of which would become mandatory (High-Level Group on Financial Supervision in the EU 2009). Two weeks after the publication of this report, a Commission communication on derivatives trading reiterated this policy line.[6] A mere three months later, the US Treasury published a lengthy communication ('Financial Regulatory Reform', 17 June 2009) that summarized the approach eventually chosen on both sides of the Atlantic: increase transparency through reporting requirements, standardize derivatives where possible (but leave room for OTC trading where necessary), and introduce CCPs. Three weeks later, the Euro-pean Commission followed with a more detailed communication containing analysis of the risks in derivatives markets, much in line with the American one and similar in its suggestions. By this time, both American and European authorities had effectively converged on the way forward in the regulation of derivatives. The approach found its way into the final communiqué of the G20 leaders in Pittsburgh in November 2009:

> All standardized OTC derivative contracts should be traded on exchanges or electronic trading platforms, where appropriate, and cleared through central counterparties by end-2012 at the latest. OTC derivative contracts should be re-ported to trade repositories. Non-centrally cleared contracts should be subject to higher capital requirements.

---

[6] The link to this report is in the original document, which in turn reflects on the De Larosière Report, published on 25 February 2009.

In the USA, these provisions were formalized in the Dodd–Frank Wall Street Reform and Consumer Protection Act (DFA, passed in July 2010); in Europe, they reappeared in the 2010 Commission proposal for a derivatives regulation (COM [2010] 484/5) which eventually became the European Market Infrastructure Regulation (EMIR, finally published in July 2012).[7] The DFA left much of the detail to be decided and implemented by the SEC and the Commodities Futures Trading Commission. These two agencies in turn coordinated intensively with European authorities on the details of how the G20 guidelines were to be implemented. CFTC Commissioner Bart Chilton reported that there were frequent staff contacts, including face-to-face meetings, between the CFTC and the Commission and ESMA.[8] In the words of Deputy Assistant Secretary Mark Sobel:

> The Dodd–Frank Act's derivatives provisions comport with G-20 and FSB principles and International Organization of Securities Commissioners (IOSCO) work. The debates we are having in the United States *strikingly resemble* those now faced in the EU under the European Market Infrastructure Regulation (EMIR). International consistency on OTC derivatives is critical to avoid gaps, and the United States and the European Commission are working hand-in-glove on a daily basis in this area.[9] (emphasis added)

At the time of writing, many of the implementing details—including the most contentious and crucial ones—remain to be decided.

While the DFA and EMIR share the same thrust, and focus on similar policy measures, they do not completely overlap. In some respects, this lack of overlap is simply due to legislative history in the two jurisdictions. The MiFID already contained provisions, particularly on the execution of trades and the duties of derivatives dealers vis-à-vis their clients, that did not exist in US legislation and are therefore part of the DFA but not included in EMIR.[10] In Europe these rules have been updated in the revised version of the MiFID (MiFID II and the accompanying regulation, MiFIR). MiFID II also covers the right of competent

---

[7] Regulation (EU) 648/2012.

[8] CFTC Commissioner Bart Chilton's testimony before the US House of Representatives Committee on Agriculture General Farm Commodities and Risk Management Subcommittee, 25 May 2011.

[9] Speech at the AIMA Policy and Regulatory Forum 2011.

[10] 'MiFID currently applies only to entities established in the EU. It does not provide for a harmonized approach across the EU to non-EU entities. The original European Commission proposal for MiFID2 and MiFIR would have harmonized the treatment of non-EU entities dealing with EU counterparties, restricting dealings except where equivalence and reciprocity requirements are met and in some circumstances requiring the non-EU entity to operate through a branch (but allowing a qualifying firm with a branch a form of "passport" to provide services across the EU). However, the Presidency compromise text makes significant changes. In particular, Member States would largely be able to continue their current treatment of non-EU entities, except that non-EU entities would be required to establish a branch to deal with retail clients.' Clifford Chance (2012: 18).

authorities to learn more about the derivatives positions that entities hold and, should it be deemed necessary, to demand that these positions be adapted (Willey and Reynolds 2011). In light of past concerns that trading in commodity derivatives may have exacerbated, or even caused, volatility and spikes in energy and food prices, this provision constitutes one of the more drastic instruments that regulatory reforms have bestowed on supervisors. In general, the MiFID review has moved EU securities trading rules closer to US rules. The main differences that remain often stem from different legislative histories (the separation of the MiFID II and EMIR in the EU), institutional legacies (the separation of the CFTC and the SEC in the US), or implementation provisions (in the EU, national authorities are by and large responsible for the implementation of directives and regulations).[11]

The Extraterritorial Application of Derivatives Rules

Even though the rules adopted in the USA and the EU coincide to a remarkable degree, they still have had the potential to generate friction and market fragmentation as both the DFA and the EMIR contain provisions that apply extraterritorially. In a nutshell, both rule-sets apply to derivatives transactions that involve at least one domestic party, or when the transaction has a 'direct and significant connection with activities or effect on commerce in the US' (DFA), or a 'direct, substantial and foreseeable effect within the EU' (EMIR).[12] Both sets of legislation contain the possibility of granting foreign rule-sets equivalent status, and the CFTC and European Commission agreed in July 2013 that they would accept each other's rules as equivalent, such that transatlantic dealing will not be disrupted. In the wake of the agreement, rules set and enforced by Japanese authorities were also granted this status, even if the political negotiations had concentrated on the transatlantic axis.

Considering the contemporary landscape of global derivatives regulation and the EU's place in it, three features are particularly remarkable. First, the discussion about regulatory reforms has for all intents and purposes been one between the EU and the USA. As they are the world's two largest markets for derivatives, this may not be surprising. But even when other financial powers enter the picture, for example, in the context of the G20, there is little evidence that their perspectives have any lasting influence on regulatory debates or on US or EU rules. Global derivatives re-regulation, in short, is a transatlantic affair. Second, and stemming from the above, international organizations such as IOSCO and the Financial Stability Forum (later the Financial Stability

---

[11] In the context of the MiFID review, the Commission has prepared a useful and comprehensive overview comparison of US and EU rules, with the overall conclusion that the overlaps are more noteworthy than the differences (EC 2011i: 330ff).

[12] EMIR, Article 4(a)(iv) and (v). Shearman & Sterling (2012).

Board) have served as forums for discussion and technical coordination. In contrast to what repeatedly happened in the Basel Committee or in IOSCO around 1990, there is no evidence that the EU and the USA at any point 'bargained' about derivatives rules in any narrow sense; what took place appeared as the coordination and adaptation of domestic rules. The guidance and commitments adopted by the G20 and IOSCO are thus better understood as epiphenomenal to EU–USA understandings than as precursors to rules adopted in either jurisdiction.[13] Third, the extraterritorial applicability of derivatives trading rules means that it will be increasingly difficult to create financial centres outside either the USA or the EU that serve clients around the world; in effect, EMIR and the DFA solidify the position of London and New York as global financial centres.

CONCLUSION

The trajectory of EU securities market regulation in the global context unfolded in three phases. The attempt in the late 1980s to create a global regime for securities trading under the auspices of IOSCO, similar to the Basel accord, ran aground as the UK opted for a European deal to unlock the single market in securities trading. Though securities markets lacked an institutionalized global rule-set like the Basel accord—as a reference point for future rules—the successful opening of the European market to cross-border securities trading did set the EU on a trajectory of financial development in which it adapted its rules to the US example, first by individual member states, later through EU-level regulation. With entrenched UK and US opposition to the tight regulation of (particularly OTC) derivatives, the EU followed the USA in its lenience towards credit derivatives, later seen as one of the seedbeds of the financial crisis.

Since the collapse of Bear Stearns and Lehman Brothers in 2008, the USA and the EU have embarked on strikingly similar trajectories of regulatory reform for derivatives. Both have eschewed more radical ideas—such as outlawing particular types of derivatives—and have instead focused on making markets work. In the bigger scheme of things, the differences between the US and EU regimes are limited. If there nevertheless remains a sense of fragmentation, it comes from elsewhere: the realization on both sides of the Atlantic that taxpayers are on the hook when things go awry. This means that public

---

[13] One exception to this point concerns margin and capital requirements for uncleared derivatives, not least because those rules impinge directly on the work of the Basel Committee. Regulators on both sides of the Atlantic have temporarily halted work on this issue to allow a BCBS–IOSCO consultation to propose a common standard. Clifford Chance (2012).

authorities desire greater control over financial markets, resulting in rules with extraterritorial implications, the tying of derivatives trading to financial system supervision, and the re-territorialization of financial service provision. If recent experience is any guide to the future, we should—for better or worse— expect no major reversals but continuing efforts to iron out the frictions generated by the extraterritorial application of domestic rules. That is, at least, until the next crisis hits.

5

Insurance

LUCIA QUAGLIA[1]

INTRODUCTION

Insurance is a bit of a Cinderella among financial services and is often not considered a financial service in the strict sense.[2] As the insurance sector weathered the global financial crisis quite well, there were no major reforms of insurance regulation either in the EU or internationally following the crisis. The only notable exception was the American insurer AIG, which experienced serious financial difficulties and needed to be rescued by the US government due to the risky investment activities of its London-based subsidiary.

This chapter analyses the EU and international regulation of insurance, addressing two key questions posed in the volume's introduction. How have European and global rules influenced each other up to the present day? Which factors inform the global influence of European regulatory efforts and the relevance of global initiatives for European rules?

Insurance is one of the few financial services where the EU was able to influence the making of international rules. The reform of insurance regulation in the EU in the 2000s enabled it to project a unified position in the main international regulatory forum for insurers. EU influence in this forum was augmented by the weak and fragmented position of the USA, where regulating insurance is a state and not a federal competence. In the EU, the reform of

[1] Lucia Quaglia wishes to acknowledge financial support from the European Research Council (204,398 FINGOVEU), the British Academy, and the Leverhulme Trust (SG120191). Research for this paper was undertaken while she was visiting fellow at the Max Planck Institute, the EUI, and the Hanse Wissenschaftskolleg. This chapter builds on material from L. Quaglia (forthcoming, 2014), *The European Union and Global Financial Regulation* (Oxford University Press).

[2] Regulation of insurance in many countries was until recently the responsibility of the social affairs or industry ministries, not the treasury or finance ministries generally responsible for financial services.

insurance regulation was possible due to the agreement of the large member states—home to reinsurers and large insurance groups which benefited from EU legislation passed in the mid-2000s.

INTERNATIONAL INSURANCE REGULATION

The main international regulatory forum for insurance is the International Association of Insurance Supervisors (IAIS). Established in 1994, it has a small secretariat hosted by the Bank for International Settlements (BIS). The IAIS has members from over 190 jurisdictions, of which 56 jurisdictions are in the US, which are represented by the state regulators, as well as the National Association of Insurance Commissioners (NAIC). This is because, unlike securities and banking, insurance in the USA is entirely a state competence; there is no federal regulator able to represent the country in international forums. The NAIC, which is not a federal regulatory body, is often unable to project a unified US position in Basel and cannot guarantee uniformity and consistency in the domestic implementation of internationally agreed rules (Singer 2007). The European Commission is a member of the IAIS, without voting power.

Since the mid-2000s, key issues in the IAIS regulatory agenda—Enterprise Risk Management (ERM), the structure of regulatory capital, the use of internal models, group supervision, and the mutual recognition of supervisory regimes[3]—have reflected EU priorities and perspectives. In the mid-2000s, the IAIS embarked on a major project to provide qualitative and quantitative benchmarks to assess insurer solvency. Three standards on solvency were adopted in October 2008: Standard No. 2.1.1 on the structure of regulatory capital requirements, Standard No. 2.2.6 on ERM for capital adequacy and solvency purposes, and Standard No. 2.2.7 on the use of Internal Models for regulatory capital purposes (IAIS 2008a). Some guidance papers, discussed below, were also issued. These documents were subsequently included in the revised Insurance Core Principles, Standards, Guidance and Assessment issued in 2012.

The IAIS standards agreed in late 2008 contained rules such as the prescribed capital requirement and the minimum capital requirement, the enterprise risk management framework, the own risk and solvency assessment, and the use of an internal model for regulatory capital purposes—all lifted from EU legislation, or more precisely the Solvency II Directive. Some terms were changed slightly. For example, the IAIS standards used 'Prescribed Capital Requirement' whereas Solvency II referred to 'Solvency Capital Requirement' (interviews, London,

---

[3] These standards can be found at: <http://www.iaisweb.org/index.cfm?pageID=40> (accessed December 2008).

30 September 2008, Basel, 19 November 2008). The IAIS in 2008 also issued a set of principles on group-wide supervision (IAIS 2008b)—the first step in its work to develop global standards and guidance on group-wide supervision, borrowed from the group regime proposed and painstakingly negotiated for the Solvency II Directive (*Financial Times*, 10 June 2008).

The IAIS paper on mutual recognition (2008c) provided guidance on cross-border recognition of reinsurance supervision with a view to convince the USA to abolish its regime for alien (non-US) insurers. Indeed, the main barrier faced by EU reinsurers wanting to expand their already significant presence in the USA was the requirement to post collaterals for the value of their commitments in the markets (US states) where they conduct business (Singer 2007). The purpose of the IAIS guidance was 'to allow a supervisor to recognise the value of the supervision exercised by another jurisdiction and thus remove significant amounts of unnecessary regulatory and supervisory requirements for re-insurers' (2008c: 1). Among these unnecessary requirements were collaterals. With the main international reinsurers headquartered in the EU, first and foremost in London, Commission and UK representatives were reportedly instrumental in pushing this issue onto the IAIS agenda.

The European Commission played a key role in preparing the rules for the new international regime for capital requirements in the insurance sector. Alongside the EU member states participating in the work of the IAIS, the Commission wanted to ensure that the new framework would resemble as much as possible the Solvency II regime then being introduced in Europe (interviews, Brussels, 28 March 2007, Frankfurt, 10 September 2007, Brussels, 9 April 2008, Rome, 27 July 2008, Basel, 19 November 2008). European policy-makers, particularly those from the UK, played key roles in chairing and driving discussions in the relevant IAIS sub-groups (House of Lords 2008: Ev 8–9).

The US authorities did not oppose the new solvency regime in the IAIS; nor were they strong supporters, as the proposed framework differed from the one used in the USA (Quaglia 2013). The US negotiating position was complicated and weakened by the fact that there was no federal supervisory authority to represent the US position (interviews, Basel, 19 November 2008; Singer 2007). Since insurance regulation is a state competence in the USA, there is limited expertise on insurance at the federal level (*Wall Street Journal*, 16 April 2008). This is in stark contrast to banking and securities markets regulation, where the US Federal Reserve and the Securities and Exchange Commission (SEC) have considerable expertise and are highly regarded in international forums (Simmons 2001; Singer 2007).

The solvency framework based on the EU directive was seen as state of the art, giving 'European companies a head start in the global economy', whereas the USA 'was stuck with highly fragmented insurance regulation' (*Financial Times*, 11 July 2007). According to the European Commission, the new rules would allow large insurance groups to save up to 40 per cent of their solvency requirements, freeing up vast sums for profitable investment (*Financial Times*, 11 July 2007). US insurers were thus concerned about the implications of Solvency II for their competitiveness. Some US policymakers and industry participants saw the new EU prudential regime as a regulatory template for reforms in the USA (interviews, Basel, 19 November 2008). In June 2008, the NAIC adopted its 'Solvency modernization work plan'[4] to study international solvency standards and the impact of Solvency II on the capital requirements of US insurers, and to propose reforms to US regulations.

Insurance Regulation in the European Union

The 'first generation' EU directives on insurance in the early 1970s focused on specific sub-sectors: life insurance, non-life insurance, motor insurance, re-insurance, etc. Directives in the 1970s and early 1980s focused on barriers to entry, abolishing restrictions on freedom of establishment subject to host country control (Story and Walter 1997). The 'second generation' insurance directives issued in the latter part of the 1980s permitted cross-border business, again subject to host country control. This was followed in the 1990s by the 'third generation' of directives establishing the single licence for insurance companies, subject to home country control and coupled with mutual recognition of 'technical provisions'[5] (the equivalent of capital for insurers), which varied considerably between member states (Story and Walter 1997: 265).

The Financial Services Action Plan (2001) envisaged two main pieces of legislation addressing issues deliberately left outside the scope of previous EU rules, namely reinsurance and solvency requirements. Financial conglomerates including their insurance businesses came to be regulated by the financial conglomerates directive issued in 2002.

Reinsurance Directive

Reinsurance—or insurance for insurers—is the practice whereby an insurance company (the insurer) transfers some of its risks to another company (the reinsurer). There were three main reasons why the EU prior to 2005 lacked a harmonized regulatory framework for reinsurance. First, the reinsurance business involves insurance companies and does not directly involve consumers (policy holders); it was assumed that professional insurers were less in need of protection by EU regulation (EC 1999b). Second, any EU

---

[4] <http://www.naic.org/index_smi.htm> (accessed June 2013).
[5] Technical provisions are the amounts an insurer needs to hold to meet its expected future obligations on insurance contracts.

regulation of reinsurers was hampered by the fact that there was no agreement on international accounting standards in the insurance sector. Third, the regulation of reinsurance varied considerably within the EU. Until the early 2000s, only reinsurers in the UK, Denmark, Finland, and Portugal were subject to the comprehensive regulation and supervision applied to direct insurers under the single market regime, including licensing and on-going financial supervision. Professional reinsurers were not subject to any supervision in Belgium, Ireland, and Greece. Germany, France, and the Netherlands applied elements of their direct insurance supervisory regime to reinsurers, while reduced licensing regimes existed in Austria, Italy, Spain, and Sweden, with only the latter two imposing a solvency margin requirement (EC 2002).

The reinsurance directive adopted in 2005 ushered in a harmonized EU regime for the regulation of reinsurers. It had three main aims. The first was to establish a 'single passport' for reinsurance companies which would henceforth be subject to supervision by competent authorities in their 'home' countries according to harmonized EU rules. The lack of an EU regulatory framework had created uncertainty for direct insurers and their policy-holders about the quality of supervision that their reinsurers were subject to. It had also created barriers to cross-border reinsurance services. For example, collaterals for outstanding claims against reinsurers were compulsory in some states such as France, but not in most others. Reinsurers were also burdened by the different supervisory rules in member states.[6]

Second, the directive aimed to contribute to international financial stability—a significant concern in international forums. The IMF in its Financial Sector Assessment Programme reviews reiterated the need for such legislation (EC 2004). Among other things, international bodies pointed out that the regulation of insurance and reinsurance worldwide had not kept pace with financial and technological innovation such as the growing use of derivatives and other complex hedging instruments.

Third, the directive was expected to strengthen the EU's bargaining power in international forums, especially vis-à-vis the USA. The IAIS, in which EU states and the Commission were members, was embarking on a project on the regulation of reinsurance. The reinsurance directive was expected to allow EU member states to speak with one voice in international forums (EC 2002).

The reinsurance directive built on the regime introduced by the third generation of insurance directives, extending to reinsurance companies the system of authorization and financial supervision by the jurisdiction in which they are headquartered, or 'home country control'. Such authorization was a 'single passport' enabling reinsurers to pursue business anywhere in the EU, either by establishing themselves in other countries or by providing services directly

[6] <http://europa.eu/rapid/pressReleasesAction.do?reference=IP/04/513&format=HTML&aged=0&language=EN&guiLanguage=en> (accessed December 2013).

from their home or another member state. This had long been the case for primary insurers.[7]

To implement home country control while ensuring the EU-wide protection of reinsurance customers (generally direct insurers), the directive set out provisions for the supervision of reinsurance to be applied by all member states. The directive outlined a licensing regime for reinsurance undertakings and the conditions to be met before licences were to be granted. It also set out prudential rules for the supervision of reinsurance undertakings, including rules on technical provisions (i.e. the amount that a reinsurance undertaking must set aside to enable it to meet its contractual obligations) and the investment of assets covering these technical provisions. One controversial issue was the abolition of national systems that obliged reinsurers to pledge assets (collaterals) to cover unearned premiums and outstanding claims when the reinsurer is based in the EU.[8] Such a regime was in place in some countries.

France and Portugal in their national legislation prescribed collaterals in the form of letters of credit or bonds. This was seen in France as a critical means of exercising insurance supervision. But the industry and the Commission reiterated that the directive's purpose was to introduce effective direct supervision at the EU level and to eliminate the need for costly collateral requirements, at least within the EU. The industry also argued that the requirement for collateral tied up capital without justification. In the end, the European Parliament and the member states in the Council agreed that such requirements should be phased out as part of the reinsurance directive (*Financial Times*, 30 March 2005).

Although preparatory work for the reinsurance directive had begun on 19 December 1998[9] the Commission tabled the legislative proposal only in 2004. The European Parliament and Council then approved it on its first reading in late 2005. That it was adopted in less than two years suggests that the main member states and the EP were happy with the legislation. The UK, which hosts the largest reinsurance market in the world, was the main sponsor of the directive; its rapporteur was the British MEP Peter Skinner. The other member states with large insurance industries supported the harmonization of EU rules and the creation of an EU passport. The reinsurance industry is dominated by big players, generally headquartered in the large member states which share similar preferences. Of the world's eight largest reinsurers, three are based in Germany, one in France, and one in the UK. They were deemed to benefit from the directive, which facilitated agreement at the EU level.

---

[7] <http://europa.eu/rapid/pressReleasesAction.do?reference=IP/04/513&format=HTML&aged=0&language=EN&guiLanguage=en> (accessed December 2013).

[8] <http://europa.eu/rapid/pressReleasesAction.do?reference=IP/04/513&format=HTML&aged=0&language=EN&guiLanguage=en> (accessed December 2013).

[9] In 1998, the Insurance Committee asked the Commission to prepare a questionnaire to be distributed to supervisory authorities with a view to map how reinsurers are regulated across the EU.

The Solvency II Directive

The Solvency II directive was one of the cornerstones of the Financial Services Action Plan. The solvency margin is the amount of capital an insurance undertaking is required to hold against unforeseen events. Such requirements, in place in the EU since the 1970s, were amended for life insurers in 2002 by the Solvency I directive which raised the minimum guarantee fund. The Solvency II directive had a much wider scope, applying to life and non-life insurance as well as re-insurance, only exempting small mutual and some small (non-mutual) insurance undertakings. The Solvency II directive also eliminated the sub-sectoral approach of past EU legislation, setting solvency requirements for all types of insurers. It did not change the regime applicable to financial conglomerates, which were regulated by a specific directive issued in 2002, subsequently revised.

Solvency II aimed to ensure policy-holder protection in all EU member states by setting requirements for solvency margins in light of the true risk of (re)insurance undertakings. The directive also aimed to increase regulatory harmonization and the convergence of supervisory tools and powers (EC 2001c).[10] It was designed to streamline EU legislation, replacing 14 existing directives regulating insurance services with a single directive.

The new approach was articulated across three pillars resembling those of the Basel II accord for banking (EC 2001d). In the first pillar of Solvency II, insurers are required to hold capital against market risk, credit risk, and operational risk. Although they were not covered by Solvency I legislation, all three potentially affect insurer solvency. Pillar 1 outlines two capital requirements which have different purposes and are calibrated accordingly: the minimum capital requirement, below which supervisory action is triggered, and the solvency capital requirement, which enables an institution to absorb significant unforeseen losses (EC 2004). The latter cannot be lower than the former. Subject to supervisory approval, insurers can use their own internal models to calculate capital requirements.

The concepts were similar to those introduced in the UK by the 2004 domestic reform of insurance regulation. The UK was the main backer of Solvency II, and to some extent was able to have its domestic rules on insurance 'uploaded' to the EU level (Quaglia 2011c). The so-called Sharma report of 1999 (CIS 2002), which did some initial groundwork for the new EU regime, was chaired by a senior British official from the Financial Services Authority (FSA). Even the terminology used in the EU legislation mirrored that of its British predecessor, though 'enhanced capital requirement' was changed to 'solvency capital requirement' in the drafting of Solvency II for political reasons (interviews, London, 23 July 2008, 30 September 2008).

---

[10] <http://europa.eu/rapid/pressReleasesAction.do?reference=IP/07/1060&format=HTML&aged=0&language=EN&guiLanguage=en> (accessed June 2008).

The second pillar of the Solvency II directive consisted of a supervisory review of the overall financial position of insurance undertakings, where, depending on the outcome of the review, supervisors could require additional capital. The second pillar also addressed the harmonization of supervisory activities. The third pillar outlined requirements for the disclosure of information to impose market discipline on insurance undertakings (EC 2001d).

Overall, Solvency II adopts a risk and principles-based approach to prudential rules for insurance companies. For the vast majority of member states, it represented a major change in their domestic regulatory frameworks. The notable exception was the UK, which had adopted a similar framework without waiting for EU rules (the so-called Tiner reform named after the FSA official who engineered it) (FSA 2005a, 2005b, 2002).

The most controversial aspect of Solvency II was group support and supervision. In group supervision, a single authority has coordination and decision-making powers for each insurance group. The group supervisor has primary responsibility for key aspects of group supervision (group solvency, intragroup transactions, etc.), to be exercised in cooperation and consultation with host supervisors (EC 2007b). Group support allows parent firms under certain conditions to use declarations of group support to meet the solvency capital requirements of its subsidiaries.

The UK is widely credited with authoring the provisions on group supervision and group support. These were first articulated in a draft document produced by the British Treasury (HMT) and the FSA in November 2006 (HMT and FSA 2006a, 2006b) and subsequently used by the Commission in its official legislative proposal of July 2007 (interviews, Brussels, 9 April 2008, Berlin, 23 April 2008, London, 23 July 2008, 30 September 2008). The other large member states—namely France, Germany, and Italy—which, like the UK and the Netherlands, are home to several large insurance groups (see Comité Européen des Assurances, CEA 2005), also supported the proposal, as did the main players in the insurance sector (CEA 2007b).

But 12 EU member states, led by Poland and Spain, which host subsidiaries and branches of insurance groups disagreed with the proposed approach (*Financial Times*, 10 June 2008; interviews, Frankfurt, 10 September 2007, Brussels, 9 April 2008, Berlin, 23 April 2008). They argued that group supervision would significantly reduce the power of host authorities to control what happens in their jurisdictions, who would then be 'left to pick up the pieces if local problems emerge' (*Financial Times*, 19 March 2008; interviews, Brussels, 9 April 2008). Towards the end of the negotiations, the outcome moved towards the inclusion of group supervision with strong limitations on group support (Council of Ministers 2008).

The Commission's draft directive, issued in April 2005, outlined three legislative approaches (EC 2005) and mirrored almost all of the main objectives set by the UK (House of Lords 2008: Ev. 36). The UK authorities subsequently proposed a single piece of legislation rather than the three proposed by the Commission, which the latter accepted. Horse trading in the final stage of negotiations (*Financial Times*, 10 June 2008) scaled down the provisions for group support and supervision.

The legislation introduced rules on the equivalence of third country solvency regimes, with consequences for groups with subsidiaries inside and outside the EU. Equivalence can only be agreed with sovereign states and not parts of such countries—a provision specifically targeting the USA. This complicated the equivalence decisions to be taken by the Commission, following the advice of the European Occupational Pension and Insurance Authority. Where the solvency regime of a third country is deemed equivalent to that of the EU, the group solvency calculation for third country subsidiaries should consider the solvency capital requirement and eligible own funds as laid down by this third country. The group supervisor is to carry out the verification of equivalence, consulting with other supervisors and the relevant authority before making a decision.

In contrast to banking, the insurance industry in Europe was never deeply divided when negotiating the requirements for solvency. The main division was between the Comité Européen des Assurances, representing the European insurance and reinsurance industry through national insurance associations (CEA 2007a, 2007c) on one side, and the Association Internationale des Sociétés d'Assurances Mutuelle and the Association of European Cooperative and Mutual Insurers, representing mutual insurers and cooperative insurance companies, on the other. Despite differences in their memberships covering diverse segments of the insurance market—there are only big players in reinsurance—the EU was able to avoid a standstill and open conflict through exemptions, proportionality clauses, and similar legislative provisions.

AN OVERALL ASSESSMENT

When we examine the links and sequencing between EU and global rules, we see that EU rules for insurance predated and contributed to the content of international rules. The main caveat here is that international rules on solvency (capital) requirements remain embryonic, unlike, for instance, in banking (Blom, this volume). As for the links between EU and global institutions, regulators from EU countries sit in the International Association of Insurance Supervisors, where the European Commission is also an observer. In both EU and international financial regulatory forums, we saw that British policymakers and the European Commission were pace-setters on solvency requirements, shaping the reform of insurance regulation in the EU and beyond.

In contrast to the regulation of hedge funds (see Howarth and Quaglia, this volume), for insurance there were no competing coalitions of nations within the EU (Quaglia 2010a, 2010b). To the extent that there was a division, it was between the home and host countries of insurance groups. On one side, the large member states—the four largest countries led by the UK and joined by other 'old' EU member states—were the 'home' countries of (generally large) insurance companies operating across borders.[11] These countries and their industries backed the principle of group support and supervision which increased the power of their 'home' supervisory authorities. On the other side were the vast majority of 'new' member states and a few old members led by Poland and Spain. These countries, which host numerous foreign insurance companies in their territories, were reluctant to relinquish or dilute the supervisory powers of their national authorities. To promote market integration, the Commission and the European Parliament (2008c)—with the exception of some MEPs from new member states (Quaglia 2011c)—tended to side with the first group, led by the four largest member states.

In contrast to the regulation for banking and hedge funds, British and American policymakers had diverging preferences for insurance. The former were keen to promote EU rules internationally; the latter tried to resist any such imposition. But the position of US policymakers was weakened by the state-by-state system of insurance regulation in that country and the fragmented external representation that ensued from it. In this sector, the EU was a 'policy-maker' rather than a 'policy-taker'; instead of waiting for international rules to be agreed, the EU set its own rules. The EU was not internally divided on insurance, which strengthened its ability to call for international rules. Similar national preferences were mostly shaped by similar configurations—the main transnational players—of the insurance industry in the main member states. Mügge (2010) has argued that cross-border integration and consolidation of the financial industry in the 1990s altered the marketplace and hence the coalitions supporting regulatory harmonization in EU securities markets. Such was also the case for insurance.

As for the factors that inform the EU's influence on global regulatory politics, explanations based on economic power (more precisely, market size) have dominated much of the literature (Simmons 2001; Drezner 2007; Dür 2011). In the case of insurance, market size is more or less the same in the USA and the EU; it thus cannot be a decisive factor in the EU–US competition for international rule-setting. But the size of the insurance industry is important for another reason: generally speaking, large insurers located in a given jurisdiction have incentives to lobby for its domestic rules to be applied internationally.

---

[11]   In 2011, the total gross premium for life and non-life insurers in the main EU countries was (in billions of euros): UK 206, France 190, Germany 178, Italy 110. The EU total was approximately 1,000 billion (source CEA 2011).

This reduces cross-border compliance costs while securing a level playing field. There is evidence that EU insurers supported EU attempts to push its regulatory templates onto the IAIS.

Prior to the Financial Services Action Plan, the EU lacked strong regulatory capacity in insurance (on the concept of regulatory capacity see Bach and Newman 2010; Posner 2009, 2010b). But unlike what prevailed for hedge funds, credit rating agencies (see Hiss and Nagel, this volume), and derivatives (see Mügge, this volume), the EU for insurance had built up its regulatory capacity before the crisis. This was reflected in its greater influence in the International Association of Insurance Supervisors. The specific character of EU multi-level governance in this sector did not weaken the international bargaining power of the EU because there were no major divisions among EU member states preventing the formulation of common policy positions in international forums (Mügge 2011c).

Since the insurance sector was only marginally affected by the global financial crisis, no substantially new regulations loom on the horizon—either for the EU or internationally. Indeed, the EU remains preoccupied by the national implementation of Solvency II in its member states.

6

Accounting Standards

BART STELLINGA

INTRODUCTION

The European and global regulation of accounting standards has witnessed remarkable changes over the past 20 years. In the early 1990s, EU accounting practices were fragmented along national lines and US accounting standards (US Generally Accepted Accounting Principles—US GAAP) were the de facto global standards. Since 2005, all EU listed companies must issue their accounts according to International Financial Reporting Standards (IFRSs) as issued by a private sector organization, the International Accounting Standards Board (IASB).[1] US GAAP lost ground as the EU and many other countries started using IFRSs. By 2013, 128 countries permitted or required the use of IFRSs.

This chapter describes and analyses how the global regulatory context has influenced the EU's policy choices over accounting standards and how EU regulatory initiatives have affected global accounting regulation. It sets out to answer three main questions. Why did the EU choose to harmonize accounting standards by adopting IFRSs? What influence did the EU have on global accounting regulation and why? How will future developments likely affect the role and position of the EU in accounting regulation? Given the subject of this book, it will pay particular attention to the EU's influence on accounting for financial instruments—of crucial importance to the regulation of financial markets.

The internationalization of business raised the urgency as well as the possibility of harmonizing accounting rules in Europe. To attract external investment,

---

[1] The IASB was founded in 2001, the successor of the International Accounting Standards Committee (IASC) which existed between 1973 and 2001. The IASB issues IFRSs but inherited the standards (International Accounting Standards—IASs) issued by the IASC. In due time, IFRSs are supposed to replace all IASs.

EU companies expanding abroad increasingly used internationally recognized standards, often US standards. Whereas governments previously saw accounting as national affairs, their preferences shifted towards European harmonization. Due to the lack of regulatory capacity in the EU to develop its own standards and the growing dominance of US GAAP in international financial reporting, the EU chose to adopt IFRSs, which appeared as a quick and easy way to harmonize accounting standards while simultaneously countering the hegemony of US standards. Alongside internal EU developments, the global regulatory and economic context crucially informed the EU's policy choices.

The EU's adoption of IFRSs triggered a remarkable shift in global accounting regulation. US GAAP lost its position as the de facto global standard, ushering in a new bi-polar situation in which US GAAP and IFRSs occupy more or less equal positions. The supranationalization of EU accounting policy (i.e. regulatory centralization) bolstered the global standing of IFRSs. Many countries followed suit, either requiring or allowing their use. But though the EU strongly influenced *which* rules became more dominant globally (i.e. IFRSs), fragmented policy preferences within the EU—combined with the IASB's relative independence and its desire to ensure US support—has meant that the EU has hitherto had only limited influence on the *content* of these rules.

The EU's future influence on global accounting regulation will depend on how its member states cope with the challenges of the financial crisis. Their divergent accounting preferences may keep the EU from formulating clear policy preferences, thereby limiting its influence. The extent of EU influence will also depend on (financial) market and regulatory developments in other regions, most notably in the USA and Asia. As the USA is expected to take a cautious approach to global harmonization, this could increase the EU's influence over IFRSs. But the growing importance of financial markets in emerging economies, especially in Asia, coupled with their recent attempts to form regional blocs in accounting matters could reduce the EU's relevance in global accounting regulation.

THE EU'S ADOPTION OF INTERNATIONAL ACCOUNTING STANDARDS

Developments Necessitating EU Harmonization of Accounting Standards

The setting of accounting standards in the EU was for a long time a national affair, generally the preserve of finance ministries or other public organizations (see Büthe and Mattli 2011: 89–94). The European Commission began its

attempts to harmonize accounting rules for limited liability companies in the
EU in the 1970s, leading to the issuance of the Fourth Council Directive in
1978 and the Seventh Council Directive in 1983. The Commission's goal was to
ensure the 'equivalence' of EU companies' financial statements (Van Hulle
2004). The Fourth Council Directive defined the types of companies required
to prepare annual accounts and their formats (Botzem 2012: 39). The Seventh
Council Directive introduced a separation between annual and consolidated
accounts: a significant distinction as only the annual accounts of listed companies were used for tax purposes. It implied that accounting harmonization
need not intervene in governments' taxation policies (Botzem 2012: 41).

The development of these directives was a painstaking process due to the
different accounting preferences of member states (see Box 6.1) (Botzem 2012:
40). The national orientation of European firms and financial markets meant
that there was little urgency to harmonize accounting rules. Although the 15
national accounting standards did converge to some extent, accounting harmonization progressed slowly due to the lack of will among member states to
wholeheartedly implement the directives and the many options they contained
(Zeff 2012: 823).

Accounting harmonization in Europe accelerated in the late 1980s due to
changes in the global and European corporate and financial landscape. The
expansion of European business abroad involved multinational firms seeking
funds in global financial markets. Due to the removal of intra-European barriers (part of the single European market programme of 1986/87), Europe saw a
rush of cross-border mergers and take-overs. The ties between the large European companies that ventured onto European and global markets and their
traditional financiers (such as creditor banks) thereby weakened, meaning that
globalizing firms increasingly had to look for funds elsewhere. Many multinational firms chose to tap into booming, deep, and liquid US financial markets
by listing on US stock exchanges. Between 1990 and 1998, the number of European companies listed in the USA rose from 50 to 250 (Camfferman and Zeff

---

Box 6.1 Accounting traditions in Europe

A distinction is usually drawn between Anglo-American and continental European
accounting practices (Nobes 1985). Accounting standards in continental Europe
were generally designed to inform a close group of interested parties. Accounting
practices in this tradition were generally conservative, allowing firms to build up
hidden reserves as part of their long-term strategies (Perry and Nölke 2006: 569).
The prime examples of countries using such accounting standards were Germany,
Italy, and France, despite differences between them. In contrast, Anglo-American
standards were more focused on (potential) outside investors and required more
openness on companies' financial positions. Key examples of EU countries in the
Anglo-American tradition were the UK, Denmark, and the Netherlands.

2007: 427). Many were high-profile companies; Daimler Benz, for example, listed on the New York Stock Exchange in 1993.

US accounting standards (US GAAP) became the de facto global standards for multinational firms as foreign firms listed in the USA were required to adopt (or reconcile statements with) US GAAP (Camfferman and Zeff 2007: 311). This heightened the urgency of European accounting harmonization. Doing nothing was no option: it would likely mean that an ever-growing number of EU companies would shift to US GAAP, the content of which the EU could not influence.

The EU, however, was not in a position to develop its own set of rules (Dewing and Russell 2004; Véron et al. 2006; Posner 2010b), primarily because it lacked regulatory capacity to do so. Apart from the Commission, the most important EU forums for accounting matters were the Contact Committee (an advisory body composed of representatives of member states) and the European Accounting Study Group (dubbed E5 + 2). Both were weak actors (Camfferman and Zeff 2007: 445–446).[2] Developing a stronger institutional framework was not a feasible strategy for the Commission as member states and private actors alike remained wary of attempts to develop a separate set of EU standards (2007: 421). In the end, the Commission came to realize the minimal chances of EU-made accounting standards being recognized in the USA—where continental European standards were generally seen as deficient (Mügge 2007: 11).

Although the Commission tried to resolve some tensions in the directives in the early 1990s, it changed its course shortly thereafter: it began to see the International Accounting Standards (IASs) issued by the International Accounting Standards Committee (IASC) as the way forward to harmonize European accounting rules and counter growing US hegemony. In 1995, the Commission formulated its preference to permit or require EU listed companies to publish their statements according to IASs.

The EU–US struggle over International Accounting Standards (1987–2001)

The IASC was founded in 1973 by national accounting standards boards and operated until the birth of the International Accounting Standards Board (IASB) in 2001. Its goal was to 'formulate and publish in the public interest, basic standards ... and to promote their worldwide acceptance and observance' (Camfferman and Zeff 2007: 500). The IASC had little impact during its first two decades: its standards (IASs) were mainly used by developing countries on a voluntary basis and it lacked enforcement power (Büthe and Mattli 2011: 69).

---

[2] The E5 + 2 forum consisted of accounting representatives from France, Germany, the Netherlands, the Nordic Federation, and the UK (E5) as well as representatives from the European Commission and the Federation of European Accountants (+ 2).

Most developed countries (and specifically the USA) saw IASs as too flexible and of doubtful quality, arguing that they contained too many options and represented the lowest common denominator of global accounting practice (Camfferman and Zeff 2007; Zeff 2012).

During the 1970s and 1980s, the European Commission—which saw the issuance of directives as the path to EU-level accounting harmonization—paid little attention to the work of the IASC (Camfferman and Zeff 2007: 16–17). This changed in the late 1980s (Posner 2010b). The EU now wanted the USA to acknowledge IASs as equivalent to US GAAP so European companies listed in the USA could use a non-US standard. The EU also wanted to prevent these standards from being fully modelled on US standards. The USA, on the other hand, stressed that international standards and standards-setting procedures would have to improve before they were deemed equivalent to US GAAP.

Reform of International Accounting Standards (1987–2001)

As the IASC strove for the recognition of its standards by national securities regulators (specifically the US SEC), it sought cooperation with the International Organization of Securities Commissions (IOSCO). While the IASC had hoped for an IOSCO endorsement of its standards, the latter (mainly due to SEC pressure) stated that its endorsement would depend on their improvement. The IASC thus embarked on projects to improve IASs, first by eliminating the many options contained in them (1987–1993), then by developing a set of high-quality 'core standards' (1993–1999) (Zeff 2012).

In this process, the Anglo-American actors, organized in the G4 + 1 group (with the SEC as *primus inter pares*), proved to be of much greater influence than their (continental) European counterparts (Eaton 2005; Camfferman and Zeff 2007; Zeff 2012).[3] US influence was mainly due to it being the world's largest and deepest financial market, and the IASC eagerly hoping for recognition of its standards by the USA (Zeff 2012). It was also due to the strong institutional framework that had developed in the USA over the previous decades, with the SEC and the Financial Accounting Standards Board (FASB) considered the expert organizations on accounting matters (Posner 2010b). As the IASC had only a small permanent staff, it depended on the resources and expertise of national, often American or other Anglo-Saxon, standards setters (Büthe and Mattli 2011: 78). Continental European countries lacked a strong institutional framework in which accounting standards were developed by independent standards setters (Camfferman and Zeff 2007: 408–416). The EU, as such, also had limited power (see Box 6.2 for an example of this).

---

[3] The G4 + 1, founded in 1993, consisted of representatives of the standards setters of the UK, US, Canada, and Australia (G4), with an IASC representative as an observer (+ 1). In 1996, New Zealand's standards setter joined as a fifth member (Zeff 2012: 816).

Box 6.2 **The development of IAS 39**

The development of the standard for financial instruments, IAS 39, exemplifies the limited EU influence on IASB standards setting. The development of IAS 39 was heavily influenced by Canadian and American actors (Camfferman and Zeff 2007: 362) and modelled on the corresponding US standard, SFAS 133. The Commission complained that the proposed standard 'has been understood by many in Europe as a clear choice in favour of US GAAP' (quoted in Camfferman and Zeff 2007: 373). The FASB, on the other hand, claimed that 'better standards than those currently adopted by FASB would be difficult for any standard setter to develop on its own' (Camfferman and Zeff 2007: 372). Although the final standard moved in the direction of EU demands—it became less detailed—the overall result was a standard more oriented towards fair value accounting (see below), conforming to the wishes of Anglo-American standards setters (although some of them thought the standard did not go far enough in this respect) (Camfferman and Zeff 2007: 361–375).

While the resulting set of core standards leaned heavily on Anglo-Saxon accounting practices (Posner and Véron 2010: 404), they cannot be seen as just another version of US GAAP, as differences remained significant (Leblond 2011). The core standards largely focused on outside investors by privileging fair value accounting (FVA) over the more traditional practice of historic cost accounting (HCA) (Perry and Nölke 2006; see Box 6.3). Historical cleavages within the EU thus re-emerged in the context of international negotiations: continental EU countries traditionally favoured accounting approaches based on prudence rather than transparency for outside investors. This explained their hesitance towards FVA (which exposes firms to shifting market prices). EU countries more inclined to Anglo-Saxon accounting practices were, however, more positive regarding the shift towards FVA.

Box 6.3 **Fair value accounting and historic cost accounting**

In fair value accounting (FVA), assets and liabilities are accounted at their current market (exit) price or, if unavailable, at their best approximation. The fair value of an instrument should usually be determined by the observable market price of identical or similar financial instruments (mark-to-market). For specific complex instruments, models may be used to determine value (mark-to-model). In historic cost accounting (HCA), assets and liabilities are recorded at the value when they were acquired. Since the 1980s both the FASB and IASB have favoured FVA over HCA, arguing that in volatile markets, the market price is more relevant to outside investors than the historic cost. Countries in the Anglo-Saxon accounting tradition were more positive about FVA than their continental European counterparts. The preferences of firms are far from clear cut: in general, they favour FVA when markets are booming and HCA when prices are falling.

The IASC completed work on its core standards in December 1998, which were then endorsed by IOSCO in May 2000. But IOSCO's endorsement constituted a 'hollow victory' for the EU (and IASC). Following the demands the SEC had made earlier that year, IOSCO allowed national regulators to impose supplementary treatments on the statements of multinational companies complying with IASs (Zeff 2012: 822–823). Rather than a full endorsement implying the equivalence of US GAAP and IASs, the SEC could continue requiring companies to conform to or reconcile with US GAAP. It meant that the US–EU struggle over mutual recognition of US GAAP/IASs would continue into the 2000s.

IASC Governance Reform (1996–2001)

The US–EU struggle over international accounting regulations involved reform of the IASC institutional framework. Both sides wanted to restructure the IASC according to their own preferences, and the USA clearly won on this issue (Camfferman and Zeff 2007; Posner 2010b; Zeff 2012). The EU's formal influence, small to begin with, remained small after the reforms to IASC governance.

The push for a new institutional framework was mainly due to SEC pressure as it had stated that its recognition of IASs equivalency would depend on the quality of standards-setting procedures at the IASC. The EU favoured a set-up based on the geographical representation of countries that had committed themselves to adopt the standards. The USA, in contrast, pushed for a governance framework involving independent experts, modelled on its own accounting framework (Zeff 2012: 819). The SEC knew that 'independent experts' selected on the basis of their professional experience would almost by default come from Anglo-Saxon accounting standards boards or from the (at that time) Big Five accounting firms, which were also inclined to the Anglo-Saxon view on accounting. The IASC sided with the USA as it feared for its own demise should the USA turn away and pursue international harmonization through the G4 + 1 (Camfferman and Zeff 2007: 443–446).

Following a painstaking process, the USA got its way: a relatively independent standards-setting board—the IASB—replaced the IASC in 2001, without any prescribed geographical representation (Camfferman and Zeff 2007: 15). The IASB inherited the International Accounting Standards (IASs) issued by IASC but would henceforth only issue International Financial Reporting Standards (IFRSs) that would eventually replace all IASs. The European Commission had little bargaining power to oppose this move. It had already formulated its preference for accepting or requiring the use of IASs in 1995 and had no alternatives. It therefore had to accept the defeat on the governance reform.

Explaining the Adoption of IASs in the EU

European leaders decided to make IASs mandatory for the consolidated accounts of all European listed companies at the Lisbon Summit in 2000. This was formalized in EU Regulation No. 1606/2002, which required shifting to IASs by 2005. It would thus seem that international rules—heavily modelled on US/Anglo-Saxon accounting standards—were influencing European rules, not vice versa.

The harmonization of accounting standards was part of a general 1990s trend in the EU to centralize financial regulation (Posner 2009, 2010b). Compared to the period before 1990, European governments and businesses had changed their positions on the desirability of a supranational strategy and a common framework was now seen as necessary to boost the European financial sector. The Financial Services Action Plan (FSAP) of March 2000 provided the legislation to integrate Europe's national financial services industries (Posner 2009: 681). Part of this plan was to harmonize accounting rules. As many public and private stakeholders found EU decision-making procedures too cumbersome to keep up with financial market developments, the Lamfalussy process provided the institutional framework to speed up regulatory reforms at the EU level. Mügge (2010) has argued that lobbying by multinational finance firms was crucial in creating consensus around regulatory centralization and liberalization among EU governments and organizations. For European governments, regulatory reform also provided an opportunity to counter the growing financial market hegemony of the USA (Donnelly 2010).

In effect, the EU's endorsement of IASs killed two birds with one stone: (1) it achieved intra-European accounting harmonization and (to some extent) global harmonization; and (2) it countered the hegemony of US standards.

Regarding the first point, neofunctionalist arguments on European regulatory integration (Leblond 2005) speak to why accounting harmonization became easier and was deemed more necessary. The globalization of business increased pressure on EU member states to harmonize their financial regulations, particularly their accounting practices. The comparability of accounts and the standardization of valuation methods became crucial as businesses sought funds abroad and listed on multiple stock exchanges: firms having to issue financial statements according to different accounting standards could, for example, post different earnings for the same year. Unfamiliarity with foreign accounting practices also made investors hesitant to invest abroad, undermining the European attempt to integrate financial markets (Leblond 2005).

Moreover, continental European domestic preferences had changed (most notably in Germany). These countries had already warmed towards the Anglo-Saxon style of accounting, resulting from the pressure of prominent companies expanding abroad. In many instances, these countries allowed the use of IASs or US GAAP for domestic companies and reformed their own institutional frameworks to more closely resemble US practices (Donnelly 2010: 227–228). The stark differences between national accounting practices had thereby weakened, easing the adoption of IASs. Multinational companies also pressured EU governments to harmonize their accounting regulations so that they could more easily attract funds (Leblond 2011).

The delegation of rule-making authority to a private, expert-based organization—in this case, the IASB—was part of a trend to present the regulation of financial markets as a technocratic, scientific enterprise (Mügge 2011a). Expert regulators, insulated from public interference, would then be able to develop rules conducive to market efficiency (Porter 2005; Martinez-Diaz 2005) or skewed towards the interests of the owners of mobile capital (Perry and Nölke 2006; Nölke 2009; Botzem 2012).

On the second point, countering the hegemony of US standards, both functionalist and expert-based arguments have less explanatory power. If the harmonization of accounting regulations to improve financial market efficiency was the ultimate goal, the EU may just as well have adopted US GAAP. To explain the adoption of IASs, arguments that focus on power politics have more traction (Posner 2010b; Leblond 2011; Büthe and Mattli 2011). The EU was reluctant to delegate rule-making authority in a crucial policy domain to its greatest financial market rival. The Commission saw the endorsement of IASs as the only viable option (Véron et al. 2006: 165). For reasons described above, the development of EU accounting standards would take too long, and in any case there was no guarantee that the USA would accept them as equivalent to US GAAP. Other countries such as Canada, South Africa, and Australia expressed support for the work of the IASC; so did international agencies, most notably IOSCO, the World Trade Organization, and, in the wake of the financial crisis in Southeast Asia in the late 1990s, the Financial Stability Forum, which adopted IASs in its Compendium of Standards and Codes (Mattli and Büthe 2005: 253). The Commission thus saw jumping on the IASB bandwagon as the best way to counter US GAAP hegemony.

DEVELOPMENTS FOLLOWING THE EU'S ADOPTION OF IFRSs

The EU's adoption of IFRSs changed the dynamics of international governance.[4] IFRSs were now seen as a viable alternative to US GAAP while the EU's backing of IASB improved the latter's standing vis-à-vis US authorities. In the struggle over the global dominance of a particular set of accounting standards,

---

[4] This section will refer to the IASB's standards as 'IFRSs', although the IASB's standards were a mix of the inherited IASs and the newly issued IFRSs.

the IASB was thus a crucial partner for the EU. However, the EU also had an interest in ensuring that the IASB's rules conformed to its wishes. In this struggle, the EU regularly clashed with the IASB. These two, sometimes conflicting, dynamics played a crucial role in the years after 2002.

The EU Institutional Framework

The EU was hesitant to fully delegate rule-making authority to a private organization over which it had only limited influence. The adoption of IFRSs in the EU was therefore conditional (Botzem 2012: 43): the standards would have to be approved by a number of EU bodies following a comitology procedure before entering into force, implying that IFRSs would not automatically become EU rules (see Box 6.4).

This formal endorsement procedure became the most powerful tool, albeit a blunt one, for the EU to influence the standards-setting process of the IASB. As a newly issued or modified standard would be scrutinized by a number of European organizations, the IASB had an interest in ensuring the acceptability of its standards by EU organizations. As the IASB was keen to present itself as an independent standards setter, uninfluenced by particularistic interests, and had many other countries and organizations to consider (especially the US SEC), it had to walk a tightrope between gaining the EU's acceptance and not appearing as a mere 'agent' of the Commission (Leblond 2011).

The EU faced a similar dilemma. It of course had an interest in ensuring standards that were acceptable within the EU, but also risked frustrating equivalence negotiations with the USA if it did not wholeheartedly implement IASB standards. In practice, this tension proved to be relatively unproblematic in the

---

Box 6.4 **EU endorsement procedures**

After the IASB issues or modifies a standard, the European Financial Reporting Advisory Group (EFRAG)—a privately financed and managed organization staffed by accounting experts—advises the Commission on its compliance to European framework directives. The Standards Advice Review Group (SARG), staffed by representatives of national accounting standards boards, then reviews whether EFRAG's advice is balanced and objective. If both organizations give their approval, the Commission issues a draft endorsement regulation which is subsequently examined by the Accounting Regulatory Committee (ARC), staffed by national representatives. If ARC considers the regulation adequate, the European Council and European Parliament have three months to oppose the endorsement. If no objection is made, the regulation is approved and the standard enters into effect in the EU. Although the Commission can reject standards, postpone adoption, or in exceptional cases 'carve out' sections of standards, it cannot modify them by adding language.

Box 6.5 The IAS 39 controversy of 2002–2005

The content of the standard on financial instruments, IAS 39, was at the centre of a dispute between the IASB and the EU. IAS 39 held that all financial instruments (including cash, loans, demand deposits, securities, and derivatives) should be on the balance sheet and that fair value should be applied to a significant part of them (Hague 2004). As the value of financial instruments like derivatives can fluctuate significantly over short periods of time, the resulting volatility in firms' financial positions was a major concern for affected firms, especially for banks whose balance sheets by and large consist of financial instruments. While EU banks and (especially continental European) governments pressed the IASB for more flexible rules on the recognition of value changes of financial instruments, the IASB claimed this flexibility would leave too much room for firms to hide mounting problems. As the controversy could not be resolved, the EU adopted a 'carved out' version of IAS 39, deleting particular sections of the standard so firms would be less exposed to financial market fluctuations.

---

period 2002–2008. The EU endorsed almost all standards without delay. As many listed companies were already familiar with international accounting practices (either US GAAP or IFRSs), most IASB standards were hardly controversial (Donnelly 2010: 227). But on a crucial issue—accounting for financial instruments—the Commission clashed with the IASB over the content of a standard and adopted a modified version (see Box 6.5).

The 'IAS 39 carve-out' means that EU accounting standards differ slightly from those issued by the IASB (for background, see Box 6.2). EU listed companies have to draw up their accounts 'in accordance with IFRSs as adopted by the EU', which in effect means that EU companies need not necessarily follow IFRSs across the board. The 'carve-out' was a clear signal to the IASB that the EU would not unconditionally adopt its standards. But it was also a controversial move, as it showed that EU IFRSs could differ from IASB IFRSs.

The EU–US struggle over International Accounting Standards (2002–2012)

The years after 2002 witnessed new dynamics in the global politics of accounting regulation (Posner 2010b). Whereas the USA was able to dictate developments in the 1990s (Simmons 2001), it now had to take a more cooperative stance. The Enron and WorldCom scandals at the beginning of the millennium did much to challenge the aura of technical superiority around US GAAP (Zeff 2012). Significantly, in 2002 the US Congress asked the SEC to review FASB's very detailed, 'rules-based' approach and to consider moving in IASB's 'principles-based' direction. The EU's adoption of IFRSs had bolstered the

IASB's bargaining position vis-à-vis the FASB. Without EU backing, it is inconceivable that the IASB would have emerged as an equal partner to FASB in the creation of a global accounting regime (Mügge 2007; Botzem 2012).

Harmonizing US GAAP and IFRSs

The key question after the EU's switch to IFRSs was whether the USA would finally (after a decade of negotiations) acknowledge IFRSs as equivalent to US GAAP, something the Commission had hoped for since the 1990s. The USA made this step conditional upon the convergence of US GAAP and IFRSs. In September 2002, the IASB and FASB reached the so-called Norwalk Agreement where the two parties committed to make US GAAP and IFRSs fully compatible and to coordinate future changes (Posner 2010b: 646).

In this convergence process, accounting standards reform was more or less a two-way street (Leblond 2011: 454). Sometimes the FASB followed IASB, at other times vice versa. This also meant that the EU could exert little influence over IASB standards in this period. The centrality of the convergence project in IASB's work seriously constrained EU efforts to influence its standards (Véron et al. 2006; Mügge 2007; Leblond 2011; Botzem 2012). But in this case, the EU's wish to ensure IFRSs–US GAAP equivalence triumphed over its wish to modify IFRSs.

The EU's adoption of IFRSs had significantly increased its bargaining position to demand recognition of these standards by the USA. Due to the introduction of regulations with equivalence determination mechanisms in 2004 (Posner 2010b: 653), the Commission could now effectively threaten the SEC with non-recognition of US GAAP, of direct consequence to some 233 US companies listed in the EU (Posner 2010b: 661).[5] The SEC finally budged in 2007 and acknowledged IFRSs (although not the EU version of IFRSs) as equivalent to US GAAP. This decision reflected the increased regulatory power of the EU and the USA's more cooperative stance (Posner 2009). The EU followed suit and decided in 2008 that US GAAP (and Japanese GAAP) were equivalent to IFRSs. The EU furthermore decided to temporarily (until 31 December 2011) allow companies from China, Canada, South Korea, and India, listed in the EU, to issue statements according to their national GAAP, thereby encouraging these countries to converge with or fully adopt IFRSs.[6]

These were major developments as they marked a turning point in the position of the USA vis-à-vis IFRSs and were reflections of the EU's increased importance in the global regulation of accounting standards. To a certain

---

[5] Before adoption of IFRSs, US GAAP were already accepted without reconciliation by all EU regulators (Posner 2010b: 643).

[6] As Canada, China, and South Korea later incorporated IFRSs into their national GAAP, the EU decided these standards to be equivalent to EU IFRSs as of 2012. The temporary equivalence agreement with India has been extended to the end of 2014.

extent, it also implied that the USA would henceforth have less bargaining power as it could no longer use the 'dangling carrot' of accepting equivalence to influence the direction of rule reform (Véron et al. 2006: 171). The waning global influence of the USA was further reflected in the SEC's adoption in 2006 of a 'road map' to investigate *if* and *when* the USA would also adopt IFRSs (Zeff 2012: 829). Certain developments, however, have slowed this process, as will be detailed below.

Rule Reform During the Financial Crisis

During the financial crisis, the EU could exercise considerable influence over the IASB's accounting standards for financial instruments. IAS 39 was again at the centre of dispute as many governments blamed its requirements to apply fair value accounting to a considerable part of banks' balance sheets for worsening the financial crisis. The EU demanded greater freedom for firms to reclassify troubled assets to the historical cost category to limit the financial damage—an obvious case of income management contrary to IASB principles. But the EU basically threatened the IASB that if it would not modify IAS 39, the Commission would do it itself, implying yet another carve-out. This would have been disastrous for the IASB, as it would set a precedent for countries using IFRSs to modify the standards as they saw fit. The IASB thus decided to modify IAS 39 itself and, given the limited time available, did so without the usual stakeholder consultation round.[7] This proved to be highly controversial as well, as many observers condemned the EU's opportunism (when market prices were rising, no complaints were heard) and criticized the IASB for giving in to the EU's demands (André et al. 2009). In contrast to the IAS 39 controversy of 2002–2005, this time the EU ensured that the IASB modified the standard itself.

This, however, was not a sign that the Commission was henceforth in a position to control the reform of standards. This was revealed when the Commission refused to endorse the new standard for financial instruments, IFRS 9, the first part of which was issued at the end of 2009. This new standard was intended to replace IAS 39 and address its shortcomings; the Commission stated that it could not endorse the standard so long as its other parts were unknown. The Commission moreover claimed that the new standard did not go far enough in limiting the application of fair value accounting. The refusal to endorse the standard was a clear signal to the IASB that it should listen carefully to the EU's concerns when drawing up the final version. But it also showed that the Commission still lacked the formal and informal powers to influence the earlier

---

[7] The IASB simultaneously modified the standard on financial disclosures (IFRS 7) so that it included the obligation to indicate the assets reclassified under the new IAS 39 rules.

phase of the standards-setting process. At the time of writing, the new standard is still unfinished and the EU has not endorsed (parts of) it (see Mügge and Stellinga 2014).

Developments during the crisis also affected the convergence project between the IASB and FASB: under EU pressure, the IASB backed away from prioritizing convergence with US GAAP. The standards setters had signed a memorandum of understanding in 2006 to reiterate their commitment to convergence and, under G20 pressure, had pledged in 2009 to 'intensify their efforts' (Zeff 2012). But the financial instrument standards controversy unveiled their reluctance to coordinate their work: IASB under EU pressure released a 'mixed measurement' standard (combining HCA and FVA) while the FASB initially released a 'full fair value' standard with no role for HCA (which it later withdrew). The boards announced that their plan for complete convergence by 2011 would not be reached. The Commission stated that the 'quality of IASB standards' was more important than 'convergence', while the IASB stated in 2012 that it would no longer prioritize convergence (Arons 2012). The USA likewise backed away from formal commitments to introduce IFRSs any time soon. That the IASB had given in to EU demands to modify IAS 39 without due process provoked serious questions in the USA about the credibility of the IASB as a viable standards setter, feeding domestic resistance to the adoption of IFRSs (Zeff 2012: 830; and see below).

EU Attempts to Increase Influence Over IASB: Governance Reform

As stated above, the EU still had few formal instruments to influence the IASB's agenda and standards-setting process. Refusing or amending (modified) standards (or threatening to do so) was the most important, but also a highly controversial, instrument. The Commission therefore tried to gain greater influence within the institutional framework of the IASB. It repeatedly stressed that countries that required IFRSs should have more structural influence over the work of the IASB than countries that did not (most importantly, the USA). Although the period 2002–2012 saw the IASB's continued integration into global financial regulatory arrangements, the EU failed to position itself as its 'principal'. Instead, the IASB generally maintained a balance between the demands of multiple (prospective) users, most importantly the USA and the EU (Leblond 2011).

Until the late 2000s, the IASB fended off the EU's demands for increased influence by pointing to its convergence project with the FASB. Reducing US representation could jeopardize American willingness to acknowledge IFRSs as equal to US GAAP. Moreover, as the IASB strove to produce standards that are *globally* acceptable, it stressed that it should not favour current over prospective users. These arguments were also put forward by the SEC. The Commission's first attempt to gain greater influence through a modified institutional framework (during the first constitution review, 2003–2005) thus largely failed (see Botzem 2012: 101–104).

The financial crisis triggered widespread discontent with the IASB's governance structure. EU member states, the European Parliament, and the Commission blamed the IASB for being unresponsive to (the EU's) financial stability concerns and demanded increased influence. But the global regulatory context frustrated the EU's attempts as the USA also demanded increased influence. In 2008, the SEC stated that its future adoption of IFRSs would be conditional upon the establishment of a public oversight body (*Journal of Accountancy* 2008). The IASB responded by speeding up the planned second constitution review (2008–2011), which resulted in the creation of a monitoring board in early 2009 to strengthen its links to public regulators.

This did not translate into increased influence for the EU. Nor did it constitute a shift towards a governance framework in which financial stability concerns would get significantly more attention. Apart from one Commission representative, the monitoring board comprised the IOSCO emerging markets committee, the IOSCO technical committee, the Japanese FSA, and the US SEC. The Basel Committee on Banking Supervision only obtained observer status. The monitoring board's mandate was moreover quite limited: it would participate in the trustee nomination and approval process, have oversight responsibilities for trustees, and could refer accounting issues to trustees and the IASB chair. As Posner (2010b: 648) points out, the creation of the monitoring board fits the overall pattern since the 1990s in which 'IASB's relative autonomy ... has been on the decline. ... The creation of the Monitoring Board ... is merely the latest and most visible manifestation of this trend'.

The EU has yet to find an adequate solution to the dilemma of implementing standards that suit its own wishes while simultaneously pushing for their global acceptance. Using IFRSs means that the EU will have to make concessions to other jurisdictions. But ensuring acceptable standards may mean moving EU IFRSs further away from IASB IFRSs.

Explaining Increased EU Influence in Global Accounting Regulation

The EU's decision to introduce IFRSs in Europe undermined US GAAP's position as the de facto world standard. Since the 2000s, the global accounting regulatory regime has been increasingly bi-polar, with IFRSs and US GAAP more or less on an equal footing (Posner 2010b). This fits the more general trend of the EU and the USA becoming increasingly equal partners in the global regulation of finance (Drezner 2007; Posner 2009). As Posner (2009, 2010b) points out, the new realities of regulatory power cannot be explained by referring to (relative) market size (e.g. Simmons 2001; Drezner 2007). The gap in size between American and European national capital markets grew in the years preceding 2000 and stabilized thereafter (Bach and Newman 2007; Posner 2009: 679; Büthe and Mattli 2011). Rather, regulatory centralization in Europe increased the EU's leverage in global financial—and particularly accounting—regulation, boosting the position of IFRSs. For the EU, the endorsement process and the equivalence determination mechanisms are its main means of leverage over the IASB and the regulatory preferences of other jurisdictions.

Alongside developments within the EU, changed circumstances in the USA explain the EU's greater influence in global accounting regulation. As stated earlier, accounting scandals in the USA and the resulting call for a more 'principles-based' approach facilitated a more cooperative FASB stance towards the IASB (Eaton 2005). US multinational firms also felt pressure to align with the rest of the world (Posner 2010b: 654), leading US regulators to pay more attention to international developments. More generally, the strict rules imposed by the Sarbanes–Oxley Act of 2002 and booming markets elsewhere raised American concerns about the continued attractiveness of its capital markets, which could be bolstered by seeking alignment with internationally accepted accounting practices.

Although the EU's backing of IFRSs made them more or less equal to US GAAP, this does not imply that the EU controls their content. This is partly because EU member states still have divergent accounting preferences, thus hampering the ability of the EU to assert itself as a bloc during the process of developing standards (Büthe and Mattli 2011). The IASB furthermore strives for global acceptability: other major countries such as China, Japan, Brazil, India, Canada, and South Korea have already adopted (or converged with) IFRSs, or have set out time-tables to do so (Büthe and Mattli 2011: 72), while important international organizations such as IOSCO, the WTO, and the FSB support their use. As of 2013, 128 countries permitted or required IFRSs for domestic listed companies (Deloitte 2013). While the EU may currently be the most important actor, it is certainly not the only 'principal' that can influence accounting standards.

THE FUTURE ROLE OF THE EU IN GLOBAL ACCOUNTING REGULATION

Global accounting regulation has witnessed remarkable changes over the past 20 years. Whereas US GAAP was long considered the global 'gold standard', its position has been challenged by the rise of IFRSs, now used around the world. The EU has succeeded in harmonizing accounting standards for EU listed companies by adopting IFRSs, but has hitherto found it difficult to influence the content of these standards. This proved challenging during the financial crisis, which politicized accounting standards and led many to call for their modification. Simultaneously, the global financial landscape is changing and emerging economies are seeking more influence in the global regulation of finance. Where is the global regulation of accounting standards heading? And what role will be played by the EU? This chapter concludes by pointing to developments that may well affect global accounting regulation in the future.

How Future EU Regulatory Activity May Matter for the Rest of the World

After the financial crisis hit, European governments became acutely aware of the importance of accounting regulation for financial market stability. Although most EU governments supported the temporary suspension of FVA to give banks breathing space, it soon became clear that fundamental differences remained between the preferences of EU member states. To some extent, cleavages re-emerged between the countries in the continental and Anglo-Saxon accounting traditions. Whereas the UK and the Netherlands, for instance, generally supported the new accounting standard for financial instruments (IFRS 9), Germany, France, and Italy were highly critical of the still significant role it contained for FVA (Sanderson 2009). A debate ensued over whether accounting standards for financial instruments should contribute to financial stability, or should focus on maximizing transparency for outside investors. EU member states seem to be divided on this issue. It therefore remains unclear whether the Commission will be able to speak with one voice during continuing deliberations on the content of the accounting standard for financial instruments, possibly hampering the EU's ability to formulate clear policy preferences and thereby undermining its influence (Mügge 2011c).

Disagreements between EU member states can become more salient with the establishment or strengthening of national organizations focused on accounting. Although the EU has made efforts to coordinate stakeholder input (Botzem 2012: 173), we see the strengthening and increasing activity of national organizations with an interest in accounting matters. EU member states are trying to distil national accounting preferences through organizational change, which may foreshadow further difficulties for the Commission to formulate clear policy preferences at the level of the IASB. The divergent preferences of EU member states combined with more centralized regulatory frameworks at the national level (decentralization viewed from the EU perspective) may well limit the coherence of EU policy positions.

At the same time, it seems unlikely that the EU will succeed in restructuring the IASB to ensure that its voice is more prominently heard. Two successive institutional reviews have only produced modest changes. Although the EU ensured that 'convergence with US GAAP' was no longer a primary IASB goal, it did little to achieve more structural influence over the IASB's agenda and rule-setting procedures. As the IASB's legitimacy will continue to stem from its output rather than input (i.e. procedural) legitimacy (Botzem 2012: 175), the EU will most likely continue to derive its leverage from its ability to adapt or refuse adoption of new or modified standards. The extent to which the IASB will give in to EU demands will depend on the EU's importance relative to those countries that have adopted or will adopt IFRSs in the future (see below). The question then will be how far the EU is willing to depart from IFRSs as published by the IASB. If IFRSs become the standard in regions where EU companies desire to list on exchanges or where the EU hopes to attract business, the EU will feel pressure to keep the differences between EU IFRSs and IASB IFRSs (or local 'dialects' of IFRSs) as small as possible.[8]

How Global Developments May Shape EU Regulatory Efforts

Regulatory and financial market developments in the USA and in emerging regions, particularly in Asia, will crucially affect the EU's future role in global accounting regulation.

The US position towards IFRSs seems more negative now than it was in the period 2002–2008. In 2009, Mary Shapiro, then head of the SEC, stated she did not feel bound by the roadmap for US adoption of IFRSs established by her predecessor, Christopher Cox (Zeff 2012). Although the FASB and IASB are still working to converge their standards, the diverging responses to the financial crisis and the subsequent difficulty to reach an agreeable mutual standard for financial instruments are indicative of the disagreements between the EU and the USA (Jones 2011). Domestic resistance against adopting IFRSs in the USA remains high as it involves ceding a degree of regulatory authority and considerable transaction costs. But as so many countries have now adopted IFRSs, it is doubtful whether US regulatory authorities can continue to resist pressure from other domestic actors (for instance US companies seeking funds abroad) and from other countries to permit or require domestic use of IFRSs. For the near future, an approach termed 'condorsement' is not unlikely, under which some US standards gradually converge with IFRSs, while others are replaced by IFRSs directly (Véron 2011).

---

[8] It may well be possible that we see a future proliferation of national or regional 'dialects' of IFRSs. As the EU has chosen to depart from IASB IFRSs, other regions or countries may take similar steps in the future. This, of course, is wholly contrary to the goal of the IASB, but it cannot prevent this as it lacks enforcement power (Véron 2011; Zeff 2012). IFRSs will then become, or continue to be (depending on one's perspective of the current situation) only a template for regional or national accounting practices, rather than *the* global accounting language. The future might then contain reemerging national/regional clashes to establish equivalence between dialects of IFRSs, depending on the extent to which local versions diverge.

That the USA is not expected to adopt IFRSs anytime soon arguably paves the way for greater EU influence over the IASB. The USA has already established equivalence between US GAAP and IFRSs, and it would be a bold move if it were to backtrack on this. But the US capital market is still the largest and most important in the world (Zeff 2012: 833). It is unlikely that the IASB, after many years of working towards the adoption of IFRSs in the USA, will simply abandon its quest. American caution may thus encourage the IASB to listen even more carefully to US demands, at the expense of EU influence.

Regulatory and financial market developments in emerging economies, most notably in Asia, will be crucial for the EU's future role in global accounting regulation (Zeff 2012). Although the past decades have witnessed bi-polar battles between the EU and the USA, the future may look very different. Other regional blocs are already forming coalitions to counter the influence of the EU and the USA. In Asia, national accounting standards setters founded the Asian-Oceanic Standard-Setters Group (AOSSG) in 2009, now consisting of 25 members. In South America, accounting bodies have formed the Group of Latin American Standard Setters (GLASS) (Zeff 2012: 832). As these countries already require or allow IFRSs—or have adopted road maps towards conversion or adoption—the IASB needs to pay close attention to their wishes. These developments indicate that the IASB will need to balance the demands of the newly formed regional bodies with those of the EU and USA, potentially limiting the latter's influence.

Particular attention should be paid to developments in China. Although China has adopted IFRSs in its national standards, it may decide to move away from them in the future. Given China's deepening and expanding capital markets and its importance in the region, other Asian countries may follow its lead rather than follow IFRSs. In that case, the IASB will come under pressure to accommodate such developments, again limiting the EU's influence over the content of IFRSs. The desirability of the EU diverging from IFRSs will then depend on Europe's wish to attract business from Asia, and European firms to attract Asian capital.

7

Auditing Standards

IAN DEWING AND PETER RUSSELL

INTRODUCTION

An early sub-section of an influential textbook on international accounting, now in its twelfth edition, is entitled 'Accounting and World Politics' (Nobes and Parker 2012: 6). Making such a link may seem puzzling to those who see accounting and auditing as obscure matters having no relation to politics and best left to technical experts. But Nobes and Parker provide an impressive list of how 'world politics'—including empires past and present—have influenced 'accounting'.

Alongside the global economic, political, and social trends that can influence the development of accounting and auditing, crises, failures, and scandals have informed significant changes to accounting and auditing institutions and practice. In the early part of the third millennium, the failures of Enron, Worldcom, and the demise of Andersen—one of the former Big Five accountancy practices—led to wide-ranging debate and the 2002 Sarbanes-Oxley Act in the USA, subsequently leading to major changes not only in the USA but in the EU and other jurisdictions (Dewing and Russell 2004). The recent major event is the financial crisis that began in 2008. As Humphrey et al. (2011: 431–432) have noted, auditors were not in 'the immediate firing line'; the auditing profession was even portrayed as having had 'a good crisis'. But the question remained: how could so many major banks collapse and need rescuing so soon after their financial statements had been audited (see Sikka 2009)? In the EU, the European Commission decided to review the role and scope of the audit in the context of post-crisis regulatory reform and issued its green paper 'Audit Policy: Lessons from the Crisis' in 2010 (EC 2010a).

This chapter explores recent EU and international developments in audit policy, and focuses on the adoption of International Standards on Auditing

(ISAs) issued by the International Auditing and Assurance Standards Board (IAASB),[1] one of the standards-setting bodies of the International Federation of Accountants (IFAC). Like the International Accounting Standards Board (IASB)[2] that sets International Financial Reporting Standards (IFRSs; see Stellinga, this volume), IFAC was established by the worldwide accountancy profession. Both the IASB (the international accounting standards setter) and the IAASB (the international auditing standards setter) are private, non-state, actors.

The IASB regime for setting IFRSs has attracted attention from outside the academic and practitioner accounting communities (e.g. Botzem and Quack 2006; Eaton 2005; Leblond 2011; Mügge 2011c; Nölke and Perry 2007; Perry and Nölke 2005, 2006; Porter 2005; Posner 2010b). But there has been much less interest, even by accounting academics and practitioners, in the regime for setting ISAs under the IAASB. The important exceptions include a series of articles by Humphrey et al. (2009), Humphrey and Loft (2009), and Loft et al. (2006), although their main focus is on the role of IFAC and the auditing profession within the international financial architecture rather than the specific role of the IAASB. Nor has there been much academic interest in the IAASB and its ISAs in the European context (although see Dewing and Russell 2004: 295–298, 308–309; Mügge 2006: 191–193; Humphrey et al. 2011: 445–446).

In discussing the development of auditing within the international financial architecture, both Loft et al. (2006) and Humphrey et al. (2009) use the term 'coordinated network governance' to refer to 'a set of regulatory arrangements that are binding together international regulators and the international profession in an on-going project pursuing global governance in the audit arena' (Humphrey et al. 2009: 812). As we will see, a crucial challenge is ensuring that IFAC and IAASB, as private bodies, act in the public interest and not in the interests of the accounting profession. This has led to a detailed—arguably obsessive—concern with governance structures to ensure that IFAC and IAASB act transparently and in the public interest.

The chapter proceeds as follows: the following section clarifies what is meant by the term audit and considers extracts from the audit reports of three companies from three different EU member states. The third section outlines European and international developments in audit policy prior to the financial crisis, particularly the debate over the adoption of ISAs. The final section considers financial crisis, post-financial crisis, and future developments.

---

[1] The IAASB was originally constituted as the International Auditing Practices Committee (IAPC) in 1978, which included the issuance of Auditing Guidelines re-codified as ISAs in 1991. The IAPC was reconstituted as the IAASB in 2002. For ease of reading, the chapter uses IAASB and ISAs throughout.

[2] The IASB was originally constituted as the International Accounting Standards Committee (IASC) in 1973 to issue International Accounting Standards (IASs). The IASC was reconstituted as the IASB in 2001 and from then new standards were designated as IFRSs. For ease of reading, the chapter uses IASB and IFRSs throughout.

WHAT IS AN AUDIT?

We begin with a general definition of an audit, originally provided by the American Accounting Association and often referred to in accounting and auditing textbooks (e.g. Nobes and Parker 2012: 495; Porter et al. 2008: 2):

> Auditing is a systematic process of objectively obtaining and evaluating evidence regarding assertions about economic actions and events to ascertain the degree of correspondence between those assertions and established criteria and communicating the results to users. (American Accounting Association 1973: 2)

A more recent definition of the objectives of the auditor and the conduct of an audit, specifically concerning the financial statements of companies, is provided by the IAASB:

> The purpose of an audit is to enhance the degree of confidence of intended users in the financial statements. This is achieved by an expression of opinion by the auditor on whether the financial statements are prepared, in all material respects, in accordance with an applicable financial reporting framework. In the case of most general purpose financial frameworks, that opinion is based on whether the financial statements are presented fairly, in all material respects, or give a true and fair view in accordance with the framework. (IAASB, ISA 200, para 3)

To understand what this means in practice, consider the extracts in Box 7.1, taken from three auditors' reports from the UK, Germany, and France of companies listed on the London, Frankfurt, and Paris stock exchanges. The extracts focus on the core responsibility of auditors, which is to provide an opinion on the financial statements (Box 7.1):

Box 7.1. **Extracts from auditors' reports**

UK: Tesco PLC
INDEPENDENT AUDITORS' REPORT TO THE MEMBERS OF TESCO PLC
We have audited the Group financial statements of Tesco PLC for the financial year ended 23 February 2013. . . . The financial reporting framework that has been applied in their preparation is applicable law and International Financial Reporting Standards (IFRS) as adopted by the European Union.

. . .

RESPECTIVE RESPONSIBILITIES OF DIRECTORS AND AUDITORS
. . . the Directors are responsible for the preparation of the Group financial statements and for being satisfied that they give a true and fair view. Our responsibility is to audit and express an opinion on the Group financial statements in accordance with applicable law and International Standards on Auditing (UK and Ireland).

. . .

OPINION ON THE FINANCIAL STATEMENTS
In our opinion the Group financial statements:

- give a true and fair view of the state of the Group's affairs as at 23 February 2013 and of its profit and cash flows for the financial year then ended;
- have been properly prepared in accordance with IFRS as adopted by the European Union; and
- have been prepared in accordance with the requirements of the Companies Act 2006 and Article 4 of the IAS Regulation.

. . .

MARK GILL (SENIOR STATUTORY AUDITOR)
For and on behalf of PricewaterhouseCoopers LLP
Chartered Accountants and Statutory Auditors
London
1 May 2013

Germany: Volkswagen AG
AUDITORS' REPORT
We have audited the consolidated financial statements prepared by VOLKSWAGEN AKTIENGESSELLSCHAFT, Wolfsburg . . . for the business year from 1 January to 31 December 2012. The preparation of the consolidated financial statements . . . in accordance with the IFRSs, as adopted by the EU, and the additional requirements of German commercial law . . . are the responsibility of the Company's Board of Management. Our responsibility is to express an opinion on the consolidated financial statements and the combined management report based on our audit.

We conducted our audit of the consolidated financial statements in accordance with §317 HGB and German generally accepted standards for the audit of financial statements promulgated by the Institut der Wirtschaftprüfer (Institute of Public Auditors in Germany) (IDW). . . .

. . .

Our audit has not led to any reservations.

In our opinion based on the findings of our audit the consolidated financial statements comply with IFRSs, as adopted by the EU, and the additional requirements of German commercial law pursuant to §315a Abs. 1 HGB and give a true and fair view of the net assets, financial position and results of the operation of the Group in accordance with these provisions. . . .

Hanover, 13 February 2013
PricewaterhouseCoopers
Aktiengesellschaft
Wirtschaftsprüfungsgesellschaft

Harald Kayser	Martin Schröder
German Public Auditor	German Public Auditor

France: L'Oreal SA
STATUTORY AUDITORS' REPORT ON THE CONSOLIDATED FINANCIAL STATEMENTS
In compliance with the assignment entrusted to us by your Annual General Meeting, we hereby report to you, for the year ended 31 December 2012. . . .

These consolidated financial statements have been approved by the Board of Directors. Our role is to express an opinion on those consolidated financial statements based on our audit.

OPINION ON THE CONSOLIDATED FINANCIAL STATEMENTS
We conducted our audit in accordance with professional standards applicable in France. . . .
In our opinion, the consolidated financial statements give a true and fair view of the assets and liabilities and of the financial position of the Group at 31 December 2012 and of the results of its operations for the year then ended in accordance with International Financial Reporting Standards as adopted by the European Union.
. . .

Neuilly-sur-Siene, 15 February 2013
The Statutory Auditors
PricewaterhouseCoopers Audit   Deloitte and Associates
Gérard Morin   David Dupont-Noel

Source: Company Annual Reports

As can be seen, the three reports are not identical. The key points in common are as follows: the reports begin by referring to the group or consolidated financial statements, and conclude by stating the names of the audit partner(s), the audit firm(s) and the relevant office(s), and date of the report. Their central sections explain that the directors are responsible for preparing the financial statements and that the auditors are responsible for performing the audit and expressing a 'true and fair' opinion about the financial statements. The auditor's opinion is then provided, and in each case the opinion is unqualified. As well as complying with UK, German, and French company law, it is important to note that the financial statements have been prepared with IFRSs 'as adopted in the EU'—that is, in accordance with *international* accounting standards. Nevertheless, the auditors' work is currently conducted in accordance with UK, German, and French *national* auditing standards, although, as may be inferred from the wording, UK auditing standards generally replicate the relevant ISAs (Porter et al. 2008: xv).

Although the financial statements have been prepared according to a common accounting framework, the question remains whether they have been audited on a common basis. As Dewing and Russell (2004: 308) point out, 'For users to have confidence in the veracity of the accounting numbers, and in auditors' opinions thereon, it is essential that financial statements of companies in Member States are not only prepared in the same way, but are audited in the same way.' The harmonization of accounting in the EU through the adoption of international accounting standards is addressed by Stellinga in this volume. The harmonization of audit policy in the EU, particularly the debate about the adoption of international auditing standards, is discussed below.

EUROPEAN AND INTERNATIONAL AUDIT POLICY DEVELOPMENTS

A series of directives for the harmonization of company law have established a common business framework within the EU. The key directives for accounting and audit are the European Council's Fourth, Seventh, and Eighth Directives (European Council 1978, 1983, 1984). The Fourth Directive introduced common rules for the preparation and presentation of a company's annual accounts such that they give 'a true and fair view of the company's assets, liabilities, financial position and profit or loss' (Article 2); the accounts are required to be audited by 'one or more persons authorized by national law to audit accounts' (Article 51). The Seventh Directive extended this to the consolidated accounts of a group of companies. The Eighth Directive set out the professional qualifications (Articles 3–19) and the requirements of professional integrity and independence (Articles 23–27) to be met for member states to approve individuals and firms to act as auditors.

The Eighth Directive failed to address certain issues, for example, guidance as to what constituted auditor independence. Following the Single European Act and the establishment of the single market, an important issue was that of ensuring common standards for assurance and coverage of the audit across member states. In addition, the free movement of services and freedom of establishment also applied to the European audit market. To consider these and other issues, the Commission published its green paper 'The Role, the Position and the Liability of the Statutory Auditor within the European Union' (EC 1996a). It concluded:

> There is no common view at EU level on the role, the position and the liability of the statutory auditor. The absence of such a common view has a negative impact on audit quality and on the freedom of establishment and freedom to provide services in the audit field. (EC 1996a: para 1.2)

The issues set out in the audit green paper remain at the centre of continuing debate. They include: the definition of a statutory audit and the contents of the audit report; the competence, independence, position, and role of governmental and professional bodies; auditor liability; and other topics such as small company audit, audit of groups of companies, and freedom of establishment and freedom to provide services by individuals and firms.

One key issue was whether auditing harmonization in the EU should follow the path announced for accounting harmonization, where the Commission (EC 1996b) proposed 'putting the Union's weight' behind the IASB and its programme of preparing a set of IFRSs that would be accepted worldwide. The green paper explained:

> There is a significant risk that the accounts and consolidated accounts by European companies will not be accepted in international capital markets unless these accounts have been audited by an independent and qualified professional

in accordance with auditing standards that are generally accepted world-wide. The International Auditing Practices Committee of the International Federation of Accountants (IFAC) has developed a number of international auditing standards. The EU will have to decide whether it wants to support these standards, and if so, how and on what basis the European influence in the development of international auditing standards can be increased. (EC 1996a: para 2.10)

The expansion of international trade, the growth of multinational enterprises, and the development of global financial markets led nationally based professional accountancy bodies to establish the International Federation of Accountants. IFAC was founded in 1977 by 63 professional bodies in 51 countries; by 2012 it had grown to include 173 members and associates from 129 countries and jurisdictions.[3] IFAC's mission is:

> To serve the public interest by: contributing to the development, adoption and implementation of high-quality international standards and guidance; contributing to the development of strong professional accountancy organizations and accounting firms, and to high-quality practices by professional accountants; promoting the value of professional accountants worldwide; and speaking out on public interest issues where the accountancy profession's expertise is most relevant. (IFAC 2012: 12)

To achieve its objectives, IFAC established a number of committees, standards-setting boards, and advisory groups, the most important for this chapter being the IAASB, which sets ISAs. The IAASB's objective is:

> To serve the public interest by setting high-quality international standards for auditing, quality control, review, other assurance, and related services, and by facilitating the convergence of international and national auditing and assurance standards, thereby enhancing the quality and consistency of practice throughout the world and strengthening public confidence in the global auditing and assurance profession. (IAASB 2012a: 1)

The membership of IAASB currently consists of a full-time chairman and 17 individual volunteers. Nine are practitioners nominated by IFAC member bodies; the other nine are non-practitioners and include the chairman and at least three public members—individuals 'expected to reflect, and are seen to reflect the wider public interest'. The remaining members are nominated by the Transnational Auditors Committee, which acts as the executive arm of the Forum of Firms, an association of international networks of accounting firms that perform transnational audits.[4] Whatever their background, all individual members of IAASB are annually required to sign a declaration

---

[3] <http://www.ifac.org/about-ifac/organization-overview/history> (accessed on 22 February 2013).

[4] <http://www.ifac.org/about-ifac/forum-firms> (accessed on 7 June 2013).

that they will act in the public interest and with integrity in discharging their responsibilities.

Following consultations on the audit green paper, the European Commission announced the creation of a Committee on Auditing composed of experts nominated by EU member states which would have special responsibilities for auditing matters. The communication 'Statutory Audit in the European Union: The Way Forward' (EC 1998a) underlined the importance of the accounting profession's involvement in the committee's work (para 3.2). The committee's principal tasks include reviewing existing ISAs and their application in the EU, and contributing to the work of the IAASB (para 3.4). The review of ISAs was a priority, to be undertaken on the basis of papers prepared by the Commission and the profession (paras 3.7–8).

A further stimulus for auditing harmonization in the EU was the aim to complete the internal market for financial services by 2005, for which the Commission developed the Financial Services Action Plan (FSAP) (EC 1998b, 1999a). Just as IFRSs—by mirroring international best practice—were seen as the way forward for financial reporting in the EU, in the realm of auditing, ISAs were judged 'to be the minimum which should be satisfied in order to give credibility to published financial statements' (EC 1999a: 7).

The views of the accounting profession were crucial to the adoption of ISAs in the EU. Professional accountants and auditors from across Europe, including the EU member states, are represented by the Fédération des Experts Comptables Européen (FEE), the 'voice of the European accountancy profession toward the EU institutions and other international organizations'.[5] Following consultations and studies on the adoption of ISAs in the EU (FEE 1998, 2000), the FEE (2001: para 1.1) proposed that:

> By 2005 national auditing standards in the European Union should require auditors of financial statements to:
>
> - Perform audit procedures that comply with International Standards on Auditing (ISAs);
> - Report on financial statements in accordance with ISAs; and
> - Perform additional audit procedures and report additional matters in response to specific legal, regulatory or other needs established at a national level.

The FEE was of the view that the proposal could be implemented without new legislation by using national arrangements for the delegation of auditing standards setting, coordinated by a European forum of national auditing standards setters (para 1.2).

---

[5] <http://www.fee.be/index.php?option=com_contentandview=articleandid=2andItemid=104> (accessed on 22 February 2013).

While auditing harmonization and the adoption of ISAs in the EU were being prepared by the Commission and the accounting profession, the collapse of Enron in December 2001 and the demise of one of the Big Five accounting firms, Andersen, led to a rethinking of accounting and auditing regulation in the USA. The Sarbanes–Oxley Act of 2002, in particular, led to a European response (see Dewing and Russell 2004). The Commission communication *Reinforcing the Statutory Audit in the EU* (EC 2003) developed a 10-point action plan for improving and harmonizing the quality of statutory audit in the EU. One of its key proposals was to modernize the Eighth Directive, originally adopted in 1984 and not amended since, to provide a comprehensive legal basis for *all* statutory audits within the EU (para 2.1). The proposal was to adopt ISAs for all EU statutory audits from 2005. But preliminary actions were required: the analysis of EU and member state audit requirements not covered by ISAs; a common audit report and high quality translations; and further improvements to the ISA standards-setting process, which was considered to lack independence from the profession (para 3.1). Regarding the last point, the Commission had acknowledged recent improvements in transparency and the inclusion of non-practitioners in the IAASB; it nevertheless remained concerned that the IAASB's activities to set audit standards were 'fundamentally conducted by and for the audit profession'. The Commission was furthermore concerned about IFAC's accountability, commenting that its 'over-arching governance structure . . . implies control by the international accounting profession'. It suggested that the public interest would be better safeguarded if the IAASB was independent of IFAC, with a membership consisting of a majority of non-practitioner stakeholders (EC 2003: 7).

In the event, insufficient progress was made to adopt ISAs from 2005 and the new audit directive was not issued until 2006. The new Statutory Audit Directive (EPC 2006) nevertheless contained a provision whereby the Commission could adopt ISAs but only if they:

a. have been developed with proper due process, public oversight and transparency, and are generally accepted internationally;

b. contribute a high level of credibility and quality to the annual or consolidated accounts in conformity with the principles set out in Article 2(3) of Directive 78/660/EEC and in Article 16(3) of Directive 83/349/EEC; and

c. are conducive to the European public good (EPC 2006: Article 26).

The new directive required EU member states to set up public oversight systems for statutory auditors and audit firms, comparable to the independent Public Company Accounting Oversight Board (PCAOB) established in the USA following the Sarbanes–Oxley Act. It also established a committee, subsequently known as the Audit Regulatory Committee (AuRC), made up of member state representatives, to advise the Commission (Article 48). In a separate decision, the Commission established a European Group of Auditors' Oversight Bodies (EGAOB) (EC 2005), whose members would be prominent non-practitioners drawn from member state oversight bodies. The main tasks of the EGAOB are to coordinate the public oversight systems of member states, assess and cooperate with the oversight systems of other countries, and advise the Commission on ISAs. Here the EGAOB is expected to 'Contribute to the technical examination of international auditing standards, including the processes for their elaboration, with a view to their adoption at the Community level' (EC 2005: Article 2).

The first key to establishing the authority of ISAs was what became known as the 'Clarity Project' (IAASB 2004). Extant ISAs had been set over a period during which business and financial reporting had become more complex and IFAC and IAASB had undergone significant changes. Following its reconstitution, IAASB reviewed the drafting conventions used in preparing ISAs to improve their clarity and enhance their consistent application. The result was the Clarity Project, a comprehensive programme which involved the application of new drafting conventions and resulted in the substantive revision or limited redrafting of all ISAs. All ISAs now have a consistent structure in which information is presented in separate sections: introduction; objective; definitions; requirements; application; and other explanatory material. In total, 36 clarified ISAs were issued and approved, entering into effect for audits of financial statements for periods beginning on or after 15 December 2009 (IAASB 2008). In response to requests from stakeholders for a period of stability, the IAASB agreed to not issue any further ISAs that would enter into effect in the following two years. Studies have since addressed the differences between ISAs and the auditing standards of the US PCAOB (MARC 2009) and the costs and benefits of adopting ISAs in the EU (Köhler et al. 2009). Both studies were broadly supportive of the EU's adoption of ISAs. Following these studies, the Commission held another consultation on the adoption of ISAs, which again revealed widespread support for their adoption (EC 2009a, 2010b).

The second key to establishing the authority of ISAs—in light of the concerns of the Commission and others—was a series of IFAC reforms designed to further strengthen the process of audit standards setting and to demonstrate more clearly that IFAC acts in the public interest (IFAC 2003). This involved the establishment of an independent Public Interest Oversight Board (PIOB) to oversee IFAC standards-setting bodies, including the IAASB, and the creation of a Monitoring Group made up of representatives from financial regulators and others constituting the international financial architecture including the International Organization of Securities Commissions (IOSCO), the Basel Committee on Banking Supervision (BCBS), the European Commission, the International Association of Insurance Supervisors (IAIS), and the World Bank (IFAC 2003: 3–4).

The PIOB was established in 2005 as a result of the 2003 IFAC reform proposals and occupies an important niche in the IFAC structure. The PIOB's mandate is due process oversight of IFAC's public interest activities, which includes oversight of the IAASB. In addition to the IAASB, IFAC's Public Interest Activities Committees (PIACs) include the International Education Standards Board (IAESB), International Ethics Standard Board for Accountants (IESBA), their respective Consultative Advisory Groups (CAGs), and the Compliance Advisory Panel (CAP).[6] The PIOB reviews and approves terms of reference; evaluates the boards' due process procedures; oversees the work of IFAC's Nominating Committee and approves its nominations; and suggests projects to be added to the boards' work programmes.

Interestingly, the European Parliament and Council decided to establish a programme to support specific activities in financial services, financial reporting, and auditing, which included providing funds to support the work of private actors such as the PIOB (EPC 2009). At the front of its Seventh (2012) Public Report, the PIOB acknowledges that it has received financial support from the European Union (DG Internal Market and Services) since 2010. Conscious of its public interest role, the PIOB states that 'The content of this report is the sole responsibility of the PIOB and should under no circumstances be regarded as reflecting the views of the European Union' (PIOB 2012a: 2).

One reason why the PIOB is of interest is that it is a private actor charged with the responsibility of ensuring that the Public Interest Activities Committees of IFAC (also private actors) act in the public interest. As described by the chairman, this principally involves attendance at PIACs meetings:

> This breadth of attendance gives the PIOB an in-depth view of the standard-setting work taking place and enables it to influence topics that raise public interest issues. The PIOB pays special attention to how the procedures and deliberations in the PIACs reflect the public interest, by ensuring that an open and free debate takes place, that all opinions are heard, and that the arguments put on the table in the consultations, especially in the CAGs, are taken into account. Apart from an overall check, these steps ensure that the standards finally adopted reflect the public interest, embodied in the diversity of opinions as expressed in the standard-setting process. (PIOB 2012a: 3)

Within its public oversight mandate, the PIOB is seeking to develop and refine an 'oversight methodology'. A seven-step assurance cycle has been developed as follows: assign team leaders for oversight activities; develop oversight assurance models; determine oversight techniques; have oversight plan approved by the board; execute oversight plan; present oversight findings to the board; and review PIOB experience (PIOB 2012a: 6–10). For the standards-setting boards

[6] <http://www.ipiob.org/print/about/piob-mandate> (accessed on 22 February 2013).

such as IAASB, PIOB also approves work plans and, for the issuance of new standards, confirms that due process has been followed. The PIOB's other main area of oversight is the approval of membership nominations by IFAC for its Public Interest Activities Committees.

Overall, the PIOB provides a model that may have wider implications for ensuring that other transnational private—and indeed public—actors consider the public interest. However, there is the question of oversight of the PIOB. This responsibility goes to the Monitoring Group, also set up as part of the 2003 IFAC reform proposals. The original members were IOSCO, BCBS, IAIS, the Commission, and the World Bank, subsequently joined by the Financial Stability Board (FSB) and the International Forum of Independent Audit Regulators (IFIAR). The Monitoring Group is based in IOSCO offices in Madrid but is not established as a separate legal entity. In 2009 it announced the adoption of a formal charter that stated its mission (Monitoring Group 2009: 2–3):

- Cooperate in the interest of promoting high-quality international auditing and assurance, ethical and education standards for accountants;
- Monitor the implementation and effectiveness of the IFAC Reforms and, in that connection, undertake an effectiveness assessment of the IFAC Reforms and other aspects of IFAC's operations that involve the public interest;
- Through its Nominating Committee, appoint the members of the Public Interest Oversight Board;
- Monitor the execution of the PIOB of its mandate;
- Consult and advise the PIOB with respect to regulatory, legal and policy developments that are pertinent to the PIOB's public interest oversight; and
- Convene to discuss issues and share views relating to international audit quality as well as to regulatory and market developments having an impact on auditing.

In addition to its oversight of the PIOB, the Monitoring Group has reviewed the implementation of the 2003 IFAC reforms (Monitoring Group 2010). It concluded that 'virtually all' of the proposed changes had been implemented, but identified other issues for further considerations including, in the near term, the need to continue enhancing public interest safeguards and, in the longer term, whether standards-setting boards should continue to operate under the auspices of accountancy professional bodies, and whether there could be synergies between the Monitoring Group, which oversees the setting of ISAs, and the Monitoring Board, which provides equivalent oversight for the setting of IFRSs (Monitoring Group 2010: 4–5).

Following a series of reviews and reforms and the creation of new advisory and oversight bodies in a process lasting over a decade, it appeared that layered international and European governance frameworks involving private and public actors had been established to enable the EU to adopt ISAs. Then came the financial crisis.

FINANCIAL CRISIS, POST-FINANCIAL CRISIS, AND FUTURE DEVELOPMENTS

Like the Enron crisis, the financial crisis beginning in 2008 led to further calls to rethink audit in the EU. The Commission issued its second audit green paper, *Audit Policy: Lessons from the Crisis* (EC 2010a), which revisited a number of long-standing issues, including: the role of the auditor; governance and the independence of audit firms; supervision of audit firms; concentration and structure of the audit market; creation of a European market; simplification for small and medium-sized enterprises and practitioners; and international cooperation. Certain elements in the green paper were controversial, particularly proposals to enhance auditor independence and to reduce the dominance of the Big Four firms through, for example, the mandatory rotation of auditors, limiting auditors' provision of non-audit services, and the compulsory joint audits of large companies.

The Commission welcomed the improvements to ISAs brought about by the IAASB's Clarity Project and acknowledged the overall support given to the adoption of ISAs by stakeholders. It continued to seek views on the adoption of ISAs in the EU as well as on how adoption should proceed, for example, by an endorsement process similar to that for IFRSs or by non-binding instruments such as a recommendation or code of conduct (EC 2010a: 9–10). Responses to the green paper once more indicated widespread support for the adoption of ISAs from the profession, investors, public authorities, and academics, while preparers, businesses, and organizations of companies had reservations. The main reservations concerned the governance and due process of the IAASB as the auditing standards setter, and the exact nature of the EU adoption and endorsement process (EC 2011d: 12–14).

The Commission has since issued a proposed regulation on the audit of public interest entities and a proposed directive amending the recent Statutory Audit Directive (EC 2011e, 2011f). The regulation proposes that auditors comply with ISAs when carrying out the statutory audit of 'public interest entities', which include EU listed companies, and that this be stated in the audit report (Articles 21, 22(f)). Significantly, the Commission is not seeking to establish a process for endorsing individual ISAs comparable to that for individual IFRSs. Instead, the proposed directive seeks to amend Article 26 of the Statutory Audit Directive by requiring individual member states to ensure that auditors comply with ISAs when carrying out statutory audits (EC 2011f: para 12: 20–21). Member states may impose additional audit procedures or requirements in addition to ISAs only if these arise from national legal requirements and they 'contribute a high level of credibility and quality to the annual financial statements' and 'are conducive to the Union public good' (EC 2011f: para 12: 20).

Previous requirements for due process, public oversight, transparency, and general international acceptance (EPC 2006: Article 26, 2(a)) were removed since oversight for the IFAC and IAASB had been strengthened by the creation of the PIOB and the Monitoring Group (of which the Commission is a member). Interestingly, the proposed amendment allows EU member states to decide on the 'Union public good' when imposing additional requirements. While generally supportive of the Commission's approach, the FEE (2012) expressed concern that seven EU member states (Austria, France, Germany, Italy, Poland, Portugal, and Spain) had not yet fully adopted ISAs, in part because the Statutory Audit Directive has not yet been transposed or implemented. Warning of the risks of these countries not adopting ISAs, the FEE advocated an alternative endorsement procedure at the EU or Commission level (FEE 2012).

At the time of writing, the proposed regulation and directive (EC 2011e, 2011f) are making their way through the co-decision procedures of the European Parliament, Council, and Commission. Although adopting ISAs for the audit of public interest entities—including listed companies—is relatively uncontroversial, progress on the directive and regulation was delayed in the European Parliament's Committee on Legal Affairs, known as JURI, which found other aspects of the proposed legislation controversial: for example, securing auditor independence through the mandatory rotation of audit firms, limiting the extent of non-audit work, and increasing competition in the audit market. JURI reported 195 amendments from the rapporteur and a further 550 amendments tabled for the regulation (JURI 2012), and 25 amendments from the rapporteur and a further 147 amendments tabled for the directive (JURI 2013a). JURI has recently voted to enter negotiations with the Council with a view to agreeing a common text; reforms were due to go before the Parliament in 2013 (JURI 2013b). The use of ISAs for statutory audits in the EU, first raised in the 1996 green paper, finally appears at hand.

At the international level, the IAASB's 'Strategy and Work Program, 2012-14' includes the development of new and a review of existing standards (IAASB 2012b). One project of wider interest is the 'auditor reporting' project. Audit reports are highly standardized and confirm that financial statements are true and fair. The auditor reporting project, which commenced before the financial crisis but was taken up in the debates following the crisis, focuses on how auditors' reports could be made to convey more information to stakeholders. The project's objectives are to:

- Appropriately enhance the communicative value and relevance of the auditor's report through proposed revisions of ISA requirements that address its structure and content; and
- Determine whether and how the IAASB's reporting ISAs, in their design, can be made to accommodate evolving national financial reporting regimes, while at the same time ensuring that common and essential content is being communicated.[7]

[7] <http://www.ifac.org/auditing-assurance/projects/auditor-reporting> (accessed on 22 February 2013).

Two consultation papers were issued (IAASB 2011, 2012c) suggesting additional content that might be included in auditors' reports such as commentary highlighting issues that, in the judgment of auditors, are likely to be important to users' understanding of the audit and the audited financial statements. This would significantly supplement the traditional 'true and fair view' audit opinion as shown in the examples in Box 7.1. Other IAASB projects of wider interest concern audit quality, disclosures, and ISA implementation.[8]

In light of the financial crisis, the Monitoring Group's main current task is public consultation on its own governance structure as well as that of the PIOB and the standards-setting boards of IFAC, including the role and composition of the various bodies and the financing of the PIOB (Monitoring Group 2012: 1–2). While satisfied with the overall three-tiered structure of IFAC standards-setting bodies, the Monitoring Group identified five 'operational improvements' to improve the accountability of standards-setting bodies and to better align their decisions with the public interest (Monitoring Group 2013: 5). The thrust of the improvements is to more clearly identify concerns of public interest and to demonstrate that they have been addressed, especially for issues conveyed by Monitoring Group members and other stakeholders, and to improve engagement and transparency more generally (Monitoring Group 2013: 5–10).

The PIOB's concurrent consultation on its future work programme (PIOB 2012b) led to a set of 14 recommendations in response to the comment letters it had received (PIOB 2013). Again, the thrust of the recommendations was to strengthen the protection of the public interest by increasing the transparency of its activities, continuing to clarify the roles of IFAC, the PIOB, and the Monitoring Group, and more actively engaging with stakeholders. Here the PIOB specifically referred to better representation of the relatively neglected small and medium-sized accountancy firms and developing countries in IFAC's standards-setting and consultative bodies (Recommendation 3).

In conclusion, the interest in the setting of ISAs from outside the accountancy and auditing profession largely stems from the fact that the standards setters—the IAASB acting under the remit of IFAC—are private actors established by the world-wide accountancy profession. They differ from other institutions comprising the international financial architecture such as the BCBS, the IMF, and the World Bank, which are public actors established by governments. The main challenge has been to ensure that the IAASB acts—and is perceived to act—in the public interest and not in the interests of the accountancy profession. The result has been the creation of linkages at the international, regional, and national levels involving a range of private, professional, and public actors. At the international level, this includes bodies such as the International Organization of Securities Commissions, the Basel Committee

---

[8] <http://www.ifac.org/auditing-assurance/projects> (accessed on 22 February 2013).

on Banking Supervision, the International Association of Insurance Supervisors, the World Bank, the Financial Stability Board, and the International Forum of Independent Audit Regulators; at the regional level, the European Commission and its advisory bodies, the Audit Regulatory Committee and the European Group of Auditor's Oversight Bodies, the Fédération des Experts Comptables Européen as the voice of the European accountancy profession, and the European Parliament and Council; and at the national level, individuals on professional accountancy bodies, associated government departments, and other bodies responsible for the oversight and regulation of auditing. At all levels, there is the influence of the international networks of accounting firms, especially the influential Big Four. The setting of ISAs is thus embedded in a complex, transnational network of private, professional, and public actors which require them individually and collectively to act transparently and in the public interest. The setting of international auditing standards is not just a technical matter but a political one.

8

Hedge Funds

DAVID HOWARTH AND LUCIA QUAGLIA[1]

INTRODUCTION

Hedge funds have exploded into prominence over the last two decades, with global assets under management growing 50-fold between 1990 and 2007, reaching approximately $2 trillion in 2007 (EC 2008d). In recent years, trading by hedge funds has accounted for over 50 per cent of the daily trading volume in equities markets. Hedge funds have become crucial providers of liquidity and drivers of price formation in global financial markets.

Prior to the international financial crisis that began in 2007, hedge funds had come under the spotlight for promoting herding behaviour during the Asian financial crisis of 1997. In the following year, the failure of the American hedge fund Long-Term Capital Management (LTCM) highlighted the potential systemic repercussions ensuing from the failure of large hedge funds. In Europe, episodes such as the failed merger between the Deutsche Börse and the London Stock Exchange highlighted the potential disruptive effects that hedge funds can have on corporate governance in continental European countries, first and foremost in Germany (*The Economist*, 23 April 2005).

The international financial crisis brought new urgency to the debate on regulating hedge funds. Although hedge funds were not the main cause of the crisis (Brunnermeier et al. 2009; High-Level Group on Financial Supervision in the EU 2009), they did play a part in its worsening, mainly through the massive selling of shares and short-selling transactions (G30 2009; FSA 2009). The large-scale fraud perpetrated by Bernard Madoff's fund[2] (widely, but perhaps incorrectly, seen as a hedge fund) had considerable political resonance within and outside the USA and further intensified the debate on regulation.

[1] Lucia Quaglia wishes to acknowledge financial support from the European Research Council (204,398 FINGOVEU) and the British Academy and Leverhulme Trust (SG120191).
[2] See https://www.hedgeco.net/blogs/2012/10/15/did-bernie-madoff-run-a-hedge-fund/

This chapter analyses the EU and the international regulation of hedge funds, addressing two key questions posed in the introduction to this volume: How have European and global rules influenced each other up to the present day? And which factors inform the global influence of European regulatory efforts and the relevance of global initiatives for European rules? We find that the absence of agreement at the EU level has weakened the EU's position internationally and increased the influence of the USA in EU policymaking. The differences within the EU are due principally to the existence of different financial systems. Countries with many hedge fund managers (the UK and, to a lesser extent, Sweden) were the most cautious regarding EU legislation, while the lobbying of financial services firms contributed to national positioning.

The main legislative response to the international financial crisis concerning hedge funds has been the EU's Alternative Investment Fund Managers Directive (AIFMD). Proposed by the Commission in April 2009 (EC 2009c) and agreed at the December 2010 European Council, it was formally adopted in June 2011 (EC 2011h) with a deadline to transpose into national legislation by 22 July 2013. The AIFMD's 'third country' provisions raised the question of 'equivalence' and sparked the direct intervention of the US federal administration—opposed to the export of EU norms in this area—in the EU policymaking process. Although the original 'third country' provisions proposed by the Commission were significantly watered down in the adopted directive, questions remained about the impact of the 11 conditions that non-EU-based funds and fund managers would have to meet in order to access the EU passport. The delay on the Level 2 implementing regulation, published by the Commission in December 2012, contributed to on-going debate and consternation over the international impact of AIFMD.

The chapter is structured as follows. The remainder of this introduction outlines some key concepts in the regulation of hedge funds. Sections 2 and 3 outline, respectively, the regulation of hedge funds internationally and in the EU, before and after the crisis. Section 4 discusses the debate surrounding third country access resulting from the AIFMD. Section 5 concludes with an overall assessment.

Some Key Concepts Concerning Hedge Fund Regulation

How to define a hedge fund is controversial, with jurisdictions employing different definitions. The International Organization of Securities Commission (IOSCO), the international body whose regulatory remit covers hedge funds, has been unable to produce a common or shared definition, noting that 'each jurisdiction has views on what a hedge fund is' (IOSCO 2006: 9). Generally speaking, hedge funds tend to have the following characteristics (EC 2008d; IOSCO 2009): (1) they focus on the delivery of absolute returns; (2) their investment strategies are typically based on a relatively high and systematic use of leverage (they are often defined as 'highly leveraged institutions'; see, for example, BCBS 1999a, 1999b) through borrowing, short-selling,[3] and derivatives positions; (3) their investor base has traditionally been confined to institutional or other sophisticated investors; (4) significant performance fees (for instance, in the form of a percentage of profits) are paid to the manager in addition to an annual management fee; and (5) managers often have their 'own funds' invested. Unlike private equity firms, hedge funds tend to invest in liquid securities rather than long-term illiquid assets and do not intervene in the management of companies in which they invest. Prior to the financial crisis, hedge funds tended to be 'unregulated'. Indeed, the IOSCO task force analysing regulatory options for hedge funds was named the 'Task Force on Unregulated Entities'.

The main actors in the hedge funds business are the hedge fund manager, the fund itself (often legally distinct from the manager), the fund's administrator (responsible for processing trades and valuing assets), and the prime brokers (investment banks and securities firms) which act as settlement agents, have custody over assets, and provide financing (EC 2008d; FSA 2005c). Although it depends on the jurisdiction, hedge fund managers and prime brokers tend to be regulated, at least in Europe.

Hedge funds are often referred to as 'unregulated' financial entities, even though this definition is only partially correct. First, one should distinguish between the direct and indirect regulation of hedge funds. Indirect regulation entails regulation of the financial institutions that interact with hedge funds, in particular the prime brokers through which hedge funds operate in securities markets, and banks (in particular investment banks) investing in or lending to hedge funds. Second, one should distinguish between the regulation of hedge funds, many of which are located offshore and thus cannot be regulated, and the regulation of fund managers in the jurisdiction in which they are based.

REGULATING HEDGE FUNDS INTERNATIONALLY

Prior to the international financial crisis, research and fact finding on hedge funds was undertaken by international financial regulatory forums, generally following policy failures. After the Asian financial crisis and the collapse of the hedge fund LTCM in the USA, a set of policy documents was issued by the Basel Committee on Banking Supervision (BCBS) (1999a, 1999b), IOSCO (1999), and subsequently by the newly created Financial Stability Forum (FSF) (2000, then updated in 2007, when the first signs of the crisis emerged).

---

[3] Naked or uncovered short selling involves the sale of an asset that the seller does not own.

The USA also conducted its own review through the President's Working Group (PWG) on Financial Markets (1999). Basically, all these documents concluded in favour of the indirect regulation of hedge funds, which was indeed strengthened.

In policy discussions in international forums, two different approaches were apparent: one in favour of direct regulation supported by Germany and France, and the other resisting such regulation supported by the USA and the UK (interviews, Basel, November 2008; Madrid, March 2009; Fioretos 2010). In 2007, German officials used their presidency of the EU and of the G8 to push for direct regulation, receiving some backing from the FSF, which the G8 had charged with studying the issue.[4] At the outset of the global financial crisis, the German finance minister Peer Steinbrück called for a formal code of conduct for hedge funds. The USA opposed a code of conduct, while the US Treasury secretary Henry Paulson Jr. supported a set of principles that informed investors, leaving them to monitor risk (*International Herald Tribune*, 23 April 2007; *Bloomberg News*, 23 April 2007). An impasse followed and no action was taken to deal with the problems posed by hedge and private-equity funds.

However, in 2007 the FSF called on the hedge fund industry to develop a code of best practices. In response, several standards were issued by private sector bodies in the UK and US jurisdictions: the Hedge Fund Working Group (HFWG)/Hedge Fund Standards Board (HFSB) and the Alternative Investment Management Association (AIMA) in the UK, and the Managed Funds Association (MFA) based in the USA (Alternative Investment Industry Association 2007, 2008). Their recommendations covered sound practices for hedge fund governance, transparency, and processes and methodologies for the valuation of hedge fund portfolios.

After the eruption of the financial crisis, the international division over how to regulate hedge funds re-emerged amid preparations for the April 2009 G20 summit. Several European countries, led by France and Germany and supported by Italy (*Reuters*, 11 October 2008), pushed for a tougher regulatory regime and for hedge funds to be overseen similarly to banks (*Financial Times*, 23 February 2009; Quaglia 2011b). In contrast, US and UK authorities favoured greater disclosure over more regulation, proposing that hedge funds be required to register with the government and disclose additional information with a view to increasing transparency (*Wall Street Journal*, 14 March 2009). European leaders also wanted to clamp down on tax havens.

[4] Previously, in July 2005, then Chancellor of Germany, Gerhard Schröder, a Social Democrat, had pressed for tighter controls on hedge funds at the G7 summit in Britain, where it was blocked by 'Wall Street and London' (Schröder in *The Independent*, 16 June 2005).

In February 2009, German Chancellor Angela Merkel hosted a summit of German, French, Italian, Spanish, Dutch, and British leaders in Berlin. The purpose of the gathering was to prepare a common EU policy in advance of London's G20 summit in April 2009. The press statement issued after the meeting pointed out that 'all financial markets, products and participants must be subject to appropriate oversight or regulation, without exception and regardless of their country of domicile. This is especially true for those private pools of capital, including hedge funds, that may present a systemic risk.'[5] The consensus was seen as a victory for France and Germany, which had championed a comprehensive regulatory architecture (*Financial Times*, 23 February 2009). The UK Chancellor of the Exchequer, Gordon Brown, reportedly agreed to restrictions on hedge funds to clear the way for an overall accord, which included strengthening the International Monetary Fund (*Daily Telegraph*, 23 February 2009).

A joint letter from French President Nicolas Sarkozy and German Chancellor Angela Merkel (2009) to the EU Council President Mirek Topolanek and President of the European Commission Jose Manuel Barroso, in preparation for the G20 summit in April 2009, reiterated the goal of a joint EU position on the 'appropriate registration, regulation, and oversight' of hedge funds and other funds presenting potential systemic risk. After protracted negotiations, the G20 in London in April 2009 agreed that:

> hedge funds or their managers will be registered and will be required to disclose appropriate information on an ongoing basis to supervisors or regulators, including on their leverage, necessary for assessment of the systemic risks that they pose individually or collectively. Where appropriate, registration should be subject to a minimum size. They will be subject to oversight to ensure that they have adequate risk management. . . .

Following the G20 recommendations, IOSCO published a report (2009) containing some rather general recommendations on the regulation of hedge funds. During preparatory discussions, participants—member state regulators—had been unable to agree on the fundamental issue of whether the hedge fund or the hedge fund manager should be regulated, as there were different views and legislation in place in the participating jurisdictions (interview, Madrid, March 2009). In the end, the IOSCO report left this issue ambiguous.

Since 2009, hedge fund managers based in the USA have been working on new industry standards under the auspices of the President's Working Group. The PWG contained two separate committees: the Asset Managers' Committee made up of institutional alternative asset managers representing diverse perspectives charged with developing guidelines that define best

[5] <http://www.diplo.de/diplo/en/WillkommeninD/D-Informationen/Nachrichten/090224-1.html> (accessed May 2009).

practices for the hedge fund industry (Asset Managers' Committee 2009), and the Investors' Committee, which also issued a set of best practice standards to reduce systemic risk and foster investor protection (Investors Committee 2009). Under the aegis of IOSCO, industry associations have worked together to produce a single summary standards document, the Hedge Fund Matrix.[6]

EU REGULATION OF HEDGE FUNDS

Prior to the international financial crisis, hedge funds (and fund managers) were not regulated at the EU level (Lutton 2008). But hedge funds, or more precisely some of their activities, were subject to EU legislation, notably the Markets in Financial Instruments Directive (MiFID), the Transparency Directive, and the Market Abuse Directive. Some prudential reporting to supervisors was required by a European Central Bank (ECB) regulation concerning statistics on the assets and liabilities of investment funds. According to this regulation, issued in 2007 in the early stages of the financial crisis, all investment funds in the EU, including hedge funds, had to provide certain information to national central banks. At the national level, hedge fund managers were regulated entities in some member states though not subject to specific legislation. In other words, they were regulated as 'normal' fund managers. In other countries such as France, Italy, Spain, and Germany, the fund itself was a regulated onshore vehicle (IOSCO 2006, 2009), though often it was domiciled in a third country.

Since the early 2000s, some EU member states, most notably Germany, as well as some members of the European Parliament (see e.g. the Kaforis report) had encouraged discussion on the regulation of hedge funds at the EU level. Partly to assuage these concerns, the Commission set up a group of experts—the Alternative Investment Expert Group—to discuss the issue. The group, which included several hedge fund managers and other alternative investment fund managers (AIFMs) among its members, issued a report in 2006, *Managing, Servicing and Marketing Hedge Funds in Europe*, which concluded against EU legislation on hedge funds (Alternative Investment Expert Group 2006). The issue was raised again by the German presidency of the EU in 2007 and during its hosting of the G8 summit (*The Economist*, 26 May 2007) but with scant support (interviews, Berlin, April 2008).

In the past, the Commission, notably the Commissioner for the Internal Market, Charles McCreevy, had ruled out EU legislation on hedge funds. According to several interviewees, the Barroso Commission and Commissioner McCreevy

---

[6] <http://www.hedgefundmatrix.com/> (accessed August 2009).

in particular favoured the 'better regulation' of financial services, which often meant 'light touch' regulation or no regulation at all, as in the case of hedge funds and credit rating agencies (interviews, Brussels, June 2007; Paris, July 2007; Rome, December 2007). But the international financial crisis shifted the political dynamics in Brussels (Buckley and Howarth 2011; Quaglia 2011b). The top echelons of the Commission, led by President Barroso, began to favour regulation—seen in the decision to propose regulation for credit rating agencies and AIFMs which the Commission had previously ruled out. The European Parliament became particularly vocal on the need to regulate hedge funds, producing two reports: the 'Rasmussen' report and the 'Lehne' report (European Parliament 2008a, 2008b). An EP resolution on 23 September 2008 requested the Commission to submit a legislative proposal or proposals covering all relevant actors and financial market participants, including hedge fund managers and private equity firms.

In December 2008, the Commission issued a consultation document discussing regulatory measures for hedge funds. Most government respondents argued that an international or global response would be superior to an EU response. But a small majority of government respondents believed that it was nevertheless appropriate to move forward with EU-level action. Many respondents, most notably the French and German governments, argued that 'Europe should play an instrumental role in shaping a global regulatory regime for hedge funds through the creation of a "European label". An EU framework could serve as a reference for global regulation of alternative investment management activity' (EC 2009d: 8).

In June 2009 the Commission presented its draft directive on AIFMs, which covered managers of hedge, private equity, and real estate funds (EC 2009c). It introduced a legally binding authorization and supervisory regime for all AIFMs in the EU, irrespective of the legal domicile of the managed alternative investment fund. AIFMs would be subject to authorization from the competent authority of the home member state and to reporting systemically important data to supervisors. The draft directive recommended a European passport for AIFMs: an AIFM authorized in its home member state would be entitled to market its funds to professional investors in other member states, which would not be permitted to impose additional requirements. The Commission's initial draft directive had extensive, potential extraterritorial effects, discussed in the following section. This was seen by some member states, especially the UK, and the hedge funds industry as protectionist and likely to result in retaliatory action from the US federal government (especially the provision on 'equivalence'). Other member states, first and foremost France and Germany, argued that such an approach was necessary to prevent Europe from becoming 'the Trojan horse for offshore funds', as the French finance minister put it (*European Voice*, 29 April 2009).

The draft directive was revised following intense lobbying from affected financial service firms (see Woll 2012, 2014) and the American and British governments. In the end, the most controversial proposals, including plans to impose fixed caps on leverage and capital requirements, were either removed or significantly watered down. The AIFMD required fund managers to appoint a separate custodian for hedge fund assets and provide independent portfolio valuations, but this provision reflected what was already standard industry practice for most funds operating in the EU. Questions remained over the power of the European Securities and Markets Authority (ESMA) in relation to national authorities in the authorization of AIFMs. While the reporting requirements imposed unwelcome, albeit limited, compliance costs on hedge funds, their existing business practices were not affected in any significant way. Provisions on third country access are considered below.

The adopted EU directive aligned closely to existing US legislation passed in the aftermath of the financial crisis, which observers have described as not onerous or likely to restrict existing business activities. The Dodd–Frank Wall Street Reform and Consumer Protection Act of July 2009 requires all hedge funds above a minimum size to register with the Securities and Exchange Commission (SEC), imposes minimal reporting requirements, and subjects funds to periodic SEC examinations and inspections.

To sum up, the main line of division on the regulation of hedge funds within the EU stemmed from the financial system. France, Germany, and Italy were worried about activist investors, such as hedge fund managers and private equity firms, loosening the traditional finance-industry ties that enabled long-term investment for manufacturing firms (*Financial Times*, 30 April 2009; for a similar argument see Zimmermann 2010). For this reason, hedge funds were subject to rather strict regulation in these countries prior to the crisis. Moreover, as Woll (2012, 2014) has pointed out, France hosted a thriving asset management industry including the largest collective investment fund (UCITS) industry in Europe that competed with hedge funds. UCITS were already heavily regulated in the EU and, in certain respects, competed for business with hedge fund managers.

Prior to the international financial crisis, the UK—which hosts four-fifths of Europe's hedge fund managers—opposed EU regulation. But in the wake of the crisis, the British government relaxed its opposition, in part to appease British public opinion (Helleiner and Pagliari 2010). But British policymakers were also concerned with how AIFMs would react to the costs of complying with EU rules and their threat to relocate, endangering the primacy of London as a global financial centre. As London competes with other financial centres worldwide to attract business, concern for international 'regulatory arbitrage'[7] has traditionally been at the forefront of British policymakers' minds (interviews, London, May 2007, July 2008).

---

[7] This expression is used frequently in policy documents produced by the British Treasury, the FSA, and the Bank of England.

THE DEBATE ON THIRD COUNTRY ACCESS IN THE EU AND EQUIVALENCE

One of the most controversial issues during negotiations on the directive was 'third country' access: the rules according to which the managers of non-EU-based funds—whether based inside or outside the EU—can obtain the 'EU passport' to market to professional investors throughout the Union (Buckley and Howarth 2011). This issue is important for the overall theme of this volume because, given the absence of robust rules on hedge funds at the international level, domestic rules in the main jurisdictions, namely the EU and the USA, are paramount for their governance. The interaction between hedge fund rules in these jurisdictions moreover poses potential problems for future regulation.

In the making of the AIFMD, the French government in particular sought to restrict the ability of funds based in low-tax jurisdictions (whether managed in the EU or not) to access its market. The French argued that the passport should be granted to the managers of non-EU-based funds only when the applicable regulatory regime is deemed equivalent to that of the EU (*Financial Times*, 14 April 2010). Many in the European Parliament, in particular Socialist MEPs, were in favour of similarly tough rules.

As noted above, the British and American governments, among others, together with the fund management industry, challenged these proposals as protectionist. The US administration made very public its opposition to the 'third country' element in the proposed directive and its perception of EU efforts to dictate the global regulatory landscape. The US SEC stated that it would probably be unable to comply with the equivalence criteria suggested in the AIFMD drafts, which would close the EU market to US-based funds (Harris 2010).

A letter dated 1 March 2010, from US Secretary of the Treasury, Timothy Geithner, to Michel Barnier, the Commissioner for the Internal Market and Services, and the Spanish chair of the Ecofin Council, was leaked to the press and published in full in the *Financial Times* (11 March 2010). So too was a 5 April letter from Mr Geithner to the UK Chancellor of the Exchequer, Alistair Darling, and the German, French and Spanish finance ministers enjoining them to reconsider the AIFMD (*Financial Times*, 6 April 2010). In the 1 March letter, Mr Geithner notes:

> ... I believe we agree that [it] is essential to fulfill our G-20 commitment to avoid discrimination and maintain a level playing field. In this context, we are concerned with various proposals that would discriminate against US firms and deny them the access to the EU market that they currently have. We strongly hope that the rule that you put in place will ensure that non-EU fund managers and global custodian banks have the same access as their EU counterparts. You will see that our approach in the US maintains full access for EU fund managers and custodians to our market. (*Financial Times*, 11 March 2010)

The USA stopped short of threatening retaliatory action. However, if the third country rules of the directive were not significantly watered down, EU-based fund managers could face reprisals in the US Congress. Senior EU officials responded to US concerns by insisting that the proposed directive was in line with G20 guidelines to improve transparency in the financial system and noted that Mr Barnier sought to work with the US administration to ensure 'robust standards' (*Financial Times*, 12 March 2010). The British Labour government joined forces with the Obama administration to water down the demands imposed on third country funds. Many British AIFMs ran funds which were based outside the EU for tax purposes. The British sought a regime that allowed non-EU funds to be marketed across the EU provided the jurisdiction in which they were based had 'equivalent' regulatory standards, with a relaxed set of criteria to determine 'equivalence'. Ireland, the Czech Republic, Malta, Sweden, and Austria adopted similar positions.

Industry associations echoed the concerns of the American Treasury secretary to the third country proposal, warning of retaliatory action in non-EU jurisdictions damaging the interests of EU-based financial services firms (*Financial Times*, 13 May 2010). The uncertainty also hit off-shore centres, including the Cayman Islands, which had already lost funds to onshore locations in Europe. Despite the recent financial crisis, hedge and other funds in the EU enjoyed significant growth in both total assets and, from early 2009, the number of funds under management (*Financial Times*, 2 May 2010). For the first time, the Channel Islands of Jersey and Guernsey established a diplomatic mission in Brussels reflecting their governments' fears that their financial services industry could be damaged by new EU regulations (*Financial Times*, 3 July 2010).

With the failure to reach a compromise deal on the third country issue at the March 2010 European Council, MEPs went ahead with their own efforts to produce a more acceptable draft. Surprisingly, the Monetary and Economic Affairs Committee responsible for the directive shifted its views. The AIFMD rapporteur, the French conservative MEP Jean-Paul Gauzès, put forward compromise solutions more popular in the UK than in France (*Financial Times*, 4 April 2010). The committee organized discussions of a possible transitional arrangement on the issue; in the intervening period, national rules would continue to apply.

In the end, the most controversial provisions of the draft directive were substantially scaled back. The French government's hard-line position on third country funds lost support from other member states. The existing system of individual market application was to continue until 2015. As before, third country managers wishing to market their funds in the EU would have to do so in accordance with the private placement regimes (PPRs) of the EU member states into which they were marketing. Yet compliance with certain aspects of the AIFMD would still be necessary (as summarized in Table 8.1) and real burdens were imposed not only on non-EU-based managers but also on third country supervisory authorities.

A dual system of national PPRs and EU passports was to exist between 2015 and 2018, when ESMA would review the passport regime and consider recommending an end to the PPRs. Nevertheless, member states would not be forced to adopt the passport in 2018. If they chose to do so, a passport to market in the EU would be required for all funds managed by third country managers.

A two-tiered system would thus almost inevitably be introduced in 2018. Funds managed within an EU member state but domiciled outside would be eligible for a passport provided the country of domicile met four conditions: that the foreign regulator supplies EU regulators with required information; that the foreign jurisdiction allows European funds to be sold there; that regulation to prevent

Table 8.1 Necessary compliance with AIFMD from 2013

	Imposition on manager	Imposition on third country authorities
EU manager with third country fund (not marketed in the EU)	Full compliance with AIFMD, except depositary and annual reporting requirements.	Cooperation arrangements between supervisory authorities and the competent authorities of the country of domicile of the EU manager.
EU manager with third country fund (marketed in the EU)	Full compliance with AIFMD, except depositary requirements.	Cooperation arrangements between supervisory authorities and the competent authorities of the country of domicile of the EU manager. Third country fund must not be domiciled in a so-called Non-Cooperative Country and Territory (NCCT) as determined by the Financial Action Task Force.
Third country manager with EU fund or third country fund (marketed in the EU)	Annual report for each fund. Rules on improved disclosure to investors on investment strategy, risk factors, service providers, and investors' fees and expenses. Regular reporting to regulators of markets where manager trades. Where a fund acquires control of a non-listed company, notification and reporting requirements to the shareholders of the company and relevant regulators.	Cooperation arrangements between supervisory authorities where the fund and manager are based and the competent authorities in each EU member state where the fund is to be marketed. Neither the fund nor the manager should be domiciled in an NCCT.

money laundering and funding terrorism is in place; and that an acceptable tax agreement exists. Were a jurisdiction to fall short on some of these standards, funds might still be able to seek country-by-country marketing approval. But should a jurisdiction fall short on all of them, the funds would be barred from being marketed in the EU.

Funds both domiciled and managed outside the EU would, after five years, have to meet a higher standard to access the EU market—to obtain a passport, they would have to show that their home jurisdiction had 'equivalent' regulation to the EU (*Financial Times*, 13 May 2010). The policy on 'equivalence' ended up reflecting policy already established in international financial forums. The home jurisdiction of the non-EU funds applying for an EU passport would have to comply with IOSCO standards on hedge fund oversight, including compliance with international tax and anti-money laundering agreements. It was very likely that the USA and other key markets would be deemed appropriately regulated jurisdictions (Plumridge 2010). While this compromise appeared to lower the hurdle for third country access, many investor and industry groups remained concerned by the definition of 'equivalent', with conditions to be clarified by a regulation implementing the AIFMD. Critics also noted that funds investing in emerging markets would find it hardest to comply, making it more difficult for EU investors to back fund managers in African and other countries, with negative implications for growth in the developing world (*Financial Times*, 13 May 2010).

The fears of EU fund managers and the US Treasury resurfaced in the spring of 2012 following a leak of the Commission's draft regulation to adopt 'Level 2' measures (supplementary rules) implementing the AIFMD, which was perceived as a hawkish departure from the more flexible position previously presented by ESMA in November 2011 (*Financial Times*, 1 April 2012, 11 July 2012). The Commission was accused of reneging on the compromises of 2010 on a range of matters (*Financial Times*, 1 April 2012, 11 July 2012), including the definition of conditions that fund managers and funds in non-EU jurisdictions would have to meet to access EU investors. From April to December 2012, industry pressure helped redirect the Commission back towards the flexibility outlined in the ESMA recommendations. On 19 December 2012, the Commission adopted the 'Level 2' implementing regulations for the AIFMD, finally approved unaltered by the Council and European Parliament on 15 May 2013 (EC 2013c, 2013d). These Level 2 regulations were long anticipated by fund managers and governments in Europe and abroad to clarify the conditions and procedures for the authorization of AIFMs and to set out the rules to be applied to third country managers, funds, and authorities, including conditions for delegation, rules on depositories, reporting requirements, leverage calculation, and rules for cooperation arrangements. But a considerable degree of uncertainty remained. In the spring of 2013, top US Treasury officials expressed broad satisfaction with the adopted Level 2 regulations, which they believed aligned roughly with the provisions of the Dodd–Frank Act (interview, Washington, 6 May 2013). However, several US hedge fund managers and their representative law firms continued to express the concern that tightened reporting requirements would result in some managers withdrawing from the EU market or opting not to enter it (*Financial Times*, 2 June 2013). There was no indication that the UK—where the bulk of EU fund managers were based—would abolish its current national PPR. But the possibility remained that the British government would apply additional AIFMD requirements on the home-based managers of non-EU-based funds and on third country-based fund managers and funds.

AN OVERALL ASSESSMENT

Prior to the financial crisis, the international regulation of hedge funds was mostly 'indirect' and the EU lacked its own rules; hence there could be no formal linkage between EU and global rules. As for ties between EU and global institutions, regulators from EU countries sat in IOSCO but this organization only endorsed the indirect regulation of hedge funds. Within the EU and in international financial regulatory forums, some national policymakers called for the regulation of hedge funds but British and American policymakers were opposed.

In this period, the EU was a 'policy-taker' rather than a policymaker, waiting for international rules to be agreed rather than setting its own rules on hedge funds. The EU, internally divided, was unable to project its influence internationally or to call for international rules. Diverging national preferences on regulating hedge funds were mostly rooted in different national financial systems, which also hampered progress towards the establishment of EU rules.

After the onslaught of the crisis, continental policymakers grew more vocal on hedge funds, while US and UK policymakers endorsed G20 commitments to regulate systemically important hedge funds. At least in the wake of the crisis, the EU was better able to coordinate its international influence, with its members meeting to agree on language prior to G20 summit meetings. The EU thus played a significant role in advancing the international regulation of hedge funds, which came to be supported by the UK and the USA mostly for domestic political reasons (Helleiner and Pagliari 2010).

Yet international rules remained 'thin'—the often cited, but very general, G20 commitment and the vague IOSCO principles notwithstanding. In contrast, the EU moved ahead with its own set of rules, the AIFM directive, while the US strengthened its own national legislation on hedge funds. Even after the international financial crisis, there are thus no formal linkages between European and global rules in the regulation of hedge funds. The main regulatory discussions have revolved around the issue of third country access envisaged by EU and US legislation.

As for the factors encouraging or hampering the ability of the EU to project its regulatory influence prior to the crisis, the literature (Simmons 2001; Drezner 2007) has most often focused on economic power (to be more precise, market size). For hedge funds, market size can be measured in various ways. If one considers hedge fund managers, most are located in the USA and, within the EU, in the UK. If one considers hedge funds, some are based in the USA but most are in tax havens. And although investment in hedge funds is more common in the USA than in continental Europe, the financial markets into which funds and managers can tap are more or less the same size in the USA and the EU. Considering all this, the market size for hedge funds is not the main determinant of EU influence—or the lack thereof—on global regulation. While market size remained constant before and after the outbreak of the international financial crisis, in the wake of the crisis the EU was able to set up its own rules on hedge funds—although it still had limited influence on the work done in IOSCO.

Other authors have argued that the cross-border integration and consolidation of the financial industry altered industry coalitions supporting or opposing regulatory harmonization both within and beyond the EU (Mügge 2010). In this case, the crucial point is that the entire hedge fund industry, regardless of where it was located, opposed EU and international rules. In the USA, it lobbied hard to maintain the weak regulatory template (based on a series of exemptions) to which it was subject (Horsfield-Bradbury 2008). However, the financial crisis weakened the industry's ability to withstand regulatory reform. Pagliari (2011) notes that the hedge fund industry deftly accepted the need for some form of public regulation and focused its efforts on shaping the content of the new rules in order to avoid burdensome requirements.

The main issue was that the EU lacked regulatory capacity (see Bach and Newman 2007; Posner 2009, 2010b). Prior to 2009, member states had very different preferences and rules on hedge funds, while there were no EU rules in place. In the aftermath of the crisis, the preferences of core states (the UK) shifted and so did their bargaining power, at least temporarily.

The specific character of EU multi-level governance weakened the EU's international bargaining power, as divisions between its members prevented the formulation of clear policy positions (Mügge 2011c). The EU was unable to project a strong voice with clearly articulated preferences in international forums. After the outbreak of the crisis, the main channel through which the EU was able to increase its international clout was through the adoption of its own set of regional rules, in particular the use of equivalence clauses. However, we have shown that the conditions imposed by the AIFMD and its two implementing regulations create very limited additional requirements on non-EU-based fund managers and supervisory authorities. The AIFMD also allows member states to maintain their own private placement regimes, ensuring the continuation of divergence within the EU.

9

Credit Rating Agencies

STEFANIE HISS AND SEBASTIAN NAGEL

INTRODUCTION

Credit rating agencies (CRAs) have been involved in the global financial crisis in multiple ways. First, their massive downgrades of too-optimistic ratings of structured finance products such as Residential Mortgage Backed Securities (RMBS) and Collateralized Debt Obligations (CDOs) triggered the subprime crisis in the summer of 2007. Later, their downgrades of sovereign ratings, as in the case of Greece, aggravated these countries' refinancing problems and worsened the crisis of the euro.

Both national and global actors have presented new proposals to regulate the credit rating industry. Most have sought to improve the quality of the ratings process to restore trust in CRAs. Some of these proposals have been enacted; others remain in the pipeline. While US regulators enacted far-reaching rules following the Enron and WorldCom scandals in 2002 and again in 2006, the EU has relied on a voluntary undertaking of the rating industry: the International Organization of Securities Commissions' Code of Conduct Fundamentals (the IOSCO code). The EU published its first proposal for credit rating regulation following the subprime crisis in 2008; enacted in 2009, it drew on existing US and IOSCO rules. In 2010, the Dodd–Frank Wall Street Reform and Consumer Protection Act realigned US regulation with its European counterpart.

This chapter explores the genealogy and dynamics of the regulation of credit ratings of corporations and structured finance products. It details how Europe was a latecomer in the regulation of CRAs, how Europe relied on the voluntary IOSCO code, and how the latter was finally delegitimized by the subprime crisis, after which the EU decided to follow the US path. After introducing the credit rating industry's main conflicts and governance structures, the chapter outlines the genealogy of rating regulation until 2004. We then explain the dynamics of regulation since 2005 and describe the contemporary situation of global and European ratings regulation. We end with some concluding remarks and implications for the future of the credit rating industry.

THE RATING INDUSTRY—ITS CRISES, CONFLICTS, AND GOVERNANCE ARENAS

The CRAs' troubles did not begin with the subprime crisis in 2007. Ten years earlier, in the Asian Crisis, CRAs were accused of misunderstanding developments and fuelling the crisis through their rapid and significant downgrades of sovereign ratings (Sinclair 2005: 139). But no major regulatory efforts were pursued before the Enron and WorldCom scandals broke in 2001 and 2002, discrediting corporate bond ratings and sparking regulatory initiatives, particularly in the USA. At the same time, the International Organization of Securities Commissions (IOSCO) developed a voluntary code of conduct for credit rating agencies to solve problems generated from conflicts of interests.

CRAs forecast the credit risks of mainly companies, securities, and sovereign units. CRAs judge and rate credit risk according to a scale ranging from, for example, AAA (prime) to D (default). These grades are not meant as investment advice; they signal creditworthiness to outside creditors. With the growing importance of financial markets since the 1970s and the worldwide reach of the Basel II accord, CRAs emerged as important intermediaries between creditors and debtors. The vast majority of creditors are moreover rated by just three agencies—Standard & Poor's (S&P), Moody's, and Fitch—which together command 97 per cent of the market (White 2010: 216f). This oligopoly is one of the main factors fuelling crises in the rating industry.

Most of the regulation has emerged over the past decade in the country where CRAs originated and are headquartered: the USA. Despite the EU's role in financial markets and major crises, the EU resisted tabling its own regulations until 2008, instead putting its faith in industry self-regulation as championed by IOSCO (Quaglia 2009). Before we turn to the genealogy of the regulation of credit ratings, we give an overview of the issues at stake.

Credit rating agencies are intermediaries within financial markets. This combined with their business model leads to serious conflicts of interest, which—together with transparency and competition issues—are the focus of most regulatory efforts. As market intermediaries, CRAs are positioned between debtors and creditors. While they should provide creditors with reliable, independent information on the creditworthiness of debtors, most CRAs are profit-oriented companies with a broad range of potentially conflicting interests. To identify these conflicts of interest is 'the single greatest concern facing CRAs' (IOSCO 2003a: 12).

Two such conflicts of interest can be readily identified. The first arises from the collaboration between CRAs and issuers of structured finance products in designing these products; in effect, CRAs are paid to tailor products that they will themselves rate. 'This constitutes a discrete conflict of interest because the agency receives a separate, often lucrative, fee for this service. In 2006, for example, consulting on structured finance deals accounted for 40 per cent of Moody's total revenue. Though a service distinct from rating, it patently calls into question the objectivity of an agency that rates a financial product it has helped construct' (Strier 2008: 537). The second conflict of interest stems from the issuer-pay model (Coffee 2006: 3). Since the mid-1970s, issuers of securities mandate and pay CRAs for their own rating (White 2010: 214).[1] CRAs are thus no longer independent but 'have an interest in generating business from the firms that seek the rating' (SEC 2008b: 45). Positive ratings are an equivocal consequence of this business model. This conflict is even greater in the field of structured finance as there are a limited number of issuers (SEC 2008a: 31f).

As both conflicts of interest can undermine independent and reliable credit ratings, they are the focus of most regulatory efforts, which often hold up greater competition between CRAs and transparency of rating processes as solutions. Other solutions have been proposed as well, ranging from non-regulation—since legal regulation would lead to further recognition of ratings (Lynch 2010: 290f)—to the abolishing of rating agencies, suggested by the German services union Ver.di (Jurczyk 2010).

Especially during the subprime crisis, conflicts of interest led to failures in the ratings process and were followed by massive downgrades. As in the case of the Asian and Enron crises, the CRAs again failed to foresee market developments and warn investors, this time for structured finance products such as RMBSs and CDOs. The rating of structured finance products is a relatively new business area for CRAs, one which grew with the housing and mortgage market, in particular the subprime mortgage market in the USA. In 2005, home ownership in the USA reached an all-time high of 69 per cent (Census Bureau 2007). Due to historically low interest rates and favourable lending conditions, the housing market took off with a long, steep increase in prices. Between 1997 and 2006, real home prices in the USA rose by 85 per cent (Shiller 2008: 32). In 2007, mortgage debt in the US stood at $11 trillion, of which 65 per cent was securitized (Keys et al. 2008). Subprime mortgages were estimated to be worth around $1.5 trillion (Agarwal and Ho 2007). As the volume of subprime mortgages increased, the rate of securitization increased as well. In 1995, it was still

---

[1] Only some smaller CRAs are paid by subscribers (Möllers 2009; Katz et al. 2009: 6).

under 30 per cent; by 2003, it had reached almost 60 per cent (Chomsisengphet and Pennington-Cross 2006), climbing further to 75 per cent by 2006 (Demyanyk and Van Hemert 2008: 6). While $65 billion worth of subprime mortgages were issued in 1995, this had climbed to $600 billion by 2006 (Chomsisengphet and Pennington-Cross 2006; Decker 2007; Ashcraft and Schuermann 2008). Over 90 per cent of subprime mortgages were issued by the top 25 players such as Countrywide Financial, HSBC, Washington Mutual, Citi Group, Wells Fargo, and Ameriquest Mortgage (Ashcraft and Schuermann 2008).

The rating of structured finance products sky-rocketed alongside these developments. In 2008, 394,635 credit ratings of asset-backed securities were outstanding, compared to 75,052 corporate bond ratings. Ninety-nine per cent of all outstanding ratings (in both asset classes) were made by S&P, Moody's, and Fitch (SEC 2008b). Within only a few years, the rating of structured finance products had become a significant business for CRAs.

With the onset of the subprime crisis—evidenced by stagnating house prices, rising interest rates and a wave of foreclosures—CRAs began a massive downgrade of the ratings of structured finance products. As the crisis developed, the CRAs had to revise their earlier assessments. The three big CRAs together took 9,496 so-called rating actions on US subprime RMBS tranches in the first 10 months of 2007, compared to 836 in 2006, and 240 in 2005, an unprecedented admission of failure (Romey and Drut 2008: 9). By April 2010, up to 93 per cent of subprime RMBS rated triple A in 2006 had been downgraded to junk status, i.e. classified as non-investment grade (Levin 2010; for a detailed description of the failing of CRAs in the subprime crisis see Rona-Tas and Hiss 2010).

The spread of the subprime crisis led to the regulation of CRAs, most notably in the US, the EU, and within IOSCO, the recognized international standard-setting body for securities markets. IOSCO supports a voluntary self-regulating code of conduct for CRAs (IOSCO 2004). In the USA, the Securities and Exchange Commission (SEC) is the driving force behind regulations for CRAs. The EU did not regulate CRAs until 2008, and sought advice from CESR (Committee of European Securities Regulators) and ESME (European Securities Markets Expert Group). CESR was established by the European Commission in 2001 as an independent committee, the successor to the Forum of European Securities Commissions. Since January 2011, CESR has been part of the new European Securities and Markets Authority (ESMA), which is part of the European System of Financial Supervisors. CESR members are national securities commissions, mandated, for example, to coordinate national initiatives and to advise the Commission. ESME (not to be confused with ESMA) provides legal and economic advice for the application of EU securities directives. It was established by the Commission in 2006 and consists of '20 high level experts with practical experience in the investment services and the securities industry' (ESME n.d.).

GENEALOGY OF RATING REGULATION—USA AND IOSCO

To better understand European efforts to regulate CRAs in the wake of the subprime crisis, we first reconstruct developments in the US and within IOSCO prior to 2005. This will provide a basis for illustrating the intertwined timelines of US and European regulation (for an overview, see Figure 9.1). Before we turn to the details, we paint the story in broad strokes. The credit rating industry was almost unregulated until the Enron and WorldCom scandals underlined the need for regulation. Whereas the USA as well as IOSCO had been developing rules for credit ratings, the EU followed a different path: even after the Parmalat corporate scandal, there was little felt need for European regulations on CRAs.

United States

Credit rating regulation evolved in the wake of the Enron and WorldCom scandals in 2001 and 2002. Both scandals discredited corporate bond ratings and sparked regulatory initiatives in the years to come. Only a few days before Enron's bankruptcy in November 2001, the three big CRAs were still rating Enron's corporate bonds as investment grade (Coffee 2006: 34f; White 2009: 7; Sinclair 2003: 157). At the time, Enron had been the seventh largest corporation in the USA with a market capitalization of $62.5 billion; by the spring of 2002, it was worth only a few cents (Sinclair 2005: 167). The CRAs justified their misjudgment by blaming Enron and its accountant Arthur Andersen for

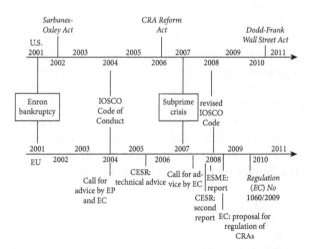

Fig. 9.1 Timeline of credit ratings regulation (Source: own illustration; Hiss and Nagel 2012).

supplying falsified financial statements. John Diaz, managing director at Moody's, defended the company's work in front of the Senate committee hearing in March 2002: 'Enron was an anomaly', he said, 'its responses to our specific requests for information were misleading and incomplete'. Moody's rating process, he observed, 'was undermined by the missing information'. Ronald M. Barone, the S&P analyst for Enron, suggested that Enron had made 'what we later learned were direct and deliberate misrepresentations to us relating to matters of great substance' (quoted in Sinclair 2003: 156).

These corporate scandals made the US an active player in the field of CRA regulation, leading to the Sarbanes–Oxley Act of 2002. The SEC in particular was already an established actor in the field; since 1975, its recognition of CRAs as Nationally Recognized Statistical Ratings Organizations (NRSROs) had led to the official use of their ratings, for example, by pension funds.[2] But although credit rating was previously part of regulation, it was itself not regulated until the Enron and WorldCom scandals shattered the field-level consensus of non-regulation.

IOSCO

IOSCO's simultaneous investigation of the role of CRAs in financial markets led to its 'Statement of Principles Regarding the Activities of Credit Rating Agencies' in 2003 (IOSCO 2003a, 2003b). The latter laid out 'high-level objectives for which ratings agencies, regulators, issuers, and other market participants should strive in order to improve investor protection and the fairness, efficiency, and transparency of the securities markets and reduce systemic risk' (IOSCO 2003b). For conflicts of interest, IOSCO stated that 'CRA ratings decisions should be independent and free from political or economic pressures and from conflicts of interest arising due to the CRA's ownership structure, business or financial activities, or the financial interests of the CRA's employees' (IOSCO 2003b). This general objective, as well as objectives concerning transparency and quality, was supported by further principles. Nevertheless, IOSCO was soon asked to clarify how these principles are to be applied in practice (IOSCO 2004: 2). A task force on CRAs, chaired by the SEC, was established, leading to the IOSCO 'Code of Conduct Fundamentals for Credit Rating Agencies':[3] 'The Code Fundamentals offer a set of robust, practical measures that serve as a guide to and a framework for implementing the Principles' objectives. These

---

[2] Since mainly the big three CRAs received NRSRO status, this regulation fostered the oligopoly of the credit ratings market by offering them a 'regulatory licence' (Coffee 2006: 288f, 326ff; Partnoy 1999: 638ff).

[3] Further contributions to these fundamentals have been made by 'IOSCO members, CRAs, representatives of the Basel Committee on Banking Supervision, the International Association of Insurance Supervisors, issuers, and the public at large' (IOSCO 2004: 2).

measures are the fundamentals which should be included in individual CRA codes of conduct . . .' (IOSCO 2004: 2). For example, ratings 'should be influenced only by factors relevant to the credit assessment' and a 'CRA should disclose the general nature of its compensation arrangements with rated entities' to avoid conflicts of interest (IOSCO 2004: 6). While the Code of Conduct Fundamentals has been 'widely recognised as a global benchmark' (CESR 2009: 10), it has not been legally enforced. Furthermore, rating agencies do 'not assume any responsibility or liability' because their codes of conduct do 'not constitute a commitment or a contractual document in terms of its relationship with customers' (AMF 2006: 7).

While the USA and IOSCO emerged as the frontrunners in credit ratings regulation, the first US response to the Enron and WorldCom scandals targeted the accounting industry. While the CRAs had clearly failed to foresee the breakdown of Enron and WorldCom, more blame was directed towards the accounting firms, in particular Enron's accountant Arthur Andersen. The Sarbanes–Oxley Act, passed in July 2002, focused on accounting firms and sought to more closely control accounting and financial statements. For CRAs, Sarbanes–Oxley directed the SEC 'to examine the role and performance of rating agencies, barriers to entry into the rating industry and conflicts of interest plaguing rating agencies' (Senate Committee on Banking, Housing, and Urban Affairs 2006: 1).

DYNAMICS OF RATING REGULATION SINCE 2005

Until the subprime crisis hit the global economy, Europe considered the voluntary IOSCO code as a legitimate and appropriate answer to the shortcomings of CRAs. This changed after 2008. The EU now decided to follow the US, at least for the main content of its rules. In this way, the EU hoped to contribute to the global, homogeneous governance of CRAs instead of to a separate, transaction cost-laden European rule-set that differed from the American one. Nevertheless, European regulation was in some ways stronger than its American counterpart until the US Dodd–Frank Act of 2010 realigned the rules.

United States

The US debate on regulating CRAs began with the Enron debacle and the Sarbanes–Oxley Act. Shortly after Enron's insolvency, the Senate Committee on Governmental Affairs, chaired by Senator Joe Lieberman, began investigating the misconduct of CRAs (Lieberman 2003). The SEC held its hearing on CRAs in November 2002, leading to its *Report on the Role and Function of*

CRAs in the Operation of the Securities Markets (SEC 2003). These investigations culminated in the US Congress passing the Credit Rating Agency Reform Act (US Congress 2006) in September 2006, which entered into effect in June 2007 and increased the influence of the SEC in regulating CRAs. The SEC, for instance, now registers and oversees CRAs. We thus see that US regulators had focused on CRAs before the subprime crisis broke out in the summer of 2007. Although the Enron case had been a corporate bond rating failure, the agenda was set. The issues dominating the regulatory debate after Enron— more transparency, more competition, better management of conflicts of interest—resurfaced with the subprime crisis.

The CRA Reform Act entered into effect in 2007 during the subprime crisis. But due to this act, the USA only had to make minor changes to the regulation of CRAs following the subprime crisis. The Dodd–Frank Act of 2010, which can be seen as a more general regulation of financial markets, only brought some minor refinements to the regulation of CRAs and realigned US regulation with its European counterpart, established in 2009.

European Union

With the implementation of new regulations in the USA, the French Autorité des marchés financiers asked whether the time had come for Europe 'to progress towards more formal regulation in the form of registration of CRAs' (AMF 2008: 6). After the subprime crisis hit Europe, the EU began studying how to best deal with CRAs. The European Commission launched its own process by asking two expert groups, CESR and ESME, for advice (EC 2008a: 3). In a nutshell, both advised the EU not to regulate CRAs as they already 'comply to a large extent' (CESR 2008a: 52) with the voluntary IOSCO code. But the Commission, and finally the European Parliament and Council, ignored this advice and enacted their own European credit ratings regulation (Regulation (EC) No. 1060/2009 of the European Parliament and of the Council on credit rating agencies). We describe this process in more detail below.

In 2004, after the Parmalat scandal and almost three years after the collapse of Enron, the Commission, urged by the Parliament, began its first move towards European regulation by asking CESR for advice. The expert group advised the Commission to follow the voluntary IOSCO code instead of inventing further binding regulations.

In 2005 CESR published its technical advice on European credit ratings regulation, based on its consultation paper and 34 responses from market participants (CESR 2005a). In its conclusions, CESR stated that 'the scope of any provisions that could be considered for CRAs should be based on the IOSCO Code. Even though there are some areas where it could be argued that the IOSCO Code will not sufficiently deal with issues brought up, the IOSCO Code strikes a balance between the different interests in the rating process; those of the agencies themselves, those of the issuers and those of investors' (CESR 2005a: 49). CESR's advice to the Commission was likewise based on the IOSCO code: 'the main question for the EU is thus to what extent the IOSCO Code should be enforced by any regulatory mechanism or whether to wait and see whether the CRAs by themselves will take sufficient steps to comply with the Code' (CESR 2005a: 50). The majority of CESR members recommended to wait and see whether the IOSCO code would be sufficient to solve existing problems (CESR 2005a: 52). Only in case of failure may there 'be a need for statutory regulation' (CESR 2005b: 1). Following Enron and WorldCom, the Commission repeatedly requested CESR to report on whether Europe-based CRAs were complying with the IOSCO code or if the regulation of CRAs was required. In each report, CESR positioned itself against the regulation of CRAs (CESR 2005a, 2006, 2008a, 2008b, 2009) as self-regulation through the IOSCO code would fulfil all necessary requirements (Stemper 2010: 212).

As a result, the Commission did not propose any new regulations but referred to the global IOSCO code as a solution for Europe: 'There are already three new financial services Directives which cover credit rating agencies. The Commission is confident that these Directives—when combined with self-regulation by the credit rating agencies themselves on the basis of the newly adopted IOSCO Code—will provide an answer to all the major issues of concern raised by the European Parliament' (EC 2006: 6). Only new developments or the unsatisfactory compliance of CRAs with the IOSCO code could lead to European regulation (CESR 2006: 6). The sole result of CESR's initial advice was a request by the Commission 'to review implementation of the IOSCO Code' by the end of 2006 (CESR 2006: 2). Over the following years, CESR published several reports on CRA compliance with the IOSCO code.

In response to the subprime crisis and in line with the Ecofin roadmap of EU finance ministers, the Commission intensified its search for solutions in the autumn of 2007. It requested both CESR and the European Securities Markets Expert Group (ESME) to 'clarify the role of the agencies and assess the need for regulatory measures' (EC 2008a: 3). In its second report of May 2008, CESR still did not think that regulation by the EU was necessary; it was uncertain, however, whether the current process was sufficient to improve the quality of ratings: 'CESR and market participants still believe that there is no evidence that regulation would have had an effect on the issues which emerged with ratings of US subprime backed securities' (CESR 2008a: 58). One reason was that European regulation would diminish the value of the 'globally recognized minimum standards' of the IOSCO code (CESR 2008a: 56). Only regulations that are closely tied to the IOSCO code could have more benefits than costs since it would reduce the risk of globally inconsistent regulations (CESR 2008a: 56).

IOSCO concurrently revised its code of conduct in light of the subprime crisis, especially in the areas of structured finance ratings and inherent conflicts of interest: 'The updated Code focuses on improving the quality of the rating process, providing transparency on rating methods and historical data, and preventing conflicts of interest, in particular "rating shopping"' (AMF 2009: 27).

In its reports, CESR balanced the benefits and drawbacks of pursuing European regulation given the existence of the IOSCO code, especially since new provisions and initiatives by several CRAs could lead to changes relevant to European regulation (CESR 2008a: 53): all these initiatives are 'steps in the right direction' even if further improvements are needed in the areas of structured finance and ancillary services by CRAs (CESR 2008a: 58). CESR did not recommend European regulation but instead proposed a new standard-setting and monitoring body to oversee new international standards close to those of IOSCO (CESR 2008a: 59f). Given the global nature of the ratings business, standards-setting and monitoring should work on a global scale: '[I]t would be desirable that supervisory authorities from other major financial centres besides the EU support the creation of such a body. However, if this international involvement cannot be achieved, CESR would still recommend the formation of such a body at EU level' (CESR 2008a: 60). Advice for formal regulation will be the next step if this monitoring body does not improve the quality of ratings.

The Commission did not rely exclusively on CESR's advice. It asked a second expert body, the European Securities Markets Expert Group (ESME), to advise the Commission 'on specific issues related to the regulation of CRAs' (ESME 2007: 2). Like CESR, ESME had to recognize the global dimension of ratings regulation; overall, 'ESME is asked to: . . . look into the functioning of the (self) regulatory framework in the EU for CRAs, taking into account the new US Credit Rating Agency Reform Act of 2006 which entered into force in June 2007' (ESME 2007: 2f).

ESME published its report in June 2008. It recommended not regulating CRAs in Europe since the 'incremental benefits of regulation would not exceed the costs' (ESME 2008: 2). There were, however, two qualifications: (1) self-regulation through the IOSCO code needed to be enhanced; and (2) there needed to be more competition between (existing and new) CRAs (ESME 2008: 2). 'Given the global nature of the business of CRAs and the existing US law, we have doubts as to whether the development of a separate EU law would produce any particular benefits. We think it is important that CRAs are subject to a global approach to their business and do not become distracted by similar laws which nevertheless have differences across a range of jurisdictions. We think that regulatory cooperation in this sphere is essential to avoid duplication of effort. Therefore, ESME believes that the SEC should be invited to join the advisory group that ESME recommends being established' (ESME 2008: 8f). Although neither CESR nor ESME recommended this, the Commission proposed new European regulation in 2008.

In November 2008, with the subprime crisis in its second year, the EU adopted the 'Proposal for a Regulation of the European Parliament and the Council on Credit Rating Agencies' (EC 2008a). CESR was particularly critical of the Commission's proposal: 'The Committee calls for the need to duly take into account such international dimension as well as the measures already adopted in other jurisdictions with the intention to avoid inconsistencies and an un-level playing field. As appears from a first analysis, on several points the EU proposal is not aligned with the US regulation on CRAs and with the international standard setters acting within IOSCO' (CESR 2008b: 1; Amtenbrink and de Haan 2009: 7ff). In April 2009, the European Parliament and the Council approved the proposal, which entered into force in December 2009 (EU 2009). From now on, 'all CRAs that wish to have their ratings used in the EU must consequently apply for registration' (AMF 2010: 14). Nevertheless, the Commission's proposal for credit ratings regulation did not rest on the demonstration of functional superiority. The new European regulation was rather seen as a 'counterbalance to other important jurisdictions' (EC 2008a: 5): 'Given the global nature of the rating business, it is important to level the playing field between the EU and the US by setting up a regulatory framework in the EU comparable to that applied in the US and based on the same principles' (EC 2008a: 3).

Elsewhere we have interpreted this development as a failure of theorization within the European Union (Hiss and Nagel 2012). We argue that the EU's approach to voluntary self-regulation fell short of how regulation was theorized in the USA. Due to the timelines involved, American thinking on the issue—encapsulated in the 2006 CRA Reform Act—was already established by the time the EU began searching for new solutions to the governance of CRAs. Given the divergent timelines, the EU followed the already successful approach of the USA.

CONTEMPORARY DESCRIPTION

Although the European Commission proposed its own regulations, these were based on ideas introduced globally some years ago. As a latecomer, the EU could not establish its own approach but followed the trends in global governance. Here we compare American and European regulatory approaches and give an overview of the main issues.

First and foremost, the IOSCO code has been a major source for European regulation, providing 'useful groundwork' for CESR (CESR 2004a: 37; CESR 2005b: 2): 'overall, the substance of the IOSCO Code is the right answer to the issues raised by the Commission's mandate' (CESR 2005a: 50). The Commission also acknowledges the importance of the IOSCO code as a global benchmark which mainly lacks enforcement mechanisms (EC 2008a: 3). The Commission's proposed regulation relied heavily on IOSCO: 'Many of its substantive provisions are inspired by the IOSCO Code. This will limit adaptation costs considerably, since many credit rating agencies already comply voluntarily with the code' (EC 2008a: 6).

Second, US rules were considered closely by the Commission, which examined 'the current legal framework for CRAs in the US' as well as 'the evolution of the proposals for changes in the US Act on CRAs implementing measures presented by the US Securities and Exchange Commission' (EC 2008b: 12).

The outcome of regulations in the USA and the EU can be seen in three main issue areas: competition, conflicts of interest, and transparency and disclosure. But comparing outcomes in the two jurisdictions is far from straightforward. For example, the relevant documents in the US cover more than 500 pages, compared to some 30 pages for the EU. We nevertheless try to highlight the general tendencies of regulation on both sides of the Atlantic (covered in greater detail in Table 9.1 in the Annex). For the US, we consider the Credit Rating Agency Reform Act of 2006, the Final Rules of 2007, and the Final Rule Amendments of February and November 2009; for the EU, we focus on the EU regulation of 2009. In comparing the mandatory rules for conflicts of interest, competition, and transparency and disclosure, it becomes obvious that the EU makes less detailed specifications than the USA.

In the aftermath of the Enron scandal, US rule-making focused on conflicts of interest. As Enron's bankruptcy was in large part due to conflicts of interest between Enron and its accountant, the issue was high on the agenda. As conflicts of interest also affect CRAs—due to the 'issuer pays' compensation scheme, for structured finance more than for corporate bond ratings—the issue was duly transferred to CRA regulation. Even before the subprime crisis broke out, conflicts of interest played a key role in the Credit Rating Agency Reform Act and the final rules accompanying it. The EU regulation also covers this issue, but provides more general obligations for reducing conflicts of interest.

Competition is another key issue in US regulation. The issuing of NRSRO status, dating from 1975, promoted an oligopoly of the big three CRAs—S&P, Moody's, and Fitch—and may have contributed to the deterioration of the quality and objectivity of ratings. By completely revising the NRSRO status and creating a formal recognition procedure for CRAs, US regulation aims to enhance competition between CRAs and the quality and objectivity of ratings. Here it needs to be seen whether the promotion of competition generates unintended side-effects. Greater competition may result in 'ratings shopping' – allowing rated entities to shop around for the 'best results'. The issue of competition has not been prominently discussed in the EU thus far.

Enhancing transparency is a key concern in the US and has resulted in the detailed description of manifold disclosure obligations. While disclosure is also an important issue in Europe, the EU mandates disclosure only when ratings are based on limited historical data.

The US and IOSCO influence on European CRA regulation can be observed in the formal networks of actors. These networks can also be seen as indicators of the possible influence of EU regulations outside Europe. The European expert group CESR has sustained a 'more regularised and intensive dialogue' (CESR 2005b: 2) with the SEC since the first call for advice in 2004, with the SEC offering to collaborate with European regulators 'to avoid conflicts of regulation' (CESR 2004b: 5; 2005b: 2). In its second report on CRA compliance with the IOSCO code in 2008, CESR again referred to its ties with the SEC, which has shown 'its willingness to collaborate with CESR' and has 'regularly updated the task force of the developments in the US' (CESR 2008a: 7). The 'CESR secretariat has been invited to the SEC to get first-hand information on the application of the new US legislation and representatives from the SEC have attended some of the task force meetings as observers' (CESR 2008a: 7).

In the same document CESR reports on the ties between CESR and IOSCO. These are more formalized since 'some of the members of IOSCO's CRAs task force are also members of CESR CRAs task force. In addition to this, contact has been maintained between the Secretariat' (CESR 2008a: 7). Further detail on the ties between CESR and IOSCO are outlined in CESR's 2009 report: 'A number of CESR's CRA Expert Group members (France, Germany, Italy, Spain, and the UK) have been actively engaged in the IOSCO Task Force on CRAs for a number of years. . . . In order to further strengthen this cooperation, the rapporteur of CESR CRA Expert Group has been invited to participate as an observer at IOSCO CRA Task Force meetings. . . . Given that CESR is undertaking work very similar to that performed by IOSCO and that such work is in relation to the same underlying firms, . . . both organizations keep each other informed about the outcome of the work they perform to discharge their respective mandates. CESR has also invited IOSCO to attend meetings of its Expert Group as an observer' (CESR 2009: 8).

CONCLUSION AND IMPLICATIONS

Until the subprime crisis hit the global economy, the European Union considered the voluntary IOSCO code as legitimate and appropriate for regulating credit rating agencies. But the subprime crisis delegitimized the IOSCO-backed voluntary approach. The US had already proposed tighter regulations in the wake of the Enron and WorldCom scandals in 2002. In 2008, the EU decided to follow the US path of regulating CRAs, at least concerning key content. Overall, the European Union has not been able to set its own priorities in the regulation of CRAs, and relies heavily on developments elsewhere.

It remains to be seen whether the EU can take a more active role in the shaping of global governance for credit ratings. Efforts to establish a new European credit ratings foundation as a counterweight to the dominant US agencies as well as new regulations on sovereign debt ratings could be the first indications of a new European approach. Both proposals were made by the European Parliament (European Parliament 2011, 2013). But which path—if any—can prevent future ratings crises remains uncertain.

Annex

Table 9.1 Outcomes of regulation in the USA and Europe

	USA	Europe
Regulation	CRA Reform Act 2006 and the Final Rules (17g 1–6) of the SEC for implementing the CRA Reform Act 2006 Final Rules: Amendments in Feb and Nov 2009 (altogether 532 pages)	Regulation (EC) No. 1060/2009 of the European Parliament and of the Council on credit rating agencies (Nov. 2009) (31 pages) (Focus on the important Articles 6 to 12) (Articles are formulated in a quite general way, accompanied by more detailed descriptions in the Appendix of the regulation)
Registration	Through formalization more open for new NRSROs, while enhancing the disclosure requirements for registration	Newly inserted a registration duty
Conflict of Interest	Detailed description of types of conflict of interest and how to proceed (prohibition, or disclosure and management)	A more general description of how to deal with conflicts of interest
Competition	Balancing between objectivity of rating through competition versus rating shopping	The term 'competition' is not used explicitly in the EU regulation, but unfair practices are addressed
Transparency and Disclosure	Detailed description of what has to be disclosed and recorded	Transparency should be enhanced

10

Money Laundering

ELENI TSINGOU

This chapter examines the role of the European Union and its member states in the regulatory and institutional framework of the global anti-money laundering (AML) regime. AML has traditionally not been a core issue for financial governance; in an era of liberalization, AML appears a paradox as it aims to impose controls on the movement of money. Moreover, thinking about money laundering has developed under the public policy objectives of law and order, seemingly far removed from debates on financial regulation. But the consolidation of the AML regime since the 1980s and the growing attention to banking activities that have a bearing on money laundering, tax evasion, sanctions, and terrorism, has made it an important issue area in the governance of finance. The renewed emphasis on more efficient tax systems by many governments since the outset of the global financial crisis provides a further dimension to the study of AML and financial crime.

The analysis in this chapter shows that we need to consider three sets of factors to understand the role of the European Union in the global AML regime and how, in turn, the regime affects practices within the EU: the motivation and policy content of the AML regime as driven by key states; the development and consolidation of particular standards through global, regional, and national organizations; and the proliferation of AML practices among both regulators and the regulated. We see that European states (though no EU coalition of states) have significant influence in the shaping of global AML standards; they are also at the vanguard of the peer review process that leads to their global diffusion. At the same time, the European Commission has developed extensive expertise on AML to guide global debates and 'translate' the resulting rules into EU policy. Paralleling these formal activities, the practices of European banks provide an additional layer of AML governance—whether as defensive reactions to enforcement actions or in proactive investments in compliance and standard-setting initiatives.

The chapter proceeds as follows. First, it provides a historical overview of the AML regime and its institutional development, including the involvement of the EU and its member states at the global level. The chapter continues with an overview of the main explanations for the creation, development, and nature of the AML regime, and expands on five specific features of AML governance as it bears on Europe: (1) rule-making; (2) building expertise; (3) global diffusion; (4) 'translating' global rules into EU policies; and (5) overcoming tensions between public and private actors both nationally and regionally. Finally, the chapter addresses continuing challenges in the governance of money laundering, including in the development of a new money laundering directive in the European Union.

DEFINITIONS, MOTIVATIONS, AND INSTITUTIONS

Money laundering is the process of disguising the illegal origin of the financial proceeds of crime. While AML rules and laws originated in law enforcement concerns with narcotics, a wide range of crimes have been added to the list of so-called predicate offences for money laundering, ranging from trafficking and smuggling to tax evasion. Attempts at quantifying money laundering have proven challenging as its secretive and illegal nature results in scarce, incomplete, and often unreliable data.[1] This makes it difficult to assess the effectiveness of AML policies, while policy rhetoric and official assessments tend to focus on detected cases of money laundering.[2] As powerful as these cases can be in highlighting the links between finance and crime, they do not address the key challenges of definition, measurement, and effectiveness. Since their beginnings in the 1980s, AML policies have thus been assessed in a broader context that includes financial governance (ensuring the integrity of the financial system and a competitive level playing field for financial institutions) and law enforcement (tackling crime in relation to drugs, trafficking, or corruption), as well as the global coordination of foreign policy and national security concerns. The latter has been particularly apparent with AML methods focusing

[1] The most recent estimates of the United Nations Office on Drugs and Crime (2011) suggest that laundered money may be equivalent to 2.7 per cent of global GDP; the report also finds that less than 1 per cent of global illicit flows are seized or frozen.
[2] The recent enforcement action against HSBC is particularly noteworthy: following a year-long investigation by the United States Senate Permanent Sub-committee on Investigations, the bank was found in 2012 to have a severely lax compliance structure which had permitted and enabled business relations with drug traffickers in Mexico as well as suspected criminal and terrorist groups in Iran, Cuba, Sudan, and North Korea, and linked to the Taliban and Hamas. The full report and related hearing documentation can be found at: <http://www.hsgac.senate.gov/subcommittees/investigations/hearings/us-vulnerabilities-to-money-laundering-drugs-and-terrorist-financing-hsbc-case-history> (accessed on 13 February 2014).

on problem countries and politically exposed persons, and the inclusion of terrorist financing in the AML framework in 2001, and the financing of the proliferation of weapons of mass destruction in 2012.

The development of the AML governance framework is also linked to questions of global taxation and, in particular, competitive pressure from offshore centres (Sharman 2006; Palan et al. 2010). The core sponsors of the AML regime are members of the Organisation for Economic Cooperation and Development (OECD). The AML regime is now also used to address falling tax revenues in advanced economies, accentuated by the global financial and economic crisis. A prominent development here is the US Foreign Account Tax Compliance Act (FATCA), which targets banks outside the United States suspected of conspiring with wealthy US citizens to hide their bank accounts from the US tax authorities (see Wigan, this volume). While not explicitly part of the AML framework, many of the tools to be employed are directly linked to AML provisions.[3]

Money laundering is a relatively recent governance issue. The first key document on money laundering was a Council of Europe initiative in 1980 promoting 'know your customer' measures for financial institutions and state coordination on the tracking of banknotes.[4] Over the ensuing decade, many countries criminalized money laundering while bodies concerned with financial governance such as the Basel Committee on Banking Supervision and organizations dealing with drug trafficking such as the United Nations sought to define and tackle the emerging policy issue.[5] This led to the creation of a specialist organization with an explicit AML mandate—the Financial Action Task Force (FATF)—by the G7 in 1989.[6] Based in Paris and hosted by the OECD, its role is to issue regularly updated recommendations that aim to set global legislative and regulatory standards for AML. The FATF has 36 members, including OECD countries, major economies and financial centres outside the OECD, the European Commission, and the Gulf Co-operation Council.[7] It is a

[3] More information on the US Foreign Account Tax Compliance Act can be found at: http://www.irs.gov/Businesses/Corporations/Foreign-Account-Tax-Compliance-Act-(FATCA) (accessed 3 March 2014). Implementation is phased in from 2014.
[4] Recommendation No. R (80) 10, Committee of Ministers to Member States, 'Measures Against the Transfer and the Safekeeping of Funds of Criminal Origin', adopted 27 June 1980.
[5] Key documents include a 1988 statement by the Basel Committee and the 1988 UN Convention Against Illicit Traffic in Narcotic Drugs and Psychotropic Substances.
[6] The FATF was first established as an 11-member task force with a one-year mandate. The original members were Australia, Austria, Canada, France, Germany, Italy, Japan, Sweden, Switzerland, the United Kingdom, the United States, and the European Commission.
[7] The full list of FATF member countries is: Argentina, Australia, Austria, Belgium, Brazil, Canada, China, Denmark, Finland, France, Germany, Greece, Hong Kong—China, Iceland, India, Ireland, Italy, Japan, Luxembourg, Mexico, Netherlands, New Zealand, Norway, Portugal, Russia, Singapore, South Africa, South Korea, Spain, Sweden, Switzerland, Turkey, the United Kingdom, and the United States. In addition, the FATF counts 22 observers and eight FATF-style regional bodies. It is estimated that over 180 jurisdictions have endorsed FATF standards.

small organization with only 12 full-time professional staff; most of its work is done in conjunction with relevant experts in the ministries of member countries.

FATF recommendations aim to provide a comprehensive framework for tackling money laundering across the financial and business sectors, offering guidance for national AML governance structures, international cooperation, and the specific content of AML rules. The recommendations define money laundering predicate offences, provide guidance on confiscation, and outline preventive measures in the areas of due diligence, reporting, correspondent banking, and 'know your customer' requirements for financial transactions and beneficial ownership (linking corporate entities to their beneficial owners). FATF recommendations also address the design of national AML frameworks (e.g. on inter-agency coordination) as well as best practice on international cooperation among national authorities. The FATF aims to produce AML standards that promote risk assessment, tailoring activities to specific types of risks in different jurisdictions, financial activities, and financial institutions.

The FATF issued its first set of 40 recommendations in 1990. In the early years, recommendations were fairly flexible in their guidance and open to interpretation. But as the FATF evolved and was able to draw on a deeper pool of expertise, its recommendations became more precise and prescriptive, leading to the issuing of Special Interpretative Notes. Following the terrorist attacks of 11 September 2001, the FATF revised its standards and produced recommendations explicitly focused on the combatting of terrorist financing. It amended its recommendations again in 2012, including proliferation of weapons of mass destruction in its remit (FATF 2012).[8] In the recent revision, the FATF consolidated and clarified previous recommendations and introduced new provisions and approaches in several areas of financial governance such as a more sustained focus on beneficial ownership, the introduction of tax offences as money laundering predicate offences, and an expansion of a risk-sensitive framework for analysing exposure to money laundering. In addition to technical compliance (often judged as mere paper compliance; see also Walter 2008), the FATF will now also assess the effectiveness of implementation.

FATF recommendations are not formally binding but are widely adopted by members and form the basis of the European Commission's money laundering directives. Comprehensive monitoring of the implementation of recommendations is a key element of AML governance and follows two forms. First, all member countries carry out self-assessment exercises. Second, a mutual evaluation procedure entails onsite visits by legal, financial, and law enforcement experts from other member governments. In 1999, the FATF took a further step, engaging in a 'naming and shaming' campaign beyond the scope of its

---

[8] A detailed overview of the recommendations and related guidance on methodology can be found at <http://www.fatf-gafi.org/> (accessed on 13 February 2014).

membership and identifying countries and territories considered guilty of non-cooperation. This resulted in the first so-called Non-Cooperative Countries and Territories (NCCTs) report being made public in 2000 (this practice was eventually wound down). The FATF then moved towards a softer approach, identifying High Risk and Non-Cooperative Jurisdictions, and calling for counter-measures from its member countries or engaging in cooperation on enhanced compliance.[9]

The FATF is unlike other international organizations in that it promotes global technical standards but is an explicitly *political* organization in its membership and practices. While its scope is global, its membership is not: to qualify for membership, a jurisdiction has to be 'strategically important', with Russia, China, and India joining in recent years. According to Drezner (2007: 145), the use of a 'club IGO' (international governmental organization) has allowed G7 states to 'cajole, coerce, and enforce a global anti-money-laundering standard into existence'. Similarly, Sharman (2008) argues that the diffusion of AML standards should not be understood as the result of a process of policy learning, but as an exercise of power through direct coercion, mimicry, and competition. Indeed, participation in the AML regime has been deliberately restricted to the proliferation of regional task forces and agencies that mirror FATF practices and evaluation processes (Jakobi 2013: Chapter 5).

The FATF's AML activities and regional networks are supplemented by the work of the Egmont Group, which brings together national AML officials in its annual meetings. The gathered officials represent the Financial Intelligence Units (FIUs) of their respective countries—special offices with assembled AML expertise, often housed within law enforcement agencies, which receive suspicious transaction reports from financial institutions. Through the Egmont Group, they have built a learning network, sharing experiences and best practice, and strengthening cross-border ties for information exchange and cooperation. Importantly, the International Monetary Fund (IMF), as part of its work on financial integrity, has also been examining AML standards in its financial sector reviews and, where appropriate, has been offering technical assistance (Johnson and Abbott 2005). The FATF, the IMF, and the World Bank all use similar assessment processes, documentation, and procedures in their AML evaluations.

This broad overview of the global AML regime reveals important formal linkages between European and global levels of governance. Several EU countries, as G7 members, were behind the creation of the FATF. Even as FATF membership has grown over the years, European countries continue to constitute a large

---

[9] The countries facing counter-measures in 2014 are Iran and North Korea. Many more countries—varying in size, commitment, and position in global governance settings—are on the list of jurisdictions needing to strengthen their AML systems. They include Algeria, Ecuador, Ethiopia, Indonesia, Myanmar, Pakistan, Syria, Turkey, and Yemen. Of these, only Turkey is a FATF member.

proportion of members and have significant potential for input into the policy content of AML governance. They also participate in monitoring diffusion, adoption, and enforcement through the FATF's mutual evaluation exercises. Formal FATF membership of the European Commission (a founding member of the FATF) adds further opportunities for input and coordination at the global level. This is especially relevant as the FATF's work forms the basis of the EU's own money laundering directives. How formal memberships and representation translate into practice is analysed in the next section.

GOVERNANCE INTERACTIONS ACROSS POLICY LEVELS

The governance of money laundering is, at first glance, a state-driven, state-focused affair. This is reflected in much of the scholarly work on money laundering, which focuses on the inter-governmental and club-like nature of the FATF (Drezner 2007). In this reading, core states have used the FATF to coordinate their standards but mostly to impose them on jurisdictions outside the club—in a manner that would have been difficult for a universal membership organization such as the IMF. Other scholars have focused on the role of the hegemon in ensuring compliance with non-binding standards and sustaining momentum through the different phases of AML policymaking and implementation (Simmons 2001). A similar focus on hegemons exists in the literature on global prohibition regimes, including the role of the United States in their development (Andreas and Nadelmann 2006). This literature is particularly useful in explaining the role of powerful states in the development, adoption, and implementation of particular prohibition norms, and the global acceptance and compliance processes that turn them into regimes. The inter-state characteristics of the AML regime are also at the heart of work exploring the legitimacy—or lack thereof—of the global scope of standards, and of policies of blacklisting beyond the standard-setting membership (see e.g. Hüllse 2008). Sharman (2008, 2011), for example, looks beyond the work of the FATF to study how the global diffusion of AML policies has taken place. He shows that AML standards have been adopted by countries large and small with little consideration for local conditions, and examines how this diffusion has been experienced—and with what consequences.

Although the governance of money laundering largely revolves around the FATF and inter-state cooperation, state interests, preferences, and policies are far from monolithic. In the governance of money laundering, they stem from the goals of different types of public actors—regulators and law enforcers who have different motivations and criteria for success. AML 'experts' may be finance professionals, lawyers, or specialists in police work. The AML governance framework is shaped by the professional knowledge of groups with different training, expertise, policy goals, and professional aspirations (Tsingou 2010). This is the case across levels of governance.

Finally, any comprehensive account of the governance of money laundering needs to address the role of the private sector. On the whole, financial institutions have clear reputational and legal incentives to take AML measures seriously (Simonova 2011). It is thus no surprise that, over time, private sector actors have become willing participants in the adoption of procedures to combat money laundering and in complying with regulatory requirements, resulting in the establishment of dedicated AML units, continuous AML training, and significant investment in compliance software. Yet, from the early stages of the global AML regime—and especially since the intensification of AML activity in the aftermath of 11 September 2001—the dominant (and predictable) private sector view is that 'when the total costs to the banking system of the myriad anti-money laundering reporting requirements are correctly measured, few anti-money laundering efforts are cost effective' (Rahn 2003). Even with attention to AML temporarily waning with the onset of the global financial crisis (particularly as a cost priority within financial institutions), compliance procedures have been maintained and reinforced, especially through their association with increasingly popular public policy concerns about tax revenue.

There are thus several distinct factors that need to be considered in order to grasp the role of the European Union and its member states in AML governance and the dynamics of interaction across policy levels.[10]

State Power and Formal Representation

As discussed above, rule-making in the FATF follows a 'big states' logic and lends itself to the state-focused analysis of international organizations. From the outset, the FATF has essentially been a US and European club. Participants from outside the OECD often point to its unofficial hierarchy: the USA on top, then Europe, with other voices remaining comparatively weak. While the USA is often seen as taking the lead on the FATF's broad directions and non-AML add-ons (terrorism, proliferation), delegates warn that US leadership on non-AML issues should not be overstated. The recent inclusion of the financing of proliferation of weapons of mass destruction is a direct response to the request of finance ministers in the FATF's 2008 mandate review and is limited to two specific recommendations, with no opportunities of cascading into other aspects of the AML regime. On the other hand, the FATF's European members

[10] The remainder of this section relies extensively on interviews with FATF delegates from European and non-European countries and industry practitioners, as well as on discussions and presentations by senior officials and FATF staff members in training conferences for AML compliance officers. The interviews took place in the autumn of 2012, and training conference participation in June 2012 and January 2013.

are seen by delegates as influential on the details of financial governance and procedural issues. This is partly due to the overwhelming European presence and the Eurocentric character of the proceedings. Nevertheless, this perception can also be misleading as the 'real' European participants are fewer than their actual number.

The FATF is consensus-driven and there have been no reported instances of members casting vetoes or being over-ruled. In practice, agreement is easy to reach as certain countries tend to dominate. The United States, Canada, the United Kingdom, France, Germany, and Switzerland are by far the most active in making proposals, leading plenary debates, and in the working groups. They have dedicated teams that have developed expert knowledge and capacity over time; they also command the resources necessary to maintain active participation in FATF activities. The USA and the leading European states are thus responsible for the content of global AML standards, with differing degrees of influence depending on the specific policy.

European states apparently do not gain any additional advantage through the power of numbers or the European Commission's membership in the FATF. Neither European nor non-European delegates report a concerted EU position, a sense of collaboration among European FATF members, or a Commission drive to advance a European agenda. European FATF members (and the Commission) can be at odds on particular issues, while several have no AML agendas of their own. The Commission delegation is also relatively small and is usually represented by five delegates. The average European country has two or three delegates, while the USA often has a team of over 70. This matters in terms of representation and perceptions of political weight, but also reflects the more comprehensive, well-researched, and professional preparation of the US delegation on a broad range of issues.

European over-representation does, however, present benefits—including to those members with little influence (and indeed interest) in rule-making. Alongside the symbolic benefits of membership in a club international organization, FATF membership also offers certain competitive advantages to the financial institutions operating in their jurisdictions: FATF membership is one of the (low) risk criteria in AML assessments of financial transactions.

The FATF as an Expert Network

Despite this focus on the role of powerful states, the FATF is sometimes seen as 'a creature that has escaped its creators' (author interview). Slippage and independence from the principal has been extensively examined in studies of international organizations (see also Nielson and Tierney 2003) and is notable in this case as the FATF is a particularly small organization that relies on networks of civil servants to pursue its work. As such, although the FATF is a *political* organization as a 'club' IGO, its operational structure depoliticizes some of its activities, especially those related to financial governance issues. On questions relating to core AML concerns, the FATF and its working groups are essentially gatherings of experts (Kerwer and Hülsse 2011), taking the total of those active within the FATF to over 600 experts and officials.

At the plenary level, expertise does not always correspond to power politics. While delegations from key member states are consistently vocal, so are other delegations on specific issues. Experts from the Scandinavian countries and the Netherlands are knowledgeable on a broad range of issues, while delegates from countries with more limited AML capacities (especially Portugal) have been active on specific themes. These patterns, coupled with the importance of consensus within the FATF, have led to the promotion of different issues associated with AML, notably financial inclusion. Other delegations have contributed little in their years of membership.[11]

The FATF's nature as an organization of experts is readily apparent in its mechanisms of mutual evaluation as peer review. In this respect, the FATF follows the long-established mechanisms of policy learning and diffusion developed by the OECD (Martens and Jakobi 2010). But whereas the OECD is often associated with cooperation and learning in policy areas where no hard law exists, the global diffusion of FATF standards and their adoption in national legal systems and regulations add a strong monitoring and sanctions dimension to the mutual evaluation process. The FATF working groups, the peer review framework, and the replication of FATF-style methods in regional AML organizations all point to the institutionalization of AML expert networks and the role of FATF recommendations in this development. As a network of experts, the FATF focuses on 'practice' (see also Stone 2012). This is in line with experimentalist explanations of governance that privilege mechanisms of peer review and participation in the production of expert knowledge (Nance and Cottrell 2014)—a governance method with a long track record in the production of internal policies in the EU (Sabel and Zeitlin 2010).

In this environment, the European Commission as a FATF member has accumulated expertise over time. Its main role has been to ensure that EU member states remain aware of the EU directives dimension of any FATF recommendations by promoting some cooperation and coordination. On other issues, the Commission has had a more modest role than its expertise would suggest. Frequent changes of personnel—with the Commission being represented by high-level officials and not necessarily by those responsible for coordinating implications for EU directives—have affected the continuity of its representation within FATF debates. Commission staff are also less likely to be

[11] Interviewees suggested some delegations contribute with only a single intervention during a week-long plenary. There is at least one delegation which no one recalled ever contributing.

involved in working group activities and have not undertaken any mutual evaluation work. As such, Commission expertise both on the content of AML policies and on the mechanisms of governance of peer review and experimentation is under-used in the FATF's work.

Global Diffusion

As discussed above, FATF activities are supplemented by the work of regional task forces that mirror the FATF in their organization and methods (see also Jakobi 2013).[12] Prominent FATF members are often members or associates in these regional organizations and responsible for capacity building. Regional leaders (also FATF members) financially support these task forces through their financial-size related membership fees, donations, and contributions in kind; their expertise, institutional capacity, and strategic interests determine the extent of their engagement with peer review activities. Officials involved in these mutual evaluations have greater influence on FATF recommendations and on matters related to practice. Their countries—by promoting the adoption of standards that may be ill-suited to local conditions against a backdrop of possible sanctions and blacklisting (see also Sharman 2011)—are also by extension participants in the coercive elements of the AML framework.

Mutual evaluations (within and beyond FATF) are almost exclusively carried out by officials from the United States and Europe on a voluntary basis. Evaluators need expertise *and* funding (they have to cover their own costs); they also need an advanced working knowledge of the English language, both for examining and drafting the relevant reports. As a result, it is estimated that officials from eight countries do 70 per cent of the work (author interview). Evaluation teams prefer to focus on countries that are seen as strategically important; in general, most jurisdictions also wish to be evaluated by teams from 'important' countries for purposes of visibility and legitimacy. This creates influence for countries whose officials are regular evaluators. It is, however, also a source of resentment for FATF members who are unhappy with what they see as free riding by some smaller European countries: 'If you are a member of a club, you participate both in its benefits and responsibilities' (author interview). With public budgets coming under pressure, some FATF members would also like to see a fairer distribution of financial responsibilities within the organization.

---

[12] These include FATF associate members (the Asia/Pacific Group on Money Laundering, the Caribbean Financial Action Task Force, the Council of Europe Committee of Experts on the Evaluation of Anti-Money Laundering Measures and the Financing of Terrorism, the Financial Action Task Force on Money Laundering in South America, and the Middle East and North Africa Financial Action Task Force) as well as FATF observer bodies (the Eurasian Group, the Eastern and Southern Africa Anti-Money Laundering Group, and the Intergovernmental Action Group against Money Laundering in Africa).

With the USA and a few European countries dominating the mutual evaluation process—and thus the monitoring of the global implementation of AML standards—there is little room for an active European Commission role. The EU instead provides global leadership through the example of its translation and adoption of regulatory and legal AML standards at the regional level.

'Translating' Global Rules into EU Policies

The main task of the European Commission in the governance of AML lies in the development of money laundering directives, always in line with FATF work—a clear example of knowledge transfer leading to policy transfer (see also Stone 2012). In the EU context, 'soft' law has been adopted into a concrete and binding legislative framework, the first to be developed at a regional level (Mitsilegas and Gilmore 2007). More broadly, the EU has been an early adopter of what has subsequently become standard AML practice. Table 10.1 provides a timeline of the EU's money laundering directives in relation to work pursued within the FATF.

The timely and enthusiastic adoption of FATF recommendations clearly reveals the significance of FATF membership of European countries and the European Commission. The directives were not merely transposed to the EU level but took shape within longer-term global processes of coordination and consensus building. The EU has thus been negotiating its own AML rules from a position of 'rule-maker' *and* 'rule-taker'. But the EU case also shows how this has involved compromises with constitutional law and EU competences (Mitsilegas and Gilmore 2007), and raised questions about competing policy

Table 10.1 The EU's money laundering directives—a timeline

FATF Recommendations: publication and revisions	Money Laundering Directive proposal	Money Laundering Directive adoption
1990: 40 Recommendations	1990	1991: First Money Laundering Directive
1996: Revision of Recommendations	1999	2001: Second Money Laundering Directive
2001: 40 + 8 Special Recommendations on Terorrist Financing		
2003: Revision of Recommendations		
2004: 40 + 9 Special Recommendations	2004	2005: Third Money Laundering Directive
2012: Revision of Recommendations Consolidation	2013	

priorities, most notably for civil liberties and the privacy of data. Successive money laundering directives have also assigned public policy roles to the private sector. The third EU directive on AML delegated risk assessment and information gathering functions to private actors, in particular to banks. The democratic implications of these developments are significant and vary across member states (Bergström, Svedberg Helgesson, and Mörth 2011).

Public Policy and Private Interests

The public policy role assumed by private actors in the governance of money laundering has led to significant changes in how AML is practised within financial institutions. Large banks in particular have the resources and organizational capacity to adjust to AML requirements; this has led to the development of an increasingly professionalized compliance industry. Whereas compliance was long seen as a necessary evil, the consolidation of AML standards has given a new veneer to the compliance function. At the senior level, we observe the phenomenon of revolving doors between law enforcement agencies and the Big Four professional services firms[13] as compliance departments look for unique skills and expertise in the areas of investigation and forensic accounting. At the same time, junior and mid-career positions are increasingly populated by staff who have followed harmonized training and have acquired globally recognized qualifications in AML. This professionalization has helped strengthen the relative standing of AML compliance departments within financial institutions, even during the financial crisis. It has also put the spotlight on the role of compliance officers straddling the public–private divide (Favarel-Garrigues, Godefroy, and Lascoumes 2011; Verhage 2009).

   Large banks have also found common ground to create a voluntary code of conduct—to harmonize principles and strengthen private sector reputation and credibility (Pieth and Aiolfi 2003)—that closely follows FATF recommendations. Created in 2000, the Wolfsberg Group of Banks[14] issues global AML guidelines for international private banks. It first focused on correspondent banking relationships but has lately expanded its work to include guidelines on matters such as the screening and monitoring of clients and transactions. While membership in the group is practically closed to new members, the initiative has evolved to include an annual 'Wolfsberg Forum' which brings together a wider spectrum of financial institutions (some of the world's largest banks) as well as representatives from national and global regulatory and supervisory

[13] The Big Four professional services firms are PwC, KPMG, Ernst & Young, and Deloitte.
[14] The group consists of banking leaders Banco Santander, Bank of Tokyo-Mitsubishi UFJ, Barclays, Citigroup, Credit Suisse, Deutsche Bank, Goldman Sachs, HSBC, J.P. Morgan Chase, Société Générale, and UBS.

agencies and from the FATF (Pieth 2006). The group regularly updates its guidance, and did so in 2012 following the announcement of the revised FATF 40 recommendations and in 2014 on the issue of correspondent banking.

These private sector developments are closely tied to the AML activities of states. Public authorities rely on the information provided by financial institutions through suspicious transaction reports, but also monitor them for wrong-doing and lapses in compliance. Governments further seek to 'protect' their own financial institutions by providing a framework that does not harm their competitiveness. Enforcement actions against 'foreign' banks (most notably HSBC and Standard Chartered) in the United States in 2012 were accompanied by polemical rhetoric, with public officials and private practitioners alike emphasizing the 'sophisticated framework' of US AML regulations and the absence of blind spots in US bank compliance. In contrast, the EU was said to have 'no teeth in their programmes' (author participant observation)—a claim that put European officials and financial institutions on the defensive.

CHALLENGES[15]

The next steps in the global governance of money laundering involve the adoption of the FATF's revised recommendations. Towards this end, the FATF issued a new methodology for compliance in 2013. It covers, as before, technical issues of process but also new ways to assess whether a jurisdiction's AML system is producing the expected results in light of predefined outcomes. The challenge for the FATF is to promote practices that are not too prescriptive and which ensure fairness. The recommendations, which result from long-standing work, need to be implemented in ways that are consistent and to overcome subjective biases. The next round of mutual evaluations will serve as a test for this ambitious exercise in coherence and consistency across jurisdictions and may well require a shift in thinking from public sector officials.

Another challenge for the FATF is to make good on its commitment to risk assessment. While the revised recommendations and the FATF's global focus have enhanced the geographical scope and the range of financial activity covered by AML provisions, there has been little attention to the risks associated with the financial sectors of core FATF countries. Though large financial systems may not need specially targeted rules, a risk-based approach implies closer scrutiny of their activities (and the complexity of these activities).

---

[15] This section draws on public expert discussions on the EU context (Conference on 'Fighting Money Laundering and Terrorist Financing: New Framework, Future Challenges', 15 March 2013, European Commission, Brussels).

These challenges, and the AML governance dynamics that underpin them, are at the forefront of AML developments within the EU and the 'translation' of the FATF recommendations into a fourth money laundering directive, proposals for which were first published in February 2013. Taking its cue from the revised FATF recommendations, the Commission has put forward two legislative proposals to address legal gaps and loopholes in the AML framework. The proposals address: non-banking activities; risk assessments that make maximum use of available resources; fighting corruption, particularly in relation to politically exposed persons; strengthening and harmonizing sanctions across member states; and improving transparency on beneficial ownership (going further than the FATF and thus the USA on this issue). The draft directive is the result of close collaboration between the Internal Market and Services Directorate General and the Home Affairs Directorate General. The latter is keen on greater cooperation between Financial Intelligence Units and Europol, harmonized standards across the EU, and stronger powers of confiscation.

As FATF recommendations are not binding, how faithfully they are adopted at the EU level is an important test for the governance of money laundering more generally. The EU is in some ways a microcosm of the global regime with its own core and periphery, as well as different-sized financial institutions across member states. The emphasis on risk assessment implies that the activities of the large financial centres of the EU, especially London, should receive special attention. It also entails a more nuanced treatment of different financial institutions and adjusting requirements according to the nature and volume of activities, while remaining sensitive to the needs of small and medium-sized entities. As on-going global disagreements over transparency on beneficial ownership show,[16] a fourth money laundering directive with greater bite will raise requirements within the EU above those of other jurisdictions. One challenge for European policymakers is to carefully negotiate the balance between AML ambitions and global competitiveness. Another challenge is to ensure that AML regulations and legislation remain 'proportional' (K.H. Lehne, Member of the European Parliament). The privacy of data, civil liberties, and confidentiality are important tenets within European policymaking and any EU-sponsored monitoring of citizens would need to be expressly justified. The European Parliament in particular is interested in questions of proportionality regarding AML targets, be they individuals, institutions, or economic sectors.

---

[16] The G8 Leaders 2013 Communiqué addresses beneficial ownership but falls short of concrete agreement on type or form of central registries and does not include a public transparency requirement as was proposed by some G8 countries. <https://www.gov.uk/government/uploads/system/uploads/attachment_data/file/207583/Lough_Erne_2013_G8_Leaders_Communique__2_.pdf> (accessed on 13 February 2014).

CONCLUSIONS

The European Union has a multifaceted role in the governance of money laundering. Focusing specifically on AML regulations and provisions related to financial governance, we can observe that the global state-centric regime has a strong European presence but not necessarily a distinct European identity. Individual member states decide on the content of the AML regime and are in charge of monitoring and evaluation; the analysis supports the common reading of the FATF as a club international organization, one led by OECD states and not solely by the United States. In this framework, the European Commission, a founding member of the FATF, essentially holds a coordinating role, building expertise and translating FATF recommendations to fit the demands of the internal market and other intra-EU policies. The European Union also serves as a location where many of the enduring challenges of the AML regime are played out and potentially resolved: tensions between large and small financial centres, larger and smaller financial institutions, and financial integrity and security policy priorities and preoccupations. As such, the EU is a regional leader but also a pioneer in implementation. Finally, the European Union—as the site where AML regulations are put into practice by some of the world's largest private sector institutions—showcases how AML compliance is internalized in banking activities. It also showcases the enduring tensions between compliance and the core business of banks.

11

Offshore Financial Centres

DUNCAN WIGAN

INTRODUCTION

In April 2009, in the immediate wake of the financial crisis, G20 leaders issued a statement promising 'to take action against non-cooperative jurisdictions, including tax havens'. They declared themselves 'ready to deploy sanctions to protect our public finances and financial systems' and claimed that 'the era of banking secrecy is over' (G20 2009b: 4). Algirdas Šemeta, European Commissioner for Taxation and Customs Union, Audit, and Anti-Fraud, expressed similarly ambitious intentions in June 2012: 'Let there be no illusion: tax evaders steal from the pockets of ordinary citizens and deprive Member States of much-needed revenue. If we want fair and efficient tax systems, we must stamp out this activity. The political will to intensify the battle is there. Now it is time to translate that into action' (quoted in EC 2012b: 1). Efforts to ensure the fairness, efficiency, and sustainability of the international political economy by tackling cross-border tax evasion and avoidance soon followed. The 2013 Lough Erne G8 leaders' communiqué—which pledged commitment to 'developing global solutions to the problems of tax evasion and tax avoidance'[1]— called on the OECD to develop a common template for country-by-country reporting and commit to a global standard for automatic information exchange (G8 2013: 6). This chapter takes stock of these developments. It sets them in the context of prior policy initiatives, and evaluates the role and impact of the European Union in creating a regulatory assemblage that promises an effective, if inchoate, multilateralism.

That this is happening now is hardly incidental. At the outbreak of the global financial crisis, tax havens attracted increased scrutiny for housing many of the

---

[1] Tax evasion is the illegal circumvention of an obligation to pay taxes, while avoidance involves using extant laws to reduce a tax contribution in a manner that is strictly legal but may transgress 'the spirit of the law'.

structured finance vehicles implicated in the meltdown. Most notoriously, the subsequently nationalized British bank, Northern Rock, had set up its special-purpose financing vehicle, Granite, in Guernsey to sell off large parts of its mortgage book to bond investors. The financial crisis in Europe soon turned into a sovereign debt crisis, leading governments to search for new streams of tax revenue. The politics of austerity borne of the crisis has cast into sharp relief the question of distributional equity in deciding who carries the greater burden in repairing crisis-hit economies. As faith in 'unfettered' markets gives way to the distributional politics of taxation, the structural difficulties of innovating policy and regulating offshore finance are being circumvented. States at the centre of the global financial crisis face both a fiscal and a political imperative to act against tax havens.[2]

Amidst the plethora of initiatives to rein in tax havens, this chapter focuses on the substantive content of policy initiatives, based on the premise that Europe's role in global financial governance can in large part be understood by examining the interactions between distinct policy innovations. The chapter first outlines the history of EU impotence in the area of direct taxation. EU policy interventions have been few, sporadic, and hamstrung by lack of consensus among member states and associated territories; until recently, the EU deferred to the limited multilateralism of the OECD. The chapter then proceeds to survey the largely failed attempts to regulate tax competition and tax havens at the multilateral level: OECD-inspired efforts have similarly foundered on the lack of consensus among its members and the 120 members of the Global Forum on Transparency and Exchange of Information for Tax Purposes.

The USA, seemingly out of frustration with the limited multilateral regime, acted unilaterally, dropping what is effectively a 'nuclear bomb' on the institutional architecture of cross-border tax evasion in the form of the Foreign Account Tax Compliance Act (FATCA 2010). At the same time, the EU has generated a series of policy proposals and is updating key directives to ameliorate what it now perceives as the harmful impact of tax havens and cross-border tax avoidance and evasion. In terms of immediate traction, EU policy palls in comparison to the recent US move. But there are signs that EU policy impotence may be reversing and what at first seem to be disparate and piecemeal approaches to regulation may coalesce into an effective multilateral regulatory assemblage. Simply put, EU policy is ambitious but hamstrung by the difficulty of generating consensus among its members. On the other hand, US FATCA is infiltrating Europe through the back door and seems to

---

[2] The term 'tax haven' is heavily politicized. Almost any state can act as a haven from another state's fiscal claims, while countries such as the UK and the Netherlands, not commonly seen as 'tax havens', may function as such. The term is deployed here in accordance with public and political discourse.

be encouraging Europe to develop its own policy agenda in forms such as country-by-country reporting.[3] Policy mechanisms on both sides of the Atlantic are converging on the practice of automatic information exchange and reducing the operational space for those seeking to game the international tax system. The OECD is secondary here but may, spurred by the initiatives of its most powerful members, regain some issue control, particularly in the guise of the base erosion and profit shifting project. Notably, the OECD follows the policy innovation of powerful states in an area where there has never been a global regulatory regime.

EU POLICY IMPOTENCE

Taxation remains one of the most fiercely guarded of EU member state competencies. As indirect taxes may undermine the free movement of goods and the supply of services within the internal market, EU power to intervene in tax matters has traditionally been restricted to indirect taxes such as VAT and excise duties. Any proposal concerning direct taxes requires unanimity at the Council of Ministers and the de facto revision of the treaties. Given this constraint, alongside the absence of exchange rate uncertainty, and integration and enlargement having created an environment where corporations and individuals can shop around, the prospects for EU success in fighting cross-border tax avoidance and evasion seem slight. Not only are there substantial legal and institutional barriers to generating EU policy in the area of direct and cross-border taxation, in matters of taxation the EU is constrained by an acute collective action problem. The EU contains within it multiple and opposed interests; many of its member states follow an offshore strategy, making the EU itself the host to the largest tax evasion industry in the world. If we include EU member state dependencies such as the former Dutch Antilles and the UK Channel Islands, Bermuda, and the Caymans, the EU hosts approximately 60 per cent of the world's tax havens.

   This is not to say that tax coordination has been absent from the EU agenda. The Neumark report proposed the harmonization of business taxation across the European Community in 1962, while the Commission had advocated a common general tax on corporate profits as early as 1967 (EC 1967). The Commission's proposal, however, was rejected by the European Council, and the first directives on direct taxation—the parent subsidiary and the mergers

---

[3] Country-by-country reporting requires firms to provide financial information for each country in which they operate. This promises to tackle the avoidance practices made possible by corporations being an economic unit rather than a legal category. As such, firms can create multiple legally separate entities and shift profits and losses across borders to reduce tax contributions.

directives[4]—only came with the onset of the single market in the 1990s (Genschel et al. 2011: 595). A convention on arbitration in international tax controversies regarding transfer pricing policies was adopted at the same time, but this was neutered by the fact that it was a convention among member states rather than a Council directive. As such, it was neither enforced by the Commission nor reviewed by the European Court of Justice (Radaelli 1999: 667). And although the 1977 directive on mutual assistance between tax authorities explicitly targeted cross-border tax evasion and avoidance (Directive 77/799/EEC), it was flawed by design.[5] While the Community adopted a significant body of legislation on VAT and excise duties in the early 1990s, this 'only highlighted the absence of a coherent policy on direct taxation' (EC 2001a: 3). Indeed, it took 30 years of discussion to produce the first direct taxation directives in 1990. Lamenting the pace of progress, the Commission in 2001 noted that there were 16 proposals for directives in the taxation domain sitting on the Council's table and 'some of these have been on the table since the early nineties' (EC 2001a: 20).

An expert report in 1992 warned of widespread corporate tax competition and proposed common restrictions on preferential tax regimes[6] and a minimum corporate tax rate of 30 per cent (EC 1992). The report was not well received by national tax administrations and ministers, who criticized it for being 'unrealistic or impracticable in the short to medium term' (Radaelli 1999: 668). But substantive movement on direct taxation followed the 1996 informal meeting of Ecofin in Verona, which identified 'harmful tax competition' as a problem to be tackled by a high-level EU working group. This led to the adoption of the 'tax package' at the December 1997 Council meeting. Under conditions of unanimity, policy change must produce gains for virtually all members. This is a formidable obstacle when a single issue is being addressed. By combining three policy areas, the tax package could conceivably generate a situation in which every member state was an overall winner (Cattoir 2006: 2). Luxembourg, which specializes in attracting overseas savings, stood to lose due to the savings tax but was compensated by the losses of Ireland and Belgium in the area of corporate tax (Radaelli 2003: 518).

---

[4] Directive 90/435/EEC on parent subsidiaries targeted the cross-border taxation of dividend payments. Directive 90/434/EEC addressed the tax treatment of mergers and acquisitions between companies of different member states.

[5] In particular, the directive left room for states subject to an information request to rely on the difficulty of obtaining information or simply delayed response to thwart its purposes. Article 8 in particular meant that for all practical purposes the directive was impotent: 'This Directive does not impose any obligation upon a Member State from which information is requested to carry out inquiries or to communicate information, if it would be contrary to its legislation or administrative practices for the competent authority of that State to conduct such inquiries or to collect the information sought' (Directive 77/799/EEC: 12).

[6] Preferential tax regimes (PTRs) aim to attract specific mobile activities into a given territory.

The three elements of the 'tax package' were the Code of Conduct on Business Taxation, the Directive on Taxation of Savings Income, and the Directive on Taxation of Interest and Royalty Payments. The third element on interest and royalty payments aimed to exempt most such payments from taxation at source (Cattoir 2006: 11). As such, it did not address tax evasion and avoidance, and sat squarely within the EU enlargement and harmonization agenda. The first two elements of the package, however, bore on the regulation of offshore finance.

The code of conduct on business taxation is soft law, used in the EU when lack of political consensus blocks policy progress.[7] By adopting the code, member states commit to rolling back existing tax measures that constitute harmful tax competition and refrain from introducing any further such measures (Cattoir 2006: 3–4). While the code explicitly recognized the benefits of tax competition, it also provided grounds for a shared understanding of harmful competition, required the participation of EU dependent territories, and led to confrontation with jurisdictions seeking to compete by distinguishing between resident and non-resident companies for tax purposes. In 2006, the Commission, citing the code, forced Luxembourg to abandon its 1929 holding companies regulation (Palan et al. 2010: 222). The code of conduct also breeds a certain synergy with the OECD efforts discussed below, as the EU can refer to international best practice to support its efforts (Radaelli 2003).

The savings tax is perhaps the most significant element within the package for assessing EU efforts to govern offshore finance. While it has limited traction on tax evasion and avoidance, it represents in the arena of tax governance the most advanced multilateral mechanism for the automatic exchange of information. Both the political limits of EU governance as well as potential remedies for these limits became apparent in its development. In a nutshell, the EU suffers from having two distinct camps in its ranks: high-tax states such as Germany and France whose fiscal systems are threatened by tax base erosion, and countries such as Luxembourg and Austria which have traditionally gained from attracting mobile capital. Negotiations over the Savings Tax Directive reflected this political divergence as some states insisted on a withholding tax option rather than the automatic exchange of information.[8]

This led to the co-existence model, where countries not party to European information exchange would be obliged to impose a withholding tax on interest earned by foreigners. Second, the proposal obliged the EU to enter into equivalent negotiations with relevant third countries. The negotiations initially stalled

---

[7] Radaelli (2003) draws parallels between the code and the EU's open method of coordination, which relies on monitoring, benchmarking, peer review, and mutual learning.

[8] A withholding option preserves the opacity upon which offshore finance thrives. Depending on the level at which it is set and the efficiency with which it is applied, it may or may not deter tax evasion and avoidance. A tax evader may take advantage of the opportunity to pay withholding once, then move the account to a non-participating jurisdiction.

as the UK, Austria, and Luxembourg argued that cooperation with all rather than some third countries should be a precondition for a European agreement. The revived proposal of 2001 (EC 2001b) retained the co-existence model but only permitted withholding for a transitional period of seven years, during which Austria, Luxembourg, and Belgium would at first impose a 15 per cent tax, and then a 20 per cent tax on interest accruing to foreign-held accounts (Holzinger 2005: 485). The final agreement in 2003 followed this trajectory and rendered the cooperation of reluctant member states dependent on the agreement of third countries such as Switzerland, Lichtenstein, and the United States. Crucially, the dichotomy built into the directive reflected the structural limitations on the EU governance of taxation—namely, the diametrically opposed interests of its members.

The agreement finally entered into force in July 2005 on the understanding that European third parties such as Monaco, Lichtenstein, and Andorra would comply. Though Switzerland struck a deal with the EU in 2004, Swiss banks subsequently began offering savings products designed to circumvent the agreement. Austria, Belgium, and Luxembourg were granted extensions until 2015; in the intervening period they could continue using the withholding model (Radaelli and Kraemer 2008). This effectively means that an agreement which explicitly seeks to tackle cross-border tax practices preserves bank secrecy—a key basis of tax evasion and avoidance. Significantly, the EU Savings Tax Directive requires the reporting of individual savings but not those held by legal entities such as trusts. Nevertheless, the agreement of certain EU member states relying on equivalent measures being adopted in non-EU member states and dependent territories such as Switzerland, the USA, and the Channel Islands gives the savings tax an institutional means of expansion. In effect, the insistence on equality of treatment by the EU's tax havens, while emblematic of the EU's collective action problem, provides a basis for EU policy to constitute a multilateral mechanism with broad geographical coverage. Amendments to the Mutual Assistance Directive (EC 2009b) reinforce this possibility. First, a most favoured nation clause was introduced obliging member states to provide other member states with the level of cooperation they have accepted in rela-tion to third parties. Second, it prohibited the reliance on bank secrecy for non-residents in refusing to supply information on taxpayers. This then provides a bridge for the transposition of US FATCA rules (discussed below) into EU practice and weakens the secrecy on which tax havens rely.

By announcing that the USA would not agree to full information-sharing on US savings accounts held by EU residents, the Bush administration in 2002 temporarily derailed the progress of EU policy. The European Union Savings Directive (2003/48/EC) which entered into force in July 2005 left EU policy in a curious halfway house. It could not capture interest payments accruing to accounts held by corporate entities; changing the beneficial owner from a natural person to a trust or limited company thus meant transparency could be circumvented. Member states could also choose to exchange information or withhold. The three European tax havens and most of the dependencies of the Netherlands and the UK chose the withholding model.

THE OECD'S MEEK MULTILATERALISM

The onset of the OECD campaign to regulate offshore finance was marked by the 1998 publication of the report *Harmful Tax Competition: An Emerging Global Issue* (OECD 1998). For a decade, multilateral efforts had been led by specialist bodies at organizations like the OECD, the Financial Action Task Force (FATF), and, occasionally, the IMF. As these organizations do not have executive powers, they must resort to persuasion and 'name and shame' tactics (Sharman 2006). A number of jurisdictions were indeed 'blacklisted'. For reasons of esteem and commercial interest, no jurisdiction aspires to be so listed, and they have largely cooperated with these organizations. But the end results have been disappointing. Most, if not all, states and jurisdictions have managed to remove themselves from such lists, while evidence of substantive changes to the role of tax havens in providing international tax arbitrage opportunities is few and far between.

The OECD[9] campaign against harmful tax competition has, since the early 2000s, proceeded on the basis of its Tax Information Exchange Agreement (TIEA). The exchange of information between tax authorities is based on two main types of bilateral agreement: Double Tax Agreements (DTAs) and TIEAs. DTAs signed under the Model Tax Convention on Income and Capital are agreements between two states which seek to prevent income or profits being taxed twice. TIEAs complement DTAs as the latter are considered inappropriate for jurisdictions with no or low taxes, where 'double non-taxation' is the pressing issue. Most TIEAs are based on the OECD Model Convention and Model Tax Information Exchange Agreement published in 2002 as part of the OECD Harmful Tax Practices Project. Both the content of these agreements and the short history of their use suggest that the OECD campaign against harmful tax competition can, to date, be considered a failure.

This failure is encapsulated in the distinction between automatic information exchange and information on request. Automatic information exchange provides for the periodic and systematic transfer of taxpayer information between jurisdictions concerning various categories of income. Simply put, automatic information exchange facilitates the detection of unsuspected tax

---

[9] The Global Forum on Transparency and Exchange of Information is formally and perhaps only ostensibly independent of both the OECD and the OECD's Centre for Tax Policy and Administration where the Forum sits.

evasion or avoidance. In contrast, the OECD Model Convention and Model Tax Information Exchange Agreement (TIEA) requires the exchange of tax information on request, and merely allows for the automatic exchange of information through separate agreement. The model was published in 2002 by the Global Forum on Taxation, formed in 2001 (OECD 2002).

Under a TIEA, a government can only request information on a named taxpayer who can be shown to have given due reason for suspicion. In effect, this means that tax havens furnish information to another state's tax authorities only when that state's tax authority has already obtained the information necessary to start building a case. Furthermore, the investigating tax administration would need to know in which jurisdiction the individual held an account. While the 2005 revision of the OECD model treaty's Article 26 overrode the prior provision that a contracting party did not have to exchange information if this violated domestic laws, such as Switzerland's strict bank secrecy laws, the OECD commentary on Article 26 specifically prohibits 'fishing expeditions' (Mcintyre 2009: 257).[10] TIEAs, then, rely on governments having in hand precisely the type of information that tax havens are designed to conceal—a clear case of placing the cart before the horse.

That TIEAs are bilateral rather than multilateral agreements poses further limitations. First, bilateral systems reduce potential benefits flowing to developing countries as these countries are likely to be hampered in identifying and tracking suspect account holders by possessing ineffective and under-resourced tax administrations. Developing countries may not have the capacity to hold prior information on suspected tax evasion and avoidance cases necessary to make valid requests. Furthermore, bilateral OECD TIEAs have only generated a few links between a limited number of players. Given that there are approximately 220 countries and territories in the world and 52 tax havens, a comprehensive lattice of agreements would entail approximately 11,000 treaties (Johannesen and Zucman 2012). The Global Forum provides a list of only 1,371 extant TIEAs, many of which have neither been reviewed nor deemed to meet the standard.

Since the majority of the world's tax havens refused to sign information exchange agreements before 2008, most of these agreements have been signed in the wake of the global financial crisis. This provides evidence not so much of a rush to compliance, but of white-washing.[11] The few agreements in place include, for instance, those between the British Crown Dependencies

---

[10] McIntyre (2009: 257) quips: 'What would happen to the fishing industry if fishermen could only catch a fish if they knew its name or if the fish had an identifying tag? The only reason I can imagine for wanting to put such a ridiculous limitation on fishermen would be to keep them from catching fish.'

[11] Before 2008 Jersey had signed two TIEAs with the USA (2001) and the Netherlands (2007). Since then, it has added 27 agreements to its list. Before 2009 the Cayman Islands had signed one agreement with the USA in 2001. It is now signatory to 29 agreements.

(Jersey, Guernsey, and Isle of Man) and the Faroe Islands and Greenland. During 2009, almost one-third of the agreements signed by tax havens were with other tax havens (Johannesen and Zucman 2012: 7). On these grounds alone, the mechanism invites charges of window dressing. In April 2009, the OECD specified that for tax havens to be removed from their list of 42 uncooperative jurisdictions, they would need to sign 12 TIEAs. Within five days all were deemed compliant, leading to the premature declaration that the 'era of bank secrecy is over'. Johannesen and Zucman's analysis of the impact of the OECD's renewed campaign on bank deposits held in tax havens shows that these remained stable between 2007 and 2011, at US$2,700bn. The authors conclude that 'The G20 initiative has caused a relocation of deposits between tax havens leaving the funds globally held offshore roughly unchanged' (Johannesen and Zucman 2012: 24).

The armoury in the war on tax havens was bolstered at the November 2009 Global Forum meeting in Mexico with the introduction of peer reviews to evaluate a country's implementation of the OECD standards. The peer review process brings in regulators from a diverse group of countries who evaluate legal and logistical provisions for tax avoidance, evasion, and regulatory compliance. The process consists of two phases. In phase one, jurisdictions' laws and regulations are analysed and graded. A successful phase one review allows countries to move into phase two. In phase two, reviewers make concrete recommendations for countries to improve their rules and regulations on the basis of an analysis of exchange of information in progress. As of April 2013, 96 peer review processes had been completed (OECD 2013a). While this process certainly represents a strengthening of the OECD's toolkit, it is far from clear that it is as robust as it might be.

That the peer review process simply aims to strengthen a process of information exchange already deemed seriously flawed limits its transformational promise. Based on the 2002 OECD Model Agreement on Exchange of Information and Article 26 of the OECD Model Tax Convention on Income and Capital, it reproduces a weak framework. Not only does the peer review process perpetuate the inadequacies of information on request, it also fails to identify information that is key to greater transparency. Meinzer (2012: 15) reports that in the case of Ireland (deemed compliant in a 2010 combined review), the peer review concluded that 'ownership and identity information for all relevant entities and arrangements is available to competent authorities'. But where companies are non-resident for tax purposes— meaning they are not centrally managed and controlled in Ireland and not subject to a double tax treaty which would require the availability of beneficial ownership information—no beneficial ownership information will be held either by the company registry or the tax administration. Compliance with OECD standards does not necessarily entail the curtailment of offshore secrecy.

Additionally, individual peer reviews may have been subject to political manipulation. A randomized experiment testing international compliance with Financial Action Task Force rules stipulating that information on the beneficial ownership of shell companies be available to 'competent authorities' produced indisputable evidence that some US states, led by Delaware, are among the most secretive jurisdictions in the world (Sharman et al. 2013). Yet the USA—considered by the Global Forum to have an adequate network of treaties and a history of information exchange with other jurisdictions—was allowed to go through a combined phase one and two review process which produced glowing results (Global Forum 2011). The UK and the Netherlands, equally dubiously, went through a combined review process. Among the countries afforded combined phase one and two reviews are some of the world's most notorious tax havens: Mauritius, Jersey, and the Isle of Man all successfully negotiated the combined review.

At this juncture, the OECD campaign against harmful tax competition seems to have borne little fruit in terms of substantive behavioural change in target jurisdictions. The volume of business booked in or routed through tax havens has remained consistent; standards of compliance, when met, are weak. As an index of compliance, the OECD maintains white, grey, and black lists which distinguish between jurisdictions that have substantially implemented OECD standards, those that have committed to implement the standards but have not yet done so, and those that have not committed to the standards at all. As of December 2012, the vast majority of Global Forum members were on the white list; only Naura and Niue were on the grey list, and the black list was empty. The index, then, seems to measure quantity—the number of information exchange agreements signed—rather than the quality of the information provided. Recent unilateral moves by both the USA and the EU seem to be rooted in frustration with the OECD standard and its results. The shift to more unilateral interventions may constitute a game changer—one which will ultimately generate a more effective, if inchoate, multilateralism.

THE US FOREIGN ACCOUNTS TAX COMPLIANCE ACT

The US Congress enacted FATCA in March 2010 to target avoidance and evasion by US taxpayers using foreign accounts. In short, the legislation requires that foreign financial institutions, from 2014, report to the Inland Revenue Service (IRS) the value and income accruing to accounts held by US taxpayers, or by foreign entities in which US taxpayers hold a substantial interest. The legislation covers accounts held both directly and by corporate entities benefiting US individuals, and deploys private financial intermediaries as guardians of US fiscal system integrity.

The regulatory principle of substituting private duties for public functions was first developed in the USA with the Qualified Intermediary (QI) system.[12] Prior to the implementation of QI in 2001, Foreign Financial Intermediaries (FFIs) did not document, collect, or report on tax matters within US jurisdiction. Under the QI system, intermediaries are required to collect withholding tax on US source payments to foreign customers and report to the IRS the US source income of US customers. But it did not target US taxpayers investing in FFIs and suffered from five debilitating weaknesses (Harvey 2012: 475–476). That only US source income was subject to reporting encouraged QI customers to shift their investments into non-US assets to avoid IRS scrutiny. QIs were not required to look through foreign shell companies[13] to establish beneficial ownership. Customers could thus avoid US reporting simply by routing investments in US assets through foreign shell companies. To reduce the administrative cost of performing due diligence on all accounts, QIs could designate only certain accounts as part of the QI system. This left room for customers who refused to identify themselves—'undeclared accounts'—to circumvent the QI system. That QIs were primarily banks also encouraged US taxpayers to invest in foreign mutual funds, private equity, or other non-QI financial firms. To compound this fragility, the QI audit merely examined QI accounts, which by definition were not a problem.

The unilateral FATCA regime was conceived amid high-profile cases involving extensive cross-border tax evasion. The leverage of FATCA pivots on the importance of the US market for intermediaries worldwide. It is, as such, both an expression and a test of the singular power of the United States. Significant coercion was required to persuade FFIs to perform the costly tasks of determining the beneficial ownership of shell companies, automatically report on both the US and foreign source income of US citizens, and review all customer accounts across an affiliated group to identify US taxpayers. FATCA places intermediaries in a position where non-participation potentially renders them uncompetitive. Since non-participating FFIs are subject to a punitive 30 per cent withholding tax on payments from US sources whether or not the payments are owned by US taxpayers, non-US customers, or the intermediary itself, they are for all practical purposes excluded from investing in the USA. Participating FFIs are also required to withhold on payments to non-participating FFIs. In contrast to the QI system, which could only police participating intermediaries, this punishment of non-participating FFIs potentially extends US regulatory reach to hundreds of thousands of intermediaries (Grinberg 2012; Harvey 2012: 481). Insofar as the ability to

---

[12] A qualified intermediary is a Foreign Financial Intermediary (FFI) or US financial intermediary abroad that has entered into a qualified intermediary withholding agreement with the Inland Revenue Service.

[13] A shell company is an entity that has no active business. It usually exists only in name as a vehicle for another company's or individual's business activities.

access US assets for clients is crucial to an intermediary's competitiveness, FATCA represents a powerful extraterritorial weapon against tax evasion and avoidance. US citizens will potentially no longer be able to cheat on taxes via foreign accounts and investments.

Effectively, a potential policy diffusion process built on the principle of the automatic exchange of information has been built into US legislative enforcement mechanisms on the basis of market power and the threat of direct or indirect market exclusion. A unilateral move by the USA has the potential to cascade through a worldwide network of financial intermediaries, including funds previously excluded from the purview of QI. Notably, any firm which is compliant in being able to identify US account holders will now necessarily have corresponding information on the accounts of other nationals. FATCA then could constitute the basis of cascading reciprocity. However, there remains the prospect that the weight of the US market alone will not be sufficient to persuade financial intermediaries that FATCA participation is worthwhile. Furthermore, a US taxpayer seeking to avoid paying US tax would still be able to invest in non-US source assets through a non-participating FFI. A truly effective FATCA may rely upon its reproduction on a multilateral basis.

The multilateral adoption of FATCA would severely curtail the range of assets available to an investor seeking to evade tax payments and relegate such investments to poor-quality institutions. To the extent that other major countries sign up as FATCA partner jurisdictions, require the same level of due diligence on intermediaries' customer bases, and impose similar penalties on non-participating intermediaries, shrinking opportunities and incentives for tax evasion and avoidance would render apposite the G20's premature announcement. A comprehensive regulatory architecture based on automatic information exchange could be built one brick at a time via bilateral agreement. Signs of this promise reaching fruition are already apparent. In November 2012, the US Treasury published the Model Intergovernmental Agreement for Cooperation to Facilitate the Implementation of FATCA, which aspires to resolve domestic legal impediments to FFIs reporting directly to the US IRS. It would render partner jurisdiction governments responsible for exchanging information with the US FFIs so that local laws would not be contravened in providing the information required by FATCA. A joint communiqué by France, Germany, Spain, Italy, the UK, and the USA on occasion of the publication of the Model Agreement stated:

> This is an important step forward in establishing a common approach to combat tax evasion based on automatic exchange of information. France, Germany, Italy, Spain, the United Kingdom and the United States will, in close cooperation with other partner countries, the OECD and where appropriate the EU, work towards common reporting and due diligence standards to support a move to a more global system to most effectively combat tax evasion while minimizing compliance burdens. (Joint Communiqué 2012: 1)

In December 2012 a US Treasury press release claimed that the USA was in negotiations with 50 jurisdictions to implement the reporting and withholding provisions of FATCA. Of these 50, the press release identified 16 jurisdictions to be in the process of finalizing an agreement, 16 jurisdictions with which the Treasury is in active dialogue towards an agreement, and a further 15 with which the Treasury is exploring options for intergovernmental engagement. In the first months of 2013, further bilateral agreements were signed with Ireland and Switzerland. On the basis of extant intergovernmental cooperation alone, it would seem reasonable to conclude that FATCA's unilateral origins belie its multilateral promise. But in light of recent EU initiatives, FATCA in fact seems to be a catalyst for a potentially game-changing regulatory assemblage. The flurry of initiatives, many now emerging and under negotiation, support this impression.

AN EMERGENT REGULATORY ASSEMBLAGE

The period following the global financial crisis has witnessed the EU producing a plethora of recommendations and policies designed to ameliorate the impact of tax avoidance and evasion. This section briefly outlines two of the most important of these initiatives, many of which are still under development, to suggest that what seems to be a series of uncoordinated and piecemeal actions may add up to being more than the sum of their parts. Catalysed by the deployment of US market power in the pursuit of unilaterally defined policy goals (Drezner 2007), EU action and now OECD deliberations promise the 'decentralized coordination' (Helleiner and Pagliari 2011) of an effectively multilateral system to regulate and re-order offshore finance. The argument here draws heavily on Perez (2011), who has suggested that for 'polycentric' soft law 'ensemble regulation', private and fragmentary regulatory mechanisms may be more efficacious than commonly understood. But a note of caution is in order. Recent scholarship has emphasized the potential for learning through peer networks and policy diffusion via best practice benchmarking (Sabel and Zeitlin 2012a). The argument of this chapter suggests that the momentum for 'experimentalist governance' even under conditions of heightened uncertainty and an acute collective action problem (Sabel and Zeitlin 2012a; Verdun 2012) may rest on the action of powerful states and a good deal of initial coercion. Whether this conclusion is valid across multiple regulatory domains is an open question – tax sovereignty is strongly guarded.

In the area of information exchange, the 2011 Directive on Administrative Cooperation in the Field of Taxation (Directive 2011/16/EU) goes beyond the 2008 proposal to extend the coverage of the EU Savings Tax Directive to include interest payments to EU residents through tax-exempted structures established in non-EU countries. The directive mandated the Commission to broaden the categories of income that member states must automatically exchange information on, and tightened procedures for doing so, thereby rendering the EU regime potentially compatible with FATCA requirements. As mentioned above, the Most Favoured Nation (MFN) clause in the amendments to the Mutual Assistance Directive (EC 2009b) underpins this compatibility by requiring member states to extend to other member states the level of cooperation they have accepted in relation to third parties. The amendments further prohibit non-residents from relying on bank secrecy in refusals to provide taxpayer information. These rules establish a bridge for the transposition of FATCA rules into EU practice. If any EU member becomes a FATCA partner country (as for instance have Austria and Luxembourg), all EU members will be empowered to demand the same treatment as that afforded the US authorities. Furthermore, so-called son of FATCA agreements, signed between member states and non-EU member jurisdictions, raise the spectre of MFN claims reaching beyond the boundaries of EU membership. Jersey, Guernsey, the Isle of Man, Switzerland, and the Cayman Islands signed 'son of FATCA' agreements with the UK between December 2012 and April 2013. As noted above, the G8 has now endorsed a system for automatic information exchange, while a 2012 OECD assessment of automatic information exchange suggests that, given the political climate, this organization may also be moving towards new standards (OECD 2012).

In March 2011 the European Commission proposed a common system for calculating the tax base of businesses operating in the EU (EC 2011g). The Common Consolidated Corporate Tax Base (CCCTB) would require firms to consolidate all profits and losses incurred across EU jurisdictions and pay taxes according to 'formulary apportionment'. The proposal maintains the sovereign rights of member states to set their own corporate tax rates. Group profits will be taxed once across the EU, and tax revenues, in contrast to systems which prioritize legal form over economic substance, will be distributed among countries according to 'real economy' criteria such as sales, capital invested, and employee numbers. While the proposal remains mired in the conflicting preferences of member states, it is notable that the Financial Transaction Tax has been established in the absence of unanimity and that a legislative template for such regulation is already available within the EU in the form of the 2013 amendments to the Accountancy and Transparency Directives (EC 2013a). These amendments mandate multinational corporations in the extractives sector to produce financial reports that show how much money they pay to host governments, a limited form of country-by-country reporting. Notably, the Capital Requirements Directive IV (EC 2013b) was revised in 2013 to mandate all European and European-listed banks to produce full financial reports on a country-by-country basis. The USA in Section 1504 of the 2010 Dodd–Frank Act had already imposed similar, though less exacting, requirements on its extractive sector companies (SEC 2010). This shift to country-by-country reporting may now also be occurring at the OECD. The ground-breaking Base Erosion and Profit Shifting (BEPS) project has led to discussions at the OECD (OECD 2013b) on the benefits of country-by-country reporting as the basis of a veritable revolution in accounting, potentially leading to unitary accounting for multinational corporations in all sectors.[14]

Perez (2011: 543) suggests that 'multiple links and cross-sensitivities between the different global private regimes have created a novel ensemble regulatory structure with positive enforcement and normative externalities'. This analysis suggests that similar links and cross-sensitivities are being constructed through apparently disparate initiatives by the USA, the EU, and now in the OECD. Pointedly, regulatory innovation is here being driven by state intervention. In the arena of tax law, cross-border tax regulation, and compliance, private initiatives may be far from optimal and jealously guarded sovereign imperatives must be overridden. Any regulatory assemblage in this policy arena will therefore depend on coercive interventions. The USA has catalysed a still-evolving regulatory assemblage by threatening private financial intermediaries with exclusion from the US market. EU actions and on-going initiatives mesh with US actions to constitute a transatlantic engine driving regulatory transformation.

CONCLUSION

This chapter has addressed the role of the EU in the global governance of offshore finance. In doing so, it has drawn attention to the interface between seemingly disparate policy initiatives. Hampered by institutional design and the divergent interests of its members, the EU has historically been slow in developing policy in the area of direct taxation. As a consequence, OECD standards until recently constituted the principal mechanism of governing offshore finance. The coming of the global financial crisis then fuelled a remarkable shift in the pace, volume, and substance of policy innovation. Here the USA has taken the clear lead, using the importance of its market to financial intermediaries worldwide to pursue unilateral action to protect its fiscal system. US action, in the form of FATCA, bypasses the obstacles to extraterritorial tax regulation—jealously guarded sovereign rights and mutually exclusive fiscal authority—by deploying private financial intermediaries to police the integrity of the US fiscal system. This system, via bilateral and limited multilateral agreements, is gradually being internationalized. This has

[14] Unitary accounting involves corporations providing financial reports on the basis of their worldwide operations. The right to tax that income is then divided between jurisdictions on the basis of real economy indicators such as sales, investment, and employee numbers. Country-by-country reporting is necessary for unitary reporting.

encouraged the EU, after creating the first multilateral system for automatic information exchange through the 2003 Saving Tax Directive, to shift gears and generate a series of new initiatives. In the shadow of the OECD's meek multilateralism, a set of seemingly diverse and disparate regulatory innovations are now restricting the space in which offshore finance can operate, limiting opportunities for tax avoidance and evasion and reinforcing the capacities of fiscally challenged states. This process of incremental policy innovation is forming a regulatory assemblage with unprecedented traction.

The chapter noted at its outset that there is no effective global regulation or governance in the area of tax. It is for this reason that effective regulation is likely to rest on the meshing of disparate initiatives. But a note of caution is in order. While the chapter has argued that the emergent regulatory assemblage it identifies comprises a sea change in the governance of offshore finance, there remain countervailing forces. First of all, China has flatly rejected FATCA; the Chinese financial system will remain outside of the regulatory space the assemblage constitutes. And while US and EU policies reduce the space for offshore finance, regulatory innovation may also rearrange the geography of offshore finance. A notable shift to developing countries and Asia is now apparent, with the rise of new centres such as Singapore (Johannesen and Zucman 2012). The changing cartography of the global economy and the rise of developing economies may thus reduce the capacity of core states to dominate global financial governance (Sharman 2012). The combined regulatory force of the EU and USA may still prove inadequate if a universal regime is necessary.

12

Macroprudential Regulation

One of the most significant financial regulatory changes following the financial crash of 2008 was the apparent international embrace of ideas about macroprudential regulation by central banks across the G20 countries. By late 2009, the United States, the European Union, and the United Kingdom were all signalling their intent to start building macroprudential regulatory regimes, and all have since created new macroprudential policy committees (Baker 2013a). This chapter begins by outlining this macroprudential ideational shift and its significance. It then examines the ties between macroprudential regulatory philosophies and European political economy more generally, and the role of EU institutions—the European Commission and the European Central Bank—in shaping the emerging international macroprudential consensus that took hold during 2009. The chapter then considers the response of EU institutions to these global developments, in particular the creation of the new European Systemic Risk Board. Finally, the chapter examines how this context affects the EU's ability to speak with one voice on macroprudential matters and the capacity of EU institutions to influence wider global debates on macroprudential policy.

THE MACROPRUDENTIAL IDEATIONAL SHIFT OF 2009

What is Macroprudential Regulation?

Macroprudential policy is a new ideology and a big idea. That befits what is, without doubt question, a big crisis. There are a great many unanswered questions before this ideology can be put into practice. These questions will shape the intellectual and public policy debate over the next several decades, just as the great depression shaped the macroeconomic policy debate from the 1940s to the early 1970s. (Haldane 2009: 1)

Macroprudential regulation is, as the Bank of England's Executive Director of Financial Stability Andrew Haldane notes, a series of new, or different, ideas about how to regulate the international financial system. At its core is the notion of systemic risk. This is the idea that the build-up of risk in the financial system has a systemic dimension that goes beyond any individual institution's risk profile to include the systemic dynamics produced by the interaction of aggregate debt exposures. Containing this build-up of risk requires a macro-systemic view and policy stance, with regulators mandated to check these systemic risks. This contrasts with the pre-crisis regulatory status quo that essentially involved supervisors assessing the risk models of individual financial institutions. That approach, referred to as 'microprudential', has subsequently been criticized for its blindness to the build-up of systemic risks and for hardwiring pro-cyclicality into the financial system (FSA 2009; Persaud 2009; Eatwell 2009). Macroprudential regulation therefore involves system-wide policies that seek to contain and constrain private sector risk-taking. According to the former director of the Bank for International Settlements, Andrew Crocket, a macro-prudential approach focuses on the financial system as a whole in order to limit the costs of financial distress in macroeconomic output (Crockett 2000).

Macroprudential thinking consists of four key interrelated concepts. First is the notion of 'fallacy of composition', or recognizing that individual institutional incentives and the courses of action that flow from these do not necessarily result in desirable aggregate or systemic outcomes (Borio 2011). Second, macroprudential thinking recognizes that prices in financial markets can be driven to extremes by an inherent 'pro-cyclicality' involving the calculation of risk following prices, so that the supply of credit fuelling investment is most plentiful when least needed (when asset prices are rising) and least plentiful when most needed (when asset prices are falling), driving asset values to extremes in both directions (Borio, Furfine, and Lowe 2001; Borio and White 2004; White 2006; BIS 2006). Third, herding entails individuals adopting behaviour close to the overall mean and deferring to the judgments of others due to the chemistry of the human brain and the propensities of the limbic system, resulting in short-term decisions and an inability to evaluate relevant information over long-term horizons (Haldane 2010b, 2012a). A fourth macro-prudential concept focuses attention on network externalities and complex systems (what BIS economists call the cross-sectional dimension), when small events can generate all kinds of systemic dislocations due to the complex and unintended interactions that ensue in complex systems (Haldane 2010a; Haldane and May 2011). These concepts draw heavily on Keynes' insights on fallacy of composition, macro dynamics, and herding, and on Hyman Minsky's findings on complexity, the endogenous nature of financial risk, and inherent financial instability (Baker 2013a; Datz 2013). They are a significant departure from the pre-crash efficient markets orthodoxy that emphasized the efficient information-processing capacity of financial markets—inhabited

by rational participants who would produce a general equilibrium through
their calculations so that prices would on the whole accurately represent
underlying fundamentals—and which claimed financial innovation and tech-
nologies had made the system as a whole more robust, durable, and stable.

The stated objective of macroprudential policy is to moderate credit supply
over the cycle, tightening policy in booms and lowering it in busts (Bank of
England 2011.) The most commonly cited macroprudential policy instrument
is the counter-cyclical capital buffer, a variant of which operated in the Spanish
and Indian banking systems in the pre-crash period. The idea behind a counter-
cyclical capital buffer is to lean against the credit cycle based on a reference
path of a normalized credit to GDP ratio. Deviations above the path involve a
tightening of capital requirements for private lending institutions while deviations below that path involve a loosening of those requirements (Haldane
2012a). Other potential macroprudential policy instruments include constraints on bank leverage levels and maximum levels being placed on bank
asset encumbrance. Empowering regulators to engage in technical calculations
and judgments is therefore one of the principal outcomes and objectives of the
macroprudential project.

However, macroprudential policy is not just about identifying and containing incipient financial booms. It also has implications for deflationary periods,
when the aim is to explore ways of stimulating private credit growth and
increased bank lending. For example, in the UK, the new macroprudential
Financial Policy Committee (FPC) is currently lending money at lower than
market rates to banks, provided that it is lent to the UK real economy, and is
also providing liquidity insurance and allowing banks greater flexibility to use
their liquid asset buffers (Turner 2012). Interventionist counter-cyclical policy
applies to both parts of the cycle and is intended to produce greater macro
stability in the supply of credit. In Haldane's words, 'if there were a benign
enlightened regulatory planner, able to redirect competitive forces, this could
potentially avert future tragedies of the financial commons. Fortunately there
is' (Haldane 2012b: 12). The implication is that macroprudential policy promises to be a good deal more interventionist in private credit and financial markets than has been the norm in most advanced economies since the 1980s. For
the EU, with its single market logic and legislation, this potentially poses some
tricky challenges.

A Short History of 'Macroprudential'

The term 'macroprudential' was first used by the Cooke Committee (an early
incarnation of the Basel Committee on Banking Supervision) in 1979 to refer to
how problems with a particular institution could have destabilizing systemic
implications (Clement 2010). Informal usage of the term continued throughout

the 1980s and 1990s at the Basel-based Bank for International Settlements (BIS), but it was after the Asian financial crisis that the research department at the BIS began to develop a fully fledged research programme and started forwarding macroprudential proposals, including a much clearer sense of the distinctive features of a macroprudential approach to financial stability (Borio, Furfine, and Lowe 2001; Borio and White 2004; White 2006; BIS 2006; Borio and Drehmann 2008). The existing literature shows that BIS staff were instrumental in developing macroprudential thinking and analysis (Maes 2009; Clement 2010; Galati and Moessner 2011; Baker 2013a). To some extent, the BIS can lay claim to the concept; initially at least, it assumed institutional ownership of the development of macroprudential thinking, analysis, and policy.

A macroprudential ideational shift emerged from the financial crash of 2008 (Baker 2013a). It largely involved technocrats from the BIS, well-networked private sector and academic economists such as Charles Goodhart, John Eatwell, Avinash Persaud, Hyun Song Shin, Markus Brunnermeier, Martin Hellwig, Jose Ocampo, and Stephanie Griffith Jones (Brunnermeier et al. 2009; Hellwig 1995; Persaud 2000; Goodhart and Segoviano 2004; Griffith Jones and Ocampo 2006), and officials from national central banks, who together exercised an 'insiders' coup d'etat' to depose the simplified efficient markets orthodoxy that had reigned over the previous two decades (Turner 2011; Baker 2013a). A number of key reports diagnosing the crisis and outlining a regulatory reform agenda advocated a macroprudential approach to regulation. These included the Turner Review (UK), the Geneva Report, the European Commission-instigated De Larosière report, the United Nations Stiglitz Commission report, a G30 report, and a report by the Financial Stability Forum (FSF) (FSA 2009; Brunnermeier et al. 2009; De Larosière Group 2009; United Nations Commission 2009; G30 2009; FSF 2009.)

Following this flood of reports, G20 leaders charged the Financial Stability Board (FSB, formerly the G7-based FSF)—comprising regulatory, central bank, and finance ministry representatives from the G20 countries—to monitor, coordinate, and report on national efforts to build macroprudential regulation and on macroprudential best practice more generally. New agencies for the evaluation of systemic risk have now been created in the form of the Financial Stability Oversight Council (FSOC) in the United States, the European Systemic Risk Board (ESRB) at the European Central Bank (ECB), and the Financial Policy Committee (FPC) at the Bank of England in the UK. The Basel III agreement has a macroprudential component involving counter-cyclical capital buffers. This ideational shift has led to the reorientation of the research machinery of the global financial architecture. When the FSB collaborated with the IMF and the BIS to produce a progress report to G20 leaders on macroprudential policy tools and frameworks in November 2011, the report referenced 22 reports and papers with a macroprudential focus produced by those three institutions since 2010. Concerted efforts are therefore underway within the international community of central bankers and regulators to construct functioning macroprudential policy regimes and build macroprudential knowledge and data sets, even if this process is proceeding on a slow and incremental basis (Baker 2013b).

In Vivien Schmidt's terms, 'macroprudential' can be conceived of as a 'coordinative' discourse that organizes experts through a 'programme' that sets the underlying principles and frames of reference that define the problems to be solved by policies, the issues to be considered, the goals to be achieved, and the norms, methods, and instruments to be applied (Schmidt 2008). The macroprudential ideational shift also fulfils Peter Hall's three criteria for third-order change (Hall 1993). First, it represents a new macroprudential policy discourse and lexicon (a new gestalt). Second, there has at least in name been a change in the hierarchy of goals behind policy, from micro surveillance assessing the safety of individual institutions towards a focus on macro dynamics and the stability of overall credit supply. Third, there was a change in causal assumptions or accounts of how the world facing policymakers actually works (Hall 1993: 280) as financial markets were no longer viewed as being efficient most of the time, but myopic, inhabited by agents with less than optimum rationality, and prone to instability (Tucker 2011).

The real significance of the macroprudential ideational shift is therefore the switch in the cognitive filter of regulators. A whole range of policy instruments, previously considered unnecessarily 'interventionist' by the efficient markets perspective, can now be placed on the table and seriously discussed. These include counter-cyclical capital requirements; dynamic loan loss provisioning; counter-cyclical liquidity requirements; administrative caps on aggregate lending; reserve requirements; limits on leverage in asset purchases; loan to value ratios for mortgages; loan to income ratios; minimum margins on secured lending; transaction taxes; constraints on currency mismatches; capital controls; and host country regulation (Elliot 2011). The terms and frames of debate over financial regulation have thus been reoriented in global and European central bankers' networks. We now examine in more detail the contribution of EU institutions and member states to this ideational shift.

THE EUROPEAN UNION AND THE MACROPRUDENTIAL IDEATIONAL SHIFT OF 2009

The genuinely transnational nature of global financial governance policy networks and their intertwined, cross-cutting nature make it very difficult to be precise about where the EU starts and stops, and whether it was influencing, or being influenced by, wider global governance debates on macroprudential regulation. The lack of formal EU representation in the key FSF working groups in 2009 that did the important analytical and foundational work for the G20's later political support and endorsement of a macroprudential approach to regulation was, however, striking. EU influence on the macroprudential ideational shift was largely indirect: through national officials linked to ECB networks participating in the FSF, or through notables writing reports for the EU and interacting with other macroprudential advocates through their own informal networks. EU institutions had minimal formal representation in the key policy forums that presided over the macroprudential ideational shift.

Despite this, it is worth noting that macroprudential concepts and ways of thinking resonate with traditional European reasoning on the role of finance in capitalist systems. From a variety of capitalism perspectives, ideas of pro-cyclicality, herding, and the notion that financial markets are prone to inherent instability are compatible with coordinated market economy structures and the acknowledged need to intervene and trammel financial systems to provide stable and reliable credit to real economy activities such as manufacturing (Hall and Soskice 2001). Leading macroprudential advocate Avinash Persaud has observed that the focus on 'too big to fail' in the United States is not really a macroprudential issue but about preserving the sanctity of the market. He notes that in Europe the focus has been much more on pro-cyclicality, which he sees as being genuinely 'macroprudential'—as opposed to the largely rhetorical use of the term in the US where half-hearted support is linked to ideological and cultural traditions that place much more faith in financial market outcomes (Persaud 2010). Claudio Borio of the BIS has reached a similar conclusion. In this sense, even if there is scant evidence of a strong EU leadership role in macroprudential thinking, there is a strong sense among a number of key pioneers that macroprudential is a 'very European' concept.

When central banks debate the broad principles and parameters around which appropriate programmes, policy, and regulation should be framed and organized (Schmidt 2008), they are much less likely to have firmly demarcated institutional and territorial identities and preferences than when they negotiate detailed policy agreements that include precise policy commitments such as the Basel III accord (Baker 2013a). As Marcussen has noted, central bank policy communities are characterized by a partial process of 'scientization'—a striking intellectualization of the world via formal analysis and mathematical abstraction (Marcussen 2006).

Modern central bankers make epistemic alliances with other members of the scientific brotherhood; their research departments finance their own scientific journals and conferences as scientific credentials enhance careers for central bankers who increasingly possess doctoral degrees in economics and engage directly with the scientific community (Marcussen 2006: 9). One of the significant consequences of this 'scientization' is that central banks' organizational, territorial, and cultural boundaries are blurring as co-equal central bankers work closely together from project to project (Marcussen 2006: 10). From this perspective, central banking is increasingly comprised of 'knowledge communities' constructed around inter-paradigmatic discussions about theory, methods, and data. The macroprudential ideational shift following the crash of 2008, and particularly how this relates to the contribution of EU institutions, provides evidence to support these somewhat tentative hypotheses.

First, those who promoted macroprudential thinking in the wake of the 2008 crash and contributed to reports advocating macroprudential regulation in the first half of 2009 were exclusively professional economists. Second, the national central bank officials engaged in developing macroprudential analysis were not simply national officials but members of wider transnational networks, exposed to repeated and enduring interactions with their peers at other central banks and the staff of institutions such as the BIS, IMF, BCBS, and the FSB. The networks of central bankers are thus intertwined; exchanges cut across one another and institutional identities are fluid. The macroprudential ideational shift provides evidence of the emergence of a transnational epistemic community that cuts across the institutions of the European Union—but one that has not always provided a specific institutional voice for the EU as a whole.

The FSF's April 2009 document 'Addressing Procyclicality in the Financial System', produced for G20 leaders, included the first significant international endorsement and elaboration of macroprudential style policies by an official body. It was driven by three working groups. One on bank capital issues was chaired by Nout Wellink, governor of Netherlands Bank and member of the ECB's governing council. Another on leverage and valuation was chaired by Jean-Pierre Landau, deputy governor of the Banque de France, a regular contributor to the ECB's research and monthly bulletins (and now chair of the ECB's International Relations Committee). Participants in key ECB committees played pivotal roles in shaping the FSF's endorsement of macroprudential forms of regulation in the aftermath of the 2008 crash. This reflected the peculiar nature of the ECB as an institution, which, although having some supranational characteristics, remains dependent on the staff of national central banks. These officials in turn participate in wider international and transnational regulatory governance structures, thereby producing intertwined, cross-cutting regulatory policy networks.

The FSF's three working groups consisted of 61 members from various national central banks, regulators, and international organizations, as well as seven secretariats. But not one of them formally represented either the ECB or the Commission. The EU did not have a formal presence in the FSF's pivotal working groups of 2009.[1] Furthermore, none of the members of the De Larosière High Level Group, asked to report on financial supervision in the EU by the Commission following the crash of 2008, had formal input into either

[1] Mario Draghi, who later became president of the ECB, was chair of the FSF during this period. But there is little evidence that he led the FSF consensus in a macroprudential direction.

the FSF report or its working groups. Two members of the EU High Level Group were, however, well networked in international financial governance and regulatory networks. The chair, Jacques De Larosière, had been IMF managing director and since 1992 a member of the G30—an influential advisory group drawn from public and private sector financial notables (Tsingou 2012). The G30 was compiling its own post-crisis regulatory report and beginning to promote macroprudential thinking, and included among its members leading macroprudential advocate Adair Turner, head of the UK's lead regulator, the Financial Services Authority (FSA) (Tsingou 2012).[2] Otmar Issing was another member of the De Larosière group who had been a prominent member of the ECB's executive board. Issing also chaired the Issing Committee, under the auspices of the University of Frankfurt's Centre for Financial Studies, which was advising the German Chancellorship on G20 issues during 2009. Another invited prominent member of the Issing Committee was BIS macroprudential pioneer William White. In other words, both De Larosière and Issing had institutional and network affiliations that brought them into regular contact with prominent macroprudential advocates.

In the G20 working group 'Enhancing Regulation'—one that BIS officials see as playing 'the key role in endorsing macroprudential thinking and concepts after the crisis'[3]—the EU was represented by one Commission official, but there was no ECB presence. Every national official in this key working group represented either a central bank, finance ministry, or regulatory agency, and had a financial or economics background. The one exception was Pierre Delsaux, the Commission representative and deputy director general for single market policy, who had a background in law, potentially placing him on the margins of the G20 working group's 'epistemic clan structure'.

Notably, the Commission's De Larosière report provided general support for the move towards a macroprudential approach. It approvingly cited Adair Turner (a leading macroprudential advocate in the UK) on a point about the excessive pro-cyclicality of the Basel II framework. The report also approvingly cited Charles Goodhart, an academic macroprudential pioneer, on the issue of cross-border resolution. As for counter-cyclical capital buffers, the report was clear that the FSF together with the BCBS should define the appropriate details. In endorsing counter-cyclical capital buffers and encouraging the BCBS to investigate further, the De Larosière report reached a similar conclusion to the FSF report. Other similar recommendations included a review of Basel II and the need to reduce the reliance on Value at Risk (VaR). Both reports highlighted the pro-cyclicality of fair value, or mark to market accounting standards. The FSF report unsurprisingly had much more to say about limiting leverage than the De Larosière report—possibly due to the De Larosière group's

---

[2] De Larosière now has the status of an emeritus member of the G30.
[3] Confidential communication between senior BIS official and the author.

close relationship with French and German banks (Buckley and Howarth 2010). The De Larosière report did call for the Commission to be given a seat at the FSF, which was later taken up and implemented. Notably, the High Level Group consulted Nout Wellink of the Dutch Central Bank, who also chaired the FSF working group on bank capital issues (and the BCBS), providing the De Larosière group with a means to influence the FSF working group while enabling the High Level group to incorporate the FSF's thinking into their own considerations.

According to one prominent BIS official, 'most of the push for macroprudential came from BIS staff and UK academics (Charles Goodhart, John Eatwell, and Avinash Persaud who were advising Adair Turner, head of the Financial Services Authority), some of whom then went to the US such as Hyun Shin'.[4] It is certainly the case that Goodhart, Eatwell, and Persaud converted Adair Turner to macroprudential thinking and that Turner became a leading macroprudential advocate in both the FSF and the G30.[5] The same BIS official also identified Tiff Macklem, the senior deputy governor of the Bank of Canada who chaired the G20 working group 'Enhancing Regulation', as a pivotal figure in overseeing the macroprudential ideational shift. Interestingly, former BIS staff member and macroprudential pioneer William White, as a Canadian citizen, was briefing both the Canadian and German G20 teams and was being referred to by Bank of Canada governor and G30 member Mark Carney as a leading prescient figure among the fraternity of economists who had predicted the crash of 2008 (Carney 2008). The UK and Canada were the two key developed country delegations driving the macroprudential ideational shift in key financial regulatory and central banking networks during 2009.

They were joined by the Reserve Bank of India (RBI), which had followed its own ad hoc version of 'dynamic provisioning', tightening capital requirements on banks in a counter-cyclical fashion. Notably, RBI chair Rakesh Mokan joined Tiff Macklem in chairing the G20 working group on regulation. The Indian approach, alongside the Spanish system of dynamic provisioning and counter-cyclical capital buffers, were often-cited examples in 2009.[6] Several EU countries also played a role in promoting the macroprudential ideational shift internationally, with Dutch, French, German, and Spanish officials making active contributions, even if they were not as active in displaying leadership as the UK, Canada, and India. In contrast, officials formally representing EU institutions were on the margins of this movement, at least in relation to wider international networks.

---

[4] Confidential conversation between author and senior BIS official.
[5] Confidential interview with anonymous macroprudential advocate, March 2010.
[6] Interview with G20 Deputy, 2010.

THE IMPLICATIONS OF THE MACROPRUDENTIAL IDEATIONAL SHIFT FOR EUROPEAN GOVERNANCE STRUCTURES

The macroprudential ideational shift in transnational regulatory networks raises the questions of how the EU responded to and was influenced by this shift, and what this means for European financial governance. Buckley and Howarth have noted how France and Germany have long track records of pushing for tighter global and European financial regulation, while the British were in favour of light-touch regulation and market opening (Buckley and Howarth 2010: 420; Zimmermann 2010). Likewise, Quaglia suggests that the EU's regulatory response to the global financial crisis has tipped the balance in favour of a more interventionist 'market shaping' coalition comprising France, Germany, Italy, and Spain, against the 'market making' coalition of the UK and the Nordic countries (Quaglia 2012b). While this may suggest that the EU would lead the move to build a macroprudential regulatory regime, the realities of how far macroprudential norms have been diffused and absorbed in particular geographical territories are a good deal more complex than a simplistic varieties of capitalism interpretation would lead us to believe. The evidence on what 'macroprudential' means for financial regulation in the EU is mixed (Buckley and Howarth 2010). Here, Young and Park's quantitative analysis of 30 OECD countries inadvertently challenges the varieties of capitalism perspective by finding strong correlations between levels of 'financialization' and strong regulatory responses to the financial crisis, with regulators acting opportunistically to take advantage of politically weakened financial sector interests to introduce more stringent financial regulations in the midst of crisis (Young and Park 2013). In this sense—and surprising from a varieties of capitalism perspective—the UK has been a leading champion of macroprudential ideas and has to date gone furthest in developing a functioning macroprudential regulatory regime in the EU.

Among the EU responses to the macroprudential ideational shift was the European Parliament's initiative to create a new European Systemic Risk Board (ESRB) on 24 November 2010. The ESRB was first proposed by the De Larosière report to monitor and assess 'systemic risk' across the European financial system. Formally it is a body without legal personality and binding powers, though it does have the power to make recommendations and issue warnings (Ferran and Alexander 2011). The ESRB has the following tasks: data collection and analysis; systemic risk assessment and prioritization; issuing systemic risk warnings and recommendations for remedial action and monitoring follow-up; issuing confidential warnings to the Council of impending emergencies; cooperating closely with and providing the European Supervisory Authorities (ESAs) with information on systemic risks; working with the ESAs in the development of quantitative and qualitative indicators to identify and measure systemic risk;

participating in the joint committee of the ESAs; coordinating with international institutions and relevant bodies in third countries on matters related to macroprudential oversight; and other related tasks as specified in EU legislation. The general board is the decision-making body of the ESRB and will be chaired by the president of the ECB for the first five years of its existence. The members of the general board who have voting rights include the president and vice-president of the ECB, national central bank governors, a member from the European Commission, the chairs of the three ESAs, the chairs and vice chairs of the two scientific advisory councils, and the chair of the advisory technical committee.

Legal scholarship has pointed out that the terms 'macroprudential' and 'systemic risk' are not well established in EU legislation. There is no comprehensive legal definition, while the term 'macroprudential' embraces concepts that are difficult to pin down from a legal perspective (Ferran and Alexander 2011: 26). Given their counter-cyclical focus, and legalistic nature of the EU regulatory order, macroprudential policies rely in part on the discretionary interventions of technocrats. But given the codified nature of the single market, macroprudential norms sit somewhat uncomfortably with conventional EU regulatory norms. The nature of the problem for the EU regulatory order is captured by Ferran and Alexander: 'The convergence trend (evident in EU regulation of the single market) could conflict with the objectives of prudential regulation and supervision, which may need diverse approaches to control systemic risk. The ESRB must somehow find a way of managing this conundrum, which touches upon potentially sensitive issues concerning the respective roles of national bodies and of the ESRB itself' (Ferran and Alexander 2011: 29).

The ESRB essentially has three objectives: to develop a macroprudential perspective to address the problem of fragmented individual risk at the national level; to act as an early warning mechanism by connecting the analysis of individual firms to the financial system as a whole; and to focus its assessments on systemic risks and issue risk warnings that are meant to be translated into national action. The ESRB's role is thus primarily analytical and advisory, monitoring developments and issuing warnings; it depends on national authorities having the powers and willingness to respond by adjusting regulatory and policy requirements to limit the build-up of systemic risk in their jurisdictions. If necessary, the ESRB can recommend specific actions to address identified risks. Although ESRB recommendations are not legally binding, they cannot be ignored. Their recipients are expected to report their actions to address the identified risk or explain their reasons for inaction. Whether recommendations are made public or not will be decided case by case. In short, the ESRB will be operating a 'comply or explain' regime (Buiter 2009).

Given their contrasting mandates and jurisdictions, the creation of the ESRB raises the possibility of inter-institutional tensions between it and the Commission (Buckley, Howarth, and Quaglia 2012: 113). The ESRB's willingness to see national authorities equipped with powers to address macro systemic issues and to go beyond Basel III requirements, if necessary for reasons of national stability, make sense from a macroprudential and financial stability perspective, but pose problems for the Commission's concern with internal market integrity (Buckley, Howarth, and Quaglia 2012). Unfortunately, this tension is unlikely to recede if EU member states are serious about developing functioning macroprudential regulatory regimes. The primary reason for this is that to become meaningfully operational, genuinely counter-cyclical macroprudential regulation requires host, rather than home, country regulation (Persaud 2010). Macroeconomic and credit cycles, even in the Eurozone, continue to follow national rhythms. The counter-cyclical tightening or loosening of capital requirements on banks requires national regulators to make discretionary judgments. While a home country regulator may not be particularly concerned about a financial institution expanding its lending activities in a way that helps inflate property bubbles in distant locations, a host country regulator most certainly would be. Here home country regulation makes sense from a microprudential perspective. But from a macro perspective, host country regulators need to be empowered to implement counter-cyclical measures that limit the threats posed to systemic stability in their jurisdictions. As Persaud notes, large banks and investment houses dislike the idea of host country regulation as it increases the number of requirements they must comply with; there is also the danger that host country regulation may slow and reduce cross border international capital flows, although from a systemic stability and macroprudential perspective this may be welcome (Persaud 2010). However, from a single market perspective, one which depends on the consistency of internal regulations, the idea of such 'unlevel playing fields' is filled with tensions and difficulties. Nevertheless, precisely such unlevel and adjustable playing fields are required if credit cycles are to be moderated and capital flows directed to where they are truly needed in the global economy (Warwick Commission 2009). For this reason, macroprudential regulation and the objective of systemic financial stability sit uncomfortably with the market-making process designed to create a single European economic space (Rosamond 2002). While the macroprudential emphasis on pro-cyclicality fits well with the notion of European managed capitalism, it creates tensions with the notion of Europe as a single market based on increasingly uniform regulation.

Such tensions were evident in the Fourth Capital Requirements Directive (CRD IV), which will implement Basel III in Europe. From a single market perspective, there is a case for having a single set of rules applicable to all. Director general of financial stability at the ECB, Mauro Grande, stated: 'it is important for banking regulation to be harmonized as much as possible across the European Union to foster the single market'. But from a macroprudential perspective, national regulators need to be able to adjust requirements for counter-cyclical purposes. Grande has noted that if national regulators want to go beyond the requirements set by CRD IV for macroprudential purposes, this should happen under a framework of constrained discretion in which prior notification is given to the ESRB so that it can assess the spill-over consequences for other countries. According to Grande, 'the national regulator should repeal the policy when the ESRB indicates that the underlying macroprudential reasons are no longer there. If this does not occur, the ESRB can issue a recommendation to the European Commission to take action against the member state.' The French position went further: a harmonized EU framework in which national regulators, under the same circumstances, do the same thing. The Commission likewise argued for a rules-based approach to CRD IV in its July 2011 draft text, which would require countries to stick to a rigid set of standards (instead of a directive which would allow national authorities to adjust requirements to suit their own macroprudential needs). The Dutch central bank favours the idea of the ESRB acting as mediator. However, the Bank of England and the Scandinavian central banks reject the idea of having to make requests to the ESRB, with the Bank of England seeking control over leverage, liquidity, funding, lending risks, and margin requirements. The CRD IV is currently in trialogue discussions with the Council of Ministers, the European Commission, and the European Parliament, led by the Irish presidency.

THE EUROPEAN UNION AND GLOBAL MACROPRUDENTIAL GOVERNANCE

These institutional tensions and uncertainties raise the questions of whether and how the EU can project itself on the global stage in macroprudential matters. In contrast to other regulatory domains, the two legal mechanisms through which EU rules have global reach—mutual recognition and equivalence (Ferran, this volume; Vogel 2013)—hardly apply to the measurement and containment of systemic financial risk in particular jurisdictions. It is therefore likely that European influence on global regulatory matters will be less pronounced in macroprudential regulation than in other areas.

But one ECB initiative should, at least in theory, enhance EU influence on the global stage. In the spring of 2010, the ECB and the European System of Central Banks (ESCB, with its 27 members) launched the Macroprudential Research Network (MaRS). Its formal mandate is to develop core conceptual frameworks, models, and tools to improve macroprudential supervision and research. As such, MaRS should provide the ECB and EU member states with a considerable analytical resource by pooling and exchanging expertise between the ESCB's 27 central banks. MaRS pursues research in three areas: macro models linking financial stability and the performance of the economy; early warning systems and system risk indicators; and assessing contagious risks. To date, the ECB has hosted two MaRS annual conferences. MaRS involves more than 180 researchers from all EU national central banks and the ECB, working on 126 individual projects and two joint cross-country projects involving multiple central banks. Participating academics are not confined to European universities, but include a range of staff from US Ivy League institutions. The MaRS network—which was envisaged to continue only until the end of 2013—encourages teaching and research in universities to reflect macroprudential concerns, particularly assessments of macroprudential regulatory instruments. With MaRS, the EU is not only reflecting but driving developments in the construction of macroprudential knowledge, ensuring that the EU, the ECB, and European central banks are technically well equipped to contribute to macroprudential debates in international settings.

In concrete terms, this raises the question of how and whether the EU was able to influence the Basel III agreement announced in September 2010, which contains a macroprudential component. Notably, Nout Wellink, who was also a member of the ECB's governing council, chaired the BCBS, which negotiated the agreement. The inter-state politics of Basel III pitched US, UK and Swiss representatives arguing for a much higher equity capital ratio against French and German representatives who feared this would disadvantage their ailing banks (Hanson, Kashyap, and Stein 2011; Mügge and Stellinga 2010). Existing scholarly accounts of Basel III also point to the influence of the Institute of International Finance (IIF) and large European banks such as BNP Paribus, arguing that higher capital ratios would result in stagnant Eurozone growth (Lall 2011: 22). Eventually, Basel III resulted in equity capital to risk weighted assets being adjusted upwards from 2 per cent to 7 per cent. There was also evidence that the BCBS caved in to industry pressure on stringent leverage ratios, resulting in a 3 per cent ratio that allowed banks to acquire assets 33 times their tier 1 capital (Lall 2011: 25). UK representatives argued for more expansive capital ratios, drawing on a macroprudential rationale that capital requirements needed to be set far above any reasonable estimate of the losses likely to be incurred by an individual bank, because what mattered was the macro systemic stability of credit supply, not just the risk of individual failure (Turner 2011; Miles, Yang, and Marcheggiano 2011). The eventual watering down of Basel III proposals and the softening of UK demands suggest that other European national delegations and European banks were successful in exerting influence in the BCBS. But this influence came through national delegations; while national central bank staff involved in ECB operations perform pivotal roles within the BCBS, the ECB itself is not a formal member of the BCBS.

One contribution to the literature on EU influence in global settings has used principal agent theory to hypothesize that European interests will be well represented in international forums when member states wholeheartedly delegate representation to EU institutions, or when member states remain entirely in charge and there is no delegation (Mügge 2011c). Problems arise with intermediate arrangements where delegation to EU institutions is half-hearted, tying the hands of member states without sufficiently empowering supranational institutions to take their place (Mügge 2011c: 384). The evidence from Basel III, where French and German delegations were effective in securing concessions for their financial sectors, appears to support Mügge's hypothesis.

Unfortunately, most of the conditions Mügge identified as undermining collective EU influence in global governance are evident in the macroprudential policy area. The internal configuration of macroprudential powers and responsibilities remains uncertain in the EU. EU member states are divided between three positions: a maximum harmonization position occupied by France, a middle compromise position with the ESRB in a mediating role favoured by the Dutch, the ECB, and the Germans, and a maximum national autonomy position occupied by the UK and Scandinavian central banks. Nor do the Commission and ECB see eye to eye. With such internal divisions on what a European regulatory regime would look like and how it would function, the external representation of the EU on macroprudential questions remains deeply uncertain. In the Financial Stability Board—the principal body assigned by G20 leaders to delineate global macroprudential best practice—we see precisely the division of responsibilities Mügge warned about, with national representatives joined by representatives of both the ECB and the Commission. The delegation of responsibility to speak for Europe on macroprudential matters is therefore not only characterized by uncertainly; external representation is similarly ambiguous, reflecting an intermediate form of delegation. While individual member states have been key players within macroprudential debates—with the UK and Spain influencing international discussions and France and Germany watering down provisions in Basel III—the prospects of Europe speaking with a common voice on global macroprudential policy seem slight.

CONCLUSION

This chapter has examined the influence of European states and the EU on the macroprudential ideational shift that took place in 2009. Here individual EU member states such as the UK and Spain made important contributions. While EU institutions had little formal role in the key G20 and FSF working groups, cross-cutting memberships in central bank networks meant that the chair of the key FSF working group, Nout Wellink of the Dutch central bank, was also a member of the governing council of the ECB. Generally speaking, the macroprudential ideational shift was pushed by an epistemic clan structure that cut across national boundaries. The UK, traditionally associated with light-touch regulation, has been one of the leading advocates of an expansive macroprudential regulatory regime, suggesting that the varieties of capitalism perspective has little explanatory power when it comes to macroprudential positions.

The task of building a macroprudential regulatory regime and implementing Basel III in Europe ignited inter-institutional tensions between EU institutions and member states. With the precise division of responsibility for macro-prudential powers still in dispute and the subject of disagreement among member states and EU institutions, it is difficult to see how the EU can project its voice and exert collective influence. EU member states have been much more influential when operating through national delegations, for example, the neg-ative influence France and Germany exerted over Basel III. On the one hand, the focus on pro-cyclicality in macroprudential thinking is a very 'European concept' because it suggests that financial market instability requires a careful trammelling of their activities. On the other hand, combatting 'pro-cyclicality' may require national macroprudential regulations that do not sit comfortably with the EU as a single market based on uniform regulation and oversight.

The divisions between member states on what the EU macroprudential reg-ulatory regime should look like, and the competition between the Commission and the ECB over turf and priorities, do not auger well for the EU's ability to intervene as a bloc within global governance debates. Who speaks for Europe in the new FSB is likewise confused and unclear, due to exactly the kinds of intermediate delegation that Mügge warns against, with responsibilities split between member states, the ECB, and the Commission (Mügge 2011c). While the EU has the ESRB and the MaRS network to articulate European macro-prudential analyses, concerns, and views, their ability to project globally remains highly uncertain.

References

Agarwal, S., and C. Ho, 2007. 'Comparing the Prime and Subprime Mortgage Markets', *Chicago Fed Letters* 241.

Alford, D. 2010. 'Supervisory Colleges: The Global Financial Crisis and Improving International Supervisory Coordination', *Emory International Law Review* 24: 57–81.

Alternative Investment Expert Group, 2006. *Managing, Servicing and Marketing Hedge Funds in Europe: Report of the Alternative Investment Expert Group to the European Commission* (July).

Alternative Investment Industry Association, 2007. *Guide to Sound Practices for Hedge Fund Valuation*.

Alternative Investment Industry Association, 2008. *Submission to the Treasury Committee, House of Commons, Banking Crisis, Written Evidence—Part 2*.

American Accounting Association, 1973. *A Statement of Basic Auditing Concepts* (Committee on Basic Auditing Concepts), Evanston: American Accounting Association.

AMF (Autorité des marchés financiers), 2006. *AMF 2005 Report on Rating Agencies*, Paris: Autorité des marchés financiers.

AMF, 2008. *AMF 2007 Report on Rating Agencies*, Paris: Autorité des marchés financiers.

AMF, 2009. *AMF 2008 Report on Rating Agencies*, Paris: Autorité des marchés financiers.

AMF, 2010. *AMF 2009 Report on Rating Agencies*, Paris: Autorité des marchés financiers.

Amtenbrink, F., and J. de Haan, 2009. 'Regulating Credit Rating Agencies in the European Union: A Critical First Assessment of the European Commission Proposal', *Fourth International Conference on Financial Regulation and Supervision*, <http://ssrn.com/abstract=1394332> (accessed on 25 February 2013).

André, P., A. Cavanaz-Jeny, W. Dick, C. Richard, and P. Walton, 2009. 'Fair Value Accounting and the Banking Crisis of 2008: Shooting the Messenger', *Accounting in Europe* 6(1): 3–24.

Andreas, P., and E. Nadelmann, 2006. *Policing the Globe—Criminalization and Crime Control in International Relations*, New York: Oxford University Press.

Armstrong, K. 2002. 'Mutual Recognition', in *The Law of the Single European Market*, edited by C. Barnard and J. Scott, Oxford: Hart Publishing.

Arons, S. 2012. 'Convergence of IFRS and US GAAP Is Not Dead, Just Dormant', *CFO Insight*, <http://www.cfo-insight.com/reporting-forecasting/accounting/convergence-of-ifrs-and-us-gaap-is-not-dead-just-dormant/> (accessed on 13 February 2013).

Ashcraft, A., and T. Schuermann, 2008. 'Understanding the Securitization of Subprime Mortgage Credit', *Federal Reserve Bank of New York, Staff Report 318*, <http://ssrn.com/abstract=1071189> (accessed on 25 February 2013).

ASIC (Australian Securities and Investments Commission), 2012. *Principles for Cross-border Financial Regulation*.

ASIC and FMA, 2012. 'Trans-Tasman Mutual Recognition of Financial Advisers Announced' (Press Release, 2 July).

Asset Managers' Committee, 2009. 'Best Practices for the Hedge Fund Industry', *Report of the Asset Managers' Committee to the President's Working Group on Financial*

Markets (January), <http://www.bankofengland.co.uk/publications/Documents/other/financialstability/discussionpaper111220.pdf> (accessed on 22 March 2014).

Avgouleas, E. 2012. *Governance of Global Financial Markets: The Law, the Economics, the Politics*, Cambridge: Cambridge University Press.

Babis, V.S. 2013. 'Abandoning Foreign Depositors in a Bank Failure? The EFTA Court Judgement in EFTA Surveillance Authority v Iceland', *Global Markets Law Journal* 1(2): 1–13.

Bach, D., and A.L. Newman, 2007. 'The European Regulatory State and Global Public Policy: Micro-institutions, Macro-influence', *Journal of European Public Policy* 14(6): 827–846.

Bach, D., and A.L. Newman, 2010. 'Transgovernmental Networks and Domestic Policy Convergence: Evidence from Insider Trading Regulation', *International Organization* 64(3): 505.

Bacon, R. 1993. 'EC Finance Rules Face Fresh Obstacles', *Euromoney* (May): 50.

Baker, A. 2006. *The Group of Seven: Finance Ministries, Central Banks and Global Financial Governance*, London: Routledge.

Baker, A. 2010. 'Deliberative International Financial Governance and Apex Policy Forums: Where We Are and Where We Should Be Headed', in *Global Financial Integration Thirty Years On*, edited by G.R.D. Underhill, G. Blom, and D. Mügge, 58–73, Cambridge: Cambridge University Press.

Baker, A. 2013a. 'The New Political Economy of the Macroprudential Ideational Shift', *New Political Economy* 18(1): 112–139.

Baker, A. 2013b. 'The Gradual Transformation? The Incremental Dynamics of Macroprudential Regulation', *Regulation and Governance*, 7(4): 417–434.

Bank of England, 2011. *Instruments of Macroprudential Policy: A Discussion Paper.*

Barnier, M. 2012. 'How to Achieve Global Convergence', *Eurofi High Level Seminar*, Speech/12/246, <http://europa.eu/rapid/press-release_SPEECH-12-246_en.htm> (accessed on 22 March 2014).

Barnier, M., G. Mantega, P. Moscovici, W. Schauble, V. Grilli, T. Aso, A. Siluanov, P. Gordhan, E. Widmer-Schlumpf, and G. Osborne, 2013. *Cross Border OTC Derivatives Regulation*, 18 April.

Barth, J.R., G. Caprio, and R. Levine, 2013. *Bank Regulation and Supervision in 180 Countries from 1999 to 2011*, <http://ssrn.com/abstract=2203516> or <http://dx.doi.org/10.2139/ssrn.2203516> (accessed on 19 January 2013).

BBA and LIBA, 2001. *Response to the Basel Committee's Second Consultation on a New Basel Accord.*

BCBS (Basel Committee on Banking Supervision), 1999a. *Banks Interactions with Highly Leveraged Institutions*, Basel.

BCBS, 1999b. *Sound Practices for Banks' Interactions with Highly Leveraged Institutions*, Basel.

BCBS, 2001. *Overview of the New Basel Capital Accord*, consultative document (CP2), January.

BCBS, 2010a. *Good Practice Principles on Supervisory Colleges*, Basel: Bank for International Settlements.

BCBS, 2010b. *The Basel Committee's Response to the Financial Crisis*: Report to the G20, October.

BCBS, 2012. *Basel III Regulatory Consistency Assessment (Level 2) Preliminary Report: European Union*, Basel: Bank for International Settlements.

Bergström, M., K. Svedberg Helgesson, and U. Mörth, 2011. 'A New Role for For-Profit Actors? The Case of Anti-Money Laundering and Risk Management', *Journal of Common Market Studies* 49(5): 1043–1064.

Bickerton, C. 2012. *From Nation States to Member States*, Oxford: Oxford University Press.

Bieling, H. 2006. 'EMU, Financial Integration and Global Economic Governance', *Review of International Political Economy* 31(3): 420–448.

Bieling, H.-J., and J. Jäger, 2009. 'Global Finance and the European Economy: The Struggle Over Banking Regulation', in *Contradictions and Limits of Neoliberal European Governance, from Lisbon to Lisbon*, edited by B. Van Apeldoorn, B.J. Drahokoupil, and L. Horn, 87–105, London: Palgrave.

BIS (Bank for International Settlements), 2006. *76th Annual Report*, Basel.

Black, J. 2012. 'Restructuring Global and EU Financial Regulation: Character, Capacities and Learning', in *Rethinking Financial Regulation and Supervision in Times of Crisis*, edited by G. Ferrarini, K.J. Hopt, and E. Wymeersch, Oxford: Oxford University Press.

Blom, J.G.W. 2011. *Banking on the Public: Market Competition and Shifting Patterns of Governance*, PhD thesis, University of Amsterdam, <http://dare.uva.nl/en/record/398055> (accessed on 22 March 2014).

Borio, C. 2003. 'Towards a Macroprudential Framework for Financial Supervision and Regulation?', *BIS Working Paper* 128, Basel.

Borio, C. 2011. 'Implementing a Macroprudential Framework: Blending Boldness and Realism', *Capitalism and Society* 6(1): 1–23.

Borio, C., and M. Drehmann, 2008. 'Towards an Operational Framework for Financial Stability: Fuzzy Measurement and its Consequences', *12th Annual Conference of the Banco Central de Chile*, Santiago 6–7 November, <http://www.bcentral.cl/eng/conferences-seminars/annual-conferences/2008/program.htm> (accessed on 22 March 2014).

Borio, C., C. Furfine, and P. Lowe, 2001. 'Procyclicality of the Financial System and Financial Stability Issues and Policy Options', *BIS Papers* 1 (March): 1–57.

Borio, C., and W. White, 2004. 'Whiter Monetary and Financial Stability: The Implications for Evolving Policy Regimes', *BIS Working Paper* 147, Basel: Bank for International Settlements.

Botzem, S. 2012. *The Politics of Accounting Regulation*, Cheltenham: Edward Elgar.

Botzem, S., and S. Quack, 2006. 'Contested Rules and Shifting Boundaries: International Standard-Setting in Accounting', in *Transnational Governance: Institutional Dynamics of Regulation*, edited by M.L. Djelic and K. Sahlin-Andersson, 266–286, Cambridge: Cambridge University Press.

Brown, P. 1997. 'The Politics of the EU Single Market for Investment Services: Negotiating the Investment Services and Capital Adequacy Directives', in *The New World Order in International Finance*, edited by G.R.D. Underhill, 124–143, Houndmills: Macmillan.

Brummer, C. 2011. *Soft Law and the Global Financial System: Rule Making in the 21st Century*, Cambridge: Cambridge University Press.

Brunnermeier, M., A. Crockett, C. Goodhart, A. Persaud, and H. Shin, 2009. 'The Fundamental Principles of Financial Regulation', *Geneva Report on the World*

Economy 11, Geneva: International Centre for Monetary and Banking Studies, London: Centre for Economic Policy Research.

Buckley, J., and D. Howarth, 2010. 'Internal Market: Gesture Politics? Explaining the EU's Response to Financial Crisis', *Journal of Common Market Studies* 48 (Annual Review): 119–141.

Buckley, J., and D. Howarth, 2011. 'Internal Market: Regulating the So Called Vultures of Capitalism', *Journal of Common Market Studies* 49 (Annual Review): 123–143.

Buckley, J., D. Howarth, and L. Quaglia, 2012. 'Internal Market? The Ongoing Struggle to Protect Europe from Its Money Men', *Journal of Common Market Studies* 50 (Annual Review): 99–115.

Buiter, W. 2009. 'The proposed European Systemic Risk Board Is Overweight Central Bankers', *Financial Times Comment*, Blog, 28 October.

Bush, J. 1990. 'Mop-up of the 1980s Mess Under Way', *Financial Times*, 25 June.

Büthe, T., and W. Mattli, 2011. *The New Global Rulers: The Privatization of Regulation in the World Economy*, Princeton and Oxford: Princeton University Press.

Camfferman, K., and S.A. Zeff, 2007. *Financial Reporting and Global Capital Markets: A History of the International Accounting Standards Committee 1973–2000*, Oxford: Oxford University Press.

Carney, M. 2008. 'From Hindsight to Foresight', Address to Women in Capital Markets, Toronto, Ontario, 17 December, <http://www.bis.org/review/r081218c.pdf> (accessed on 22 March 2014).

Casey, J., and K. Lannoo, 2005. *Europe's Hidden Capital Markets: Evolution, Architecture and Regulation of the European Bond Market*, Brussels: Centre for European Policy Studies.

Casey, J., and K. Lannoo, 2009. *The MiFID Revolution*, Cambridge: Cambridge University Press.

Cattoir, P. 2006. 'A History of the "Tax Package": The Principles and Issues Underlying the Community Approach', *Taxation Papers*, Working Paper 10.

CEA (Comité Européen des Assurances), 2005. *Topography of EU25: Description of Markets, Products and Distribution*, Brussels.

CEA, 2007a. *Solvency II, Diversification and Specialisation, Briefing Note 1* (May), Brussels.

CEA, 2007b. *The Insurance Groups and Solvency II, Briefing Note 2* (May), Brussels.

CEA, 2007c. *The Small and Medium-Sized Undertakings and Solvency II, Briefing Note 3* (May), Brussels.

CEA, 2011. *European Insurance in Figures*, Brussels.

CEBS (Committee of European Banking Supervisors), 2010. *Guidelines for the Operational Functioning of Colleges*.

CEBS and CEIOPS (Committee of European Insurance and Occupational Pensions Supervisors), 2009. *Ten Principles for the Functioning of Supervisory Colleges*.

Census Bureau, 2007. *Housing Vacancies and Home Ownership*, <http://www.census.gov/housing/hvs/files/qtr107/q107tab5.txt> (accessed on 25 February 2013).

CESR (Committee of European Securities Regulators), 2004a. *CESR's Technical Advice to the European Commission on Possible Measures Concerning Credit Rating Agencies*, Ref: CESR/04-612b, Paris: Committee of European Securities Regulators.

CESR, 2004b. *Concept Paper on Equivalence of Certain Third Country GAAP.* CESR/ 4–509C.

CESR, 2005a. *CESR's Technical Advice to the European Commission on Possible Measures Concerning Credit Rating Agencies,* Ref: CESR/05–139b, Paris: Committee of European Securities Regulators.

CESR, 2005b. 'CESR Favours Self-Regulation of Credit Rating Agencies Established Around an Internationally Agreed Code for the Time Being' (Press Release), Ref: CESR/05–198, Paris: Committee of European Securities Regulators.

CESR, 2006. *CESR's Report to the European Commission on the Compliance of Credit Rating Agencies with the IOSCO Code,* Ref: CESR/06–545, Paris: Committee of European Securities Regulators.

CESR, 2008a. *CESR's Second Report to the European Commission on the Compliance of Credit Rating Agencies with the IOSCO Code and the Role of Credit Rating Agencies in Structured Finance,* Ref: CESR/08–277, Paris: Committee of European Securities Regulators.

CESR, 2008b. *CESR's Response to the Consultation Document of the Commission Services on a Draft Proposal for a Directive/Regulation on Credit Rating Agencies,* Ref: CESR/08–671, Paris: Committee of European Securities Regulators.

CESR, 2009. *Report by CESR on Compliance of EU Based Credit Rating Agencies with the 2008 IOSCO Code of Conduct,* Ref: CESR/09–417, Paris: Committee of European Securities Regulators.

CESR, 2010. *Technical Advice to the European Commission on the Equivalence Between the Japanese Regulatory and Supervisory Framework and the EU Regulatory Regime for Credit Rating Agencies,* CESR/10–333.

CFCT (Commodities Futures Trading Commission), 2005. *The U.S. Commodity Futures Trading Commission and the Committee of European Securities Regulators Met to Facilitate Transatlantic Derivatives Business and to Appoint Task Force to Develop Further Efforts,* Chicago: CFTC.

CFTC, 2012. *Interpretive Guidance on Cross-Border Application of the Swaps Provisions of the Dodd–Frank Act.*

CFTC and SEC (Securities and Exchange Commission), 2012. *Joint Report on International Swap Regulation.*

Chomsisengphet, S., and A. Pennington-Cross, 2006. 'The Evolution of the Subprime Mortgage Market', *Federal Reserve Bank of St. Louis Review* 88(1): 31–56.

Christopoulos, D.C., and L. Quaglia, 2009. 'Network Constraints in EU Banking Regulation: The Capital Requirements Directive', *Journal of Public Policy* 29(2): 179–200.

CIS (Conference of Insurance Supervisors), 2002. *Report Prudential Supervision of Insurance Undertakings* (Sharma Report), December.

Claessens, S., G.R.D. Underhill, and X. Zhang, 2008. 'The Political Economy of Basel II: The Costs for Poor Countries', *World Economy* 31: 313–344.

Clement, P. 2010. 'The Term "Macroprudential": Origins and Evolution', *BIS Quarterly Review* (March), 59–67.

Clifford Chance, 2012. *Regulation of OTC Derivatives Markets: A Comparison of EU and US Initiatives,* London, <http://www.cliffordchance.com/publicationviews/publications/ 2012/09/regulation_of_otcderivativesmarkets-.html> (accessed on 24 May 2013).

Cline, W.R. 1995. *International Debt Re-examined*, Institute for International Economics.

Coffee, J.C. 2006. *Gatekeepers. The Professions and Corporate Governance*, Oxford: Oxford University Press.

Corrigan, T. 1992. 'SEC and Regulators Deadlocked Over Capital Requirements', *Financial Times*, 30 October.

Council of Ministers, 2008. *Amended Proposal for a Directive on the European Parliament and the Council on the Taking up and Pursuit of the Business of Insurance and Reinsurance: SOLVENCY II—Progress Report*, Brussels, 27 May.

Crockett, A. 2000. 'Marrying the Micro and Macroprudential Dimensions of Financial Stability', *BIS Speeches*, 21 September.

Dallara, C. 2008. 'How banks can put their house in order', *Financial Times*, 13 May.

Das, S. 2006. *Traders, Guns and Money: Knowns and Unknowns in the Dazzling World of Derivatives*, London: Financial Times Press.

Datz, G. 2013. 'The Narrative of Complexity in the Crisis of Finance: Epistemological Challenge and Macroprudential Policy Response', *New Political Economy* 18(4): 459–479.

Davies, H., and D. Green, 2008. *Global Financial Regulation: The Essential Guide*, Cambridge: Polity.

Davis Polk, 2012. *Governor Tarullo Foreshadows Proposal to Ring-Fence Large U.S. Operations of Foreign Banks*, Client Memorandum, <http://www.davispolk.com/files/Publication/b022e425-640f-4a4f-b71a-003f32a5d0c3/Presentation/Publication Attachment/d0db24b6-59c6-4f2b-87a4-0062094d8f9a/120312_Tarullo.pdf> (accessed on 22 March 2014).

Decker, M. 2007. *Statement of Michael Decker, Senior Managing Director, Research and Public Policy, Before the Committee on Finance United States Senate, Hearing on the Housing Decline: The Extent of the Problem and Potential Remedies*, December 13, Washington, DC: SIFMA.

De Larosière Group, 2009. *Report of the High Level Group on Financial Supervision in the EU*, Brussels.

Deloitte, 2013. *Use of IFRS by Jurisdiction*, <http://www.iasplus.com/en/resources/use-of-ifrs> (accessed on 6 September 2013).

de Lombaerde, P., F. Söderbaum, L. van Langenhove, and F. Baert, 2010. 'The Problem of Comparison in Comparative Regionalism', *Review of International Studies* 36: 731–756.

De Meester, B. (2008) 'Multilevel Banking Regulation: An Assessment of the Role of the EC in the Light of Coherence and Democratic Legitimacy', in *Multilevel Regulation and the EU: The Interplay Between Global, European and National Normative Processes*, edited by A. Follesdal, R.A. Wessel, and J. Wouters, 101–143, The Hague: Martinus Nijhoff Publishers.

Demyanyk, Y., and O. Van Hemert, 2008. *Understanding the Subprime Mortgage Crisis*, <http://ssrn.com/abstract=1020396> (accessed on 25 February 2013).

Deutsche Bank, 2013. *Post Trade Integration in the ASEAN—Challenges and Opportunities*, <https://www.db.com/en/content/company/headlines-capital-market-integration-in-south-east-asia—challenges-and-opportunities.htm> (accessed on 7 March 2013).

de Visscher, C., O. Maiscocq, and F. Varone, 2007. 'The Lamfalussy Reform in EU Securities Markets', *Journal of Public Policy* 28(1): 19–47.

Dewing, I., and P.O. Russell, 2004. 'Accounting, Auditing and Corporate Governance of European Listed Countries: EU Policy Developments Before and After Enron', *Journal of Common Market Studies* 42(2): 289–319.

Dierick, F., et al., 2005. 'The New Basel Capital Framework and Its Implementation in the European Union', *ECB Occasional Paper* 42 (December).

Directive 77/799/EEC of 19 December 1977 concerning mutual assistance by the competent authorities of the Member States in the field of direct taxation and taxation of insurance premiums.

Directive 90/434/EEC of 23 July 1990 on the common system of taxation applicable to mergers, divisions, transfers of assets and exchanges of shares concerning companies of different Member States.

Directive 90/435/EEC of 23 July 1990 on the common system of taxation applicable in the case of parent companies and subsidiaries of different Member States.

Directive 2003/48/EC of 3 June 2003 on taxation of savings income in the form of interest payments.

Directive 2011/16/EU of 15 February 2011 on administrative cooperation in the field of taxation and repealing Directive 77/799/EEC.

Donnelly, S. 2010. *The Regimes of European Integration: Constructing Governance of the Single Market*, Oxford: Oxford University Press.

Dougan, M. 2000. 'Minimum Harmonisation and the Internal Market', *Common Market Law Review* 37: 853–885.

Drezner, D. 2007. *All Politics Is Global: Explaining International Regulatory Regimes*, Princeton: Princeton University Press.

Dür, A. 2011. 'Fortress Europe or Open Door Europe? The External Impact of the EU's Single Market in Financial Services', *Journal of European Public Policy* 45(5): 771–787.

Eaton, S. 2005. 'Crisis and the Consolidation of International Accounting Standards: Enron, the IASB and America', *Business and Politics* 3(4): 1–18.

Eatwell, J. 2009. 'Practical Proposals for Regulatory Reform', in *New Ideas for the London Summit: Recommendations to the G20 Leaders*, edited by P. Subacchi and A. Monsarrat, 11–15, London: Royal Institute for International Affairs Chatham, The Atlantic Council.

EBA, 2013. *Compliance Table: Guidelines on the Assessment of the Suitability of Members of the Management Body and Key Function Holders* (EBA/GL/2012/06).

EC (European Commission), 1967. 'Program for the Harmonisation of Direct Taxes: Communication by the Commission', *Bulletin of the EC*, Supplement 8: 6–22.

EC, 1992. 'Report of the Committee of Independent Experts on Company Taxation', *Ruding Committee Report*.

EC, 1996a. *Green Paper. The Role, the Position and the Liability of the Statutory Auditor Within the European Union*, Brussels: EC.

EC, 1996b. *Accounting Harmonisation: A New Strategy vis-à-vis International Harmonisation*, Brussels: EC.

EC, 1998a. *Communication from the Commission on the Statutory Audit in the European Union: The Way Forward*, Brussels: EC.

EC, 1998b. *Financial Services: Building a Framework for Action*, Brussels: EC.

EC, 1999a. *Financial Services: Implementing the Framework for Action: Action Plan*, Brussels: EC.

References

EC, 1999b. *The Review of the Overall Financial Position of an Insurance Undertaking (Solvency II Review)*, Brussels, December.

EC, 2001a. *Communication from the Commission to the Council, the European Parliament and the Economic and Social Committee: Tax Policy in the European Union—Priorities for the Years Ahead*, COM(2001) 260 final.

EC, 2001b. *Proposal for a Council Directive to Ensure a Minimum of Effective Taxation of Savings Income in the Form of Interest Payments Within the Community*, COM(01) 0400 final.

EC, 2001c. *Solvency II: Presentation of the Proposed Work*, Brussels, 13 March.

EC, 2001d. *Banking Rules: Relevance for the Insurance Sector*, Brussels, 12 June.

EC, 2002. *Considerations on the Design of a Future Prudential Supervisory System*, Brussels, 28 November.

EC, 2003. *Reinforcing Statutory Audit in the EU*, Brussels: EC.

EC, 2004. *Framework for Consultation on Solvency II*, Brussels, 14 July.

EC, 2005. *Commission Decision of 14 December 2005 Setting up a Group of Experts to Advise the Commission and to Facilitate Cooperation Between Public Oversight Systems for Statutory Audits and Audit Firms*, Brussels: EC.

EC, 2006. 'Communication from the Commission on Credit Rating Agencies (2006/C 59/02)'. *Official Journal of the European Union* (11 March).

EC, 2007a. *European Financial Integration Report 2007*, SEC(2007) 1696.

EC, 2007b. *Proposal for a Directive of the European Parliament and of the Council on the Taking-up and Pursuit of the Business of Insurance and Reinsurance—Solvency II*, Brussels, 10 July.

EC, 2008a. *Proposal for a Regulation of the European Parliament and the Council on Credit Rating Agencies*, COM(2008) 704 final. Brussels: EC.

EC, 2008b. *Commission Staff Working Document Accompanying the Proposal for a Regulation of the European Parliament and of the Council on Credit Rating Agencies. Impact Assessment*, SEC(2008) 2745, 12.11.2008. Brussels: Commission of the European Communities.

EC, 2008c. CRD II Impact Assessment SEC(2008) 2532.

EC, 2008d. *Consultation Paper on Hedge Funds*, 18 December.

EC, 2009a. *Consultation on the Adoption of International Standards on Auditing*, Brussels: EC.

EC, 2009b. *Proposal for a Council Directive on Administrative Cooperation in the Field of Taxation*, COM(2009) 29 final.

EC, 2009c. *Proposal for a Directive of the European Parliament and of the Council on Alternative Investment Fund Managers*, 30 April.

EC, 2009d. *Feedback Statement—Summary of Responses to Hedge Fund Consultation Paper*, 12 March.

EC, 2010a. *Green Paper. Audit Policy: Lessons from the Crisis*, Brussels: EC.

EC, 2010b. *Summary of Comments: Consultation on the Adoption of International Standards on Auditing*, Brussels: EC.

EC, 2011a. *Proposal for a Directive of the European Parliament and of the Council on Markets in Financial Instruments*, COM(2011) 656.

EC, 2011b. *Proposal for a Regulation of the European Parliament and of the Council on Markets in Financial Instruments*, COM(2011) 652.

EC, 2011c. *Proposal for a Regulation of the European Parliament and of the Council on Prudential Requirements for Credit Institutions and Investment Firms*, COM(2011) 452.

EC, 2011d. *Summary of Responses. Green Paper. Audit Policy: Lessons from the Crisis*, Brussels: EC.

EC, 2011e. *Proposal for a Regulation of the European Parliament and of the Council on Specific Requirements Regarding Statutory Audit of Public-Interest Entities*, Brussels: EC.

EC, 2011f. *Proposal for a Directive of the European Parliament and of the Council Amending Directive 2006/43/EC on Statutory Audits of Annual Accounts and Consolidated Accounts*, Brussels: EC.

EC, 2011g. *Proposal for a Council Directive on a Common Consolidated Corporate Tax Base (CCCTB)*, COM(2011) 121/4.

EC, 2011h. *Directive 2011/61/EU of the European Parliament and of the Council on Alternative Investment Fund Managers and Amending Directives 2003/41/EC and 2009/65/EC and Regulations (EC) No. 1060/2009 and (EU) No. 1095/2010*, 8 June, <http://eur-lex.europa.eu/LexUriServ/LexUriServ.do?uri=OJ:L:2011:174:0001:01:EN:PDF> (accessed on 22 March 2014).

EC, 2011i. SEC(2011), 1226 final, Brussels, 20 October.

EC, 2012a. *Communication From the Commission to the European Parliament and the Council on Concrete Ways to Reinforce the Fight Against Tax Fraud and Tax Evasion Including in Relation to Third Countries*, COM(2012) 351 final.

EC, 2012b. 'Tackling Tax Fraud and Evasion: Commission Sets out Concrete Measures' (Press Release IP/12/697, 27 June), <http://europa.eu/rapid/press-release_IP-12-697_en.htm> (accessed on 29 June 2013).

EC, 2013a. *New Disclosure Requirements for the Extractive Industry and Loggers of Primary Forests in the Accounting (and Transparency) Directives (Country by Country Reporting)–Frequently Asked Questions*, 12 June 2013 MEMO/13/541, <http://europa.eu/rapid/press-release_MEMO-13-541_en.htm> (accessed on 29 June 2013).

EC, 2013b. *CRD IV/CRR—Frequently Asked Questions*, 21 March 2013 MEMO/13/272, <http://europa.eu/rapid/press-release_MEMO-13-272_en.htm> (accessed on 29 June 2013).

EC, 2013c. *Implementing Regulation (EU) No. 447/2013 of 15 May 2013 Establishing the Procedure for AIFMs Which Choose to Opt in Under Directive 2011/61/EU of the European Parliament and of the Council*, <http://ec.europa.eu/internal_market/investment/docs/alternative_investments/2013/regulation-2013-447_en.pdf> (accessed on 22 March 2014).

EC, 2013d. *Implementing Regulation (EU) No. 448/2013 of 15 May 2013 Establishing a Procedure for Determining the Member State of Reference of a Non-EU AIFM Pursuant to Directive 2011/61/EU of the European Parliament and of the Council*, <http://ec.europa.eu/internal_market/investment/docs/alternative_investments/2013/regulation-2013-448_en.pdf> (accessed on 22 March 2014).

ECB (European Central Bank), 2001. *The New Basel Capital Accord: Comments of the European Central Bank*, 31 May.

ECB, 2003. *The New Basel Capital Accord: Reply of the European Central Bank to the Third Consultative Proposals (CP3)*, August.

Egan, M. 2001. *Constructing a European Market: Standards, Regulation and Governance*, Oxford: Oxford University Press.

Eichengreen, B. 2012. 'European Monetary Integration with Benefit of Hindsight', *Journal of Common Market Studies* 50: 123–136.

Elliot, D. 2011. 'Choosing Among Macroprudential Tools', *The Brookings Institute*, <http://www.brookings.edu/~/media/Files/rc/papers/2011/0607_macroprudential_tools_elliott/0607_macroprudential_tools_elliott.pdf> (accessed on 22 March 2014).

EPC (European Parliament and Council), 2006. *Directive 2006/43/EC of the European Parliament and of the Council of 17 May 2006 on Statutory Audits of Annual Accounts and Consolidated Accounts Amending Council Directives 78/660/EC and 83/349/EEC and Repealing Council Directive 84/253/EEC [Statutory Audit Directive]*, Brussels: EPC.

EPC, 2009. *Decision No. 716/2009/EC of the European Parliament and of the Council Establishing a Community Programme to Support Specific Activities in the Field of Financial Services, Financial Reporting and Auditing*, Brussels.

ESMA (European Securities Markets Authority), 2012. *Technical Advice on CRA Regulatory Equivalence—US, Canada and Australia* (ESMA/2012/259).

ESMA, 2013. *Framework for Third Country Prospectuses under Article 20 of the Prospectus Directive* (ESMA/2013/317).

ESME (European Securities Markets Expert Group), n.d.: Terms of Reference.

ESME, 2007. *Mandate to ESME for Advice: Role of Credit Rating Agencies.*

ESME, 2008. 'Role of Credit Rating Agencies', ESME's Report to the European Commission.

EU, 2009. 'Regulation (EC) No. 1060/2009 of the European Parliament and of the Council of 16 September 2009 on Credit Rating Agencies', *Official Journal of the European Union* (17 November).

EU–US Coalition on Financial Regulation, 2012. *Inter-jurisdictional Regulatory Recognition: Facilitating Recovery and Streamlining Regulation.*

European Asset Management Association, 2001. *The New Basel Capital Accord [response to CP2]*, 1 May, London.

European Council, 1978. *Fourth Council Directive of 25 July 1978 Based on Article 54 (3) (g) of the Treaty on the Annual Accounts of Certain Types of Companies* (78/660/EEC), Brussels: European Council.

European Council, 1983. *Seventh Council Directive of 13 June 1983 Based on Article 54 (3) (g) of the Treaty on the Approval of Persons Responsible for Carrying out the Statutory Audits of Accounting Documents* (83/349/EEC), Brussels: European Council.

European Council, 1984. *Eighth Council Directive of 10 April 1984 Based on Article 54 (3) (g) of the Treaty on the Approval of Persons Responsible for Carrying out the Statutory Audits of Accounting Documents* (84/253/EEC), Brussels: European Council.

European Parliament, 2008a. *Report of the European Parliament with Recommendations to the Commission on Hedge Funds and Private Equity* (the 'Rasmussen' report), A6–0338/2008.

European Parliament, 2008b. *Report of the European Parliament with Recommendations to the Commission on Transparency of Institutional Investors* ('Lehne' report), A6–0296–2008.

European Parliament, 2008c. *Working Document on Insurance and Reinsurance (Solvency II): On Group Supervision, MCR and Own Funds*, Brussels: Committee on Economic and Monetary Affairs, 21 February.

European Parliament, 2011. 'Beefing up Credit Rating Agency Rules. Plenary Sessions' (Press Release, Ref: 20110606IPR20812, 8 June).

European Parliament, 2013. 'Tougher Credit Rating Rules Confirmed by Parliament's Vote. Plenary Sessions' (Press Release, Ref:20130114IPR05310, 16 January).

European Union Committee, 2012. *MiFID II: Getting it Right for the City and EU Financial Services Industry*, London: UK Parliament.

Faerman, S., D. McCaffrey, and D. van Slyke, 2001. 'Understanding Interorganizational Cooperation: Public–Private Collaboration in Regulating Financial Market Innovation', *Organization Science* 12(3): 372–388.

FATF (Financial Action Task Force) 2012. *International Standards on Combating Money Laundering and the Financing of Terrorism & Proliferation—the FATF Recommendations*, February, <http://www.fatf-gafi.org/topics/fatfrecommendations/documents/internationalstandardsoncombatingmoneylaunderingandthefinancingofterrorismproliferation-thefatfrecommendations.html> (accessed on 22 March 2014).

Faull, J. 2012. *Comment Letter Proposed CFTC Rules*, <http://comments.cftc.gov/PublicComments/ViewComment.aspx?id=58431&SearchText=> (accessed on 13 Feburary 2014).

Favarel-Garrigues, G., T. Godefroy, and P. Lascoumes, 2011. 'Reluctant Partners? Banks in the Fight Against Money Laundering and Terrorism Financing in France', *Security Dialogue* 42(2): 179–196.

FDIC (Federal Deposit Insurance Corporation), 2013. *Deposit Insurance Regulations: Definition of Insured Deposit*, 12 CFR Part 330.

Federal Reserve System, 2012. *Enhanced Prudential Standards and Early Remediation Requirements for Foreign Banking Organizations and Foreign Nonbank Financial Companies*, Proposed Rule, 12 CFR Part 252.

FEE (Fédération des Experts Comptables Européen), 1998. *Setting the Standards: Statutory Audit in Europe*, Brussels: FEE.

FEE, 2000. *The Auditor's Report in Europe*, Brussels: FEE.

FEE, 2001. *Proposal on International Standards on Auditing in the EU*, Brussels: FEE.

FEE, 2012. *FEE Policy Statement on the Adoption of International Standards on Auditing (ISAs) in the European Union*, Brussels: FEE.

Ferran, E. 2004. *Building an EU Securities Market*, Cambridge: Cambridge University Press.

Ferran, E. 2012. 'Crisis-Driven Regulatory Reform: Where in the World is the EU Going?', in *The Regulatory Aftermath of the Global Financial Crisis*, edited by E. Ferran, N. Moloney, J.G. Hill, and J.C. Coffee, Cambridge: Cambridge University Press.

Ferran, E., and K. Alexander, 2010. 'Can Soft Law Bodies be Effective? Soft Systemic Risk Oversight Bodies and the Special Case of the European Systemic Risk Board', *University of Cambridge Faculty of Law Research Paper* No. 36/2011, <http://ssrn.com/abstract=1676140> (accessed on 22 March 2014).

Ferran, E., and K. Alexander, 2011. 'Can Soft Law Bodies Be Effective? The Special Case of the European Systemic Risk Board', University of Cambridge Faculty of Law Research Paper, No. 36/, <http://www.rwi.uzh.ch/lehreforschung/alphabetisch/alexander/person/publikationen/KACSLBBE.pdf> (accessed on 13 February 2014).

Ferran, E., and V.S. Babis, 2014. 'The Single Supervisory Mechanism', *Journal of Corporate Law Studies* (forthcoming).

Filipovic, M. 1997. *Governments, Banks and Global Capital*, Aldershot: Ashgate.

Finnish Bankers' Association, 2001. *The New Basel Capital Accord [response to CP2]*, 31 May, London.

Fioretos, K.O. 2010. 'Capitalist Diversity and the International Regulation of Hedge Funds', *Review of International Political Economy* 17(4): 696–723.

Foreign Account Tax Compliance Act (FATCA), 2010. Part of *Hiring Incentives to Restore Employment Act*, <http://www.gpo.gov/fdsys/pkg/PLAW-111publ147/html/PLAW-111publ147.htm> (accessed on 29 June 2013).

Frieden, J. 2006. *Global Capitalism: Its Fall and Rise in the Twentieth Century*, New York: W.W.Norton.

FSA (Financial Services Authority), 2001. *The Future Regulation of Insurance*, London, November.

FSA, 2002. *The Future Regulation of Insurance: A Progress Report*, London, October.

FSA, 2005a. *Delivering the Tiner Insurance Reforms*, London, April.

FSA, 2005b. *Insurance Sector Briefing: ICAS—One Year On*, London, November.

FSA, 2005c. *Hedge Funds: A Discussion of Risk and Regulatory Engagement*, June 05/4.

FSA, 2009. *The Turner Review, A Regulatory Response to the Global Banking Crisis*, London, March.

FSB (Financial Stability Board), 2011. *Key Attributes of Effective Resolution Regimes for Financial Institutions*.

FSB, 2012. *Increasing the Intensity and Effectiveness of SIFI Supervision: Progress Report to the G20 Ministers and Governors*.

FSF (Financial Stability Forum), 2000. *Report of the Working Group on Highly Leveraged Institutions*, 5 April.

FSF, 2007. *Report on Highly Leveraged Institutions*, 19 May.

FSF, 2008. *Report on Enhancing Market and Institutional Resilience*, Basel: FSF.

FSF, 2009. *Report on Addressing Procyclicality in the Financial System*, Basel: FSF, April 2009, <http://www.financialstabilityboard.org/publications/r_0904a.pdf> (accessed on 22 March 2014).

G8, 2013. *2013 Lough Erne G8 Leaders' Communiqué*, <https://www.gov.uk/government/publications/2013-lough-erne-g8-leaders-communique> (accessed on 29 June 2013).

G20, 2009a. *London Summit—Leaders' Statement*, 3 April.

G20, 2009b. *London Summit: Leaders' Statement*, 2 April 2009, <http://www.g20.org/documents/final-communique.pdf#p5> (accessed on 29 June 2013).

G30, 2009. *Financial Reform: A Framework for Financial Stability*, Washington DC.

Galati, G., and R. Moessner, 2011. 'Macroprudential Policy: A Literature Review'. *BIS Working Paper* 337.

Genschel, P., A. Kemmerling, and E. Seils, 2011. 'Accelerating Downhill: How the EU Shapes Corporate Tax Competition in the Single Market', *Journal of Common Market Studies* 49(3): 585–606.

Global Forum on Transparency and Exchange of Information for Tax Purposes, 2011. *Purposes Peer Reviews: United States 2011*, <http://www.eoi-tax.org/jurisdictions/US#peerreview> (accessed on 29 June 2013).

Goldbach, R., and D. Kerwer, 2012. 'New Capital Rules? Reforming Basel Banking Standards After the Financial Crisis', in *Crisis and Control: Institutional Change in*

Financial Market Regulation, edited by R. Maintz, 247–262, Frankfurt: Campus Verlag.

Goodhart, C., and M.A. Segoviano, 2004. 'Basel and Procyclicality: A Comparison of the Standardised and IRB Approaches to an Improved Credit Risk Method', *Discussion Paper* 524, London: Financial Markets Group, London School of Economics and Political Science.

Graham, G. 1990. 'Tuffier Collapse Highlights Decline in Commission Rates', *Financial Times*, 22 October.

Griffith Jones, S., and J. Ocampo, 2006. 'A Countercyclical Framework for a Development Friendly International Financial Architecture', *Institute of Development Studies Working Paper*.

Grinberg, I. 2012. 'Beyond FATCA: An Evolutionary Moment for the International Tax System', *Georgetown Law Faculty Working Papers*, Working Paper 160.

Grossman, E. 2004. 'Bringing Politics Back In: Rethinking the Role of Economic Interest Groups in European Integration', *Journal of European Public Policy* 11(4): 637–654.

Grossman, E., and P. Leblond, 2011. 'European Financial Integration: Finally the Great Leap Forward?', *Journal of Common Market Studies* 49(2): 413–435.

Guevarra, V. 2012. 'U.S. Swaps Rules Trigger International Backlash', *Wall Street Journal Europe*, October 19.

Haas, P. 1992. 'Introduction: Epistemic Communities and International Policy Coordination', *International Organization* 46(1): 1–35.

Hague, I. 2004. 'IAS 39: Underlying Principles', *Accounting in Europe* 1(1): 21–26.

Haldane, A. 2009. 'Small Lessons From a Big Crisis', Remarks at the Federal Reserve Bank of Chicago, 45th Annual Conference, 'Reforming Financial Regulation', 8 May, <http://www.bankofengland.co.uk/archive/Documents/historicpubs/speeches/2009/speech397.pdf> (accessed on 13 February 2014).

Haldane, A. 2010a. 'The $100 Billion Question', *Bank of England Discussion Paper*. Originally presented at the Institute of Regulation & Risk, Hong Kong, March 2010.

Haldane, A. 2010b. 'Patience and Finance', *Bank of England Discussion Paper*, <http://www.bis.org/review/r100909e.pdf> (accessed on 13 February 2014).

Haldane, A. 2012a. 'The Short Long', *Speech at the 29th Société Universitaire Européene de Recherches Financières Colloquium*: New Paradigms in Money and Finance?, Brussels, May 2011.

Haldane A. 2012b. 'Towards a common financial language', <http://www.bankofengland.co.uk/publications/Documents/speeches/2012/speech552.pdf> (accessed on 13 February 2014).

Haldane, A., and V. Madouros, 2012. 'The Dog and the Frisbee', *speech at Federal Reserve Bank of Kansas City's 36th economic policy symposium, The Changing Policy Landscape*, Jackson Hole, Wyoming, <http://www.bankofengland.co.uk/publications/Documents/speeches/2012/speech596.pdf> (accessed on 13 February 2014).

Haldane, A., and R. May, 2011. 'Systemic Risk in Banking Ecosystems', *Nature* 469, 351–355.

Hall, P., 1993. 'Policy Paradigm, Social Learning and the State: The Case of Economic Policy Making in Britain', *Comparative Politics* 25(3): 275–296.

Hall, P., and D. Soskice, 2001. *Varieties of Capitalism: The Institutional Foundations of Comparative Advantage*, Oxford: Oxford University Press.

Hanson, S., A. Kashyap, and J. Stein, 2011. 'A Macroprudential Approach to Financial Regulation', *Journal of Economic Perspectives* 1: 1–26.

Harris, J. 2010. 'SEC says US Unable to Meet Equivalence Criteria', *Hedge Funds Review*, 10 June, <http://www.hedgefundsreview.com/hedge-funds-review/news/1653845/sec-us-unable-meet-eu-equivalence-criteria> (accessed on 13 February 2014).

Harvey, J.R. 2012. 'Offshore Accounts: Insider's Summary of FATCA and Its Potential Future', *Villanova Law Review* 57: 471–498.

Hedge Fund Standards Board Ltd (HFSB) and Hedge Fund Working Group (HFWG), 2008. *Hedge Fund Standards: Final Report*, January.

Helleiner, E., and S. Pagliari, 2010. 'The End of Self-regulation? Hedge Funds and Derivatives in Global Financial Governance', in *Global Finance in Crisis: The Politics of International Regulatory Change*, edited by E. Helleiner, S. Pagliari, and H. Zimmermann, 74–90, London: Routledge.

Helleiner, E., and S. Pagliari, 2011. 'The End of an Era in International Financial Regulation? A Postcrisis Research Agenda', *International Organization* 65(1), 169–200.

Hellwig, M. 1995. 'Systemic Aspects of Risk Management in Banking and Finance', *Swiss Journal of Economics and Statistics* 131: 723–737.

Héritier, A. 2002. 'New Modes of Governance in Europe: Policy-Making Without Legislating?', in *Common Goods: Reinventing European and International Governance*, edited by A. Héritier, Lanham: Rowman & Littlefield.

High-Level Group on Financial Supervision in the EU, 2009. *Report [De Larosière Report]*, Brussels.

Hill, J.G. 2012. 'Why Did Australia Fare So Well in the Global Financial Crisis?', in *The Regulatory Aftermath of the Global Financial Crisis*, edited by E. Ferran, N. Moloney, J.G. Hill, and J.C. Coffee, Cambridge: Cambridge University Press.

Hiss, S., and S. Nagel, 2012. *Ratingagenturen zwischen Krise und Regulierung*, Baden-Baden: Nomos.

HMT (HM Treasury) and FSA (Financial Services Authority), 2006a. *Solvency II: A New Framework for Prudential Regulation of Insurance in the EU*, London, February.

HMT and FSA, 2006b. *Supervising Insurance Groups Under Solvency II—A Discussion Paper*, London, November.

Holzinger, K. 2005. 'Tax Competition and Tax Co-operation in the EU: The Case of Savings Taxation', *Rationality and Society* 17(4): 475–510.

Horsfield-Bradbury, 2008. 'Hedge Fund Self-Regulation in the US and the UK', *Victor Brudney Prize in Corporate Governance*.

House of Lords, 2008. *Solvency II: Report with Evidence*, London: European Union Committee, 6 February.

Howarth, D., and L. Quaglia, 2013. 'Banking on Stability: The Political Economy of New Capital Requirements in the European Union', *Journal of European Integration* 35(3): 333–346.

Hülsse, R. 2008. 'Even Clubs Can't Do Without Legitimacy: Why the Anti-Money Laundering Blacklist Was Suspended', *Regulation and Governance* 2: 459–479.

Humphrey C., A. Kausar, A. Loft, and M. Woods, 2011. 'Regulating audit beyond the crisis: a critical discussion of the EU Green Paper', *European Accounting Review* 20 (3), 431–457.

Humphrey C., and A. Loft, 2009. 'Governing Audit Globally: IFAC, the New International Financial Architecture and the Auditing Profession', in *Accounting, Organizations and Institutions: Essays in Honour of Anthony Hopwood*, edited by P. Chapman, D. Cooper, and P. Miller, 205–232, Oxford: Oxford University Press.

Humphrey C., A. Loft, and M. Woods, 2009. 'The Global Audit Profession and the International Financial Architecture: Understanding Regulatory Relationships at a Time of Financial Crisis', *Accounting, Organizations and Society* 34: 810–825.

Hüpkes, E. 2012. 'The International Financial Cooperation—Recent Reforms', *European Company and Financial Law Review* 9: 179–193.

IAASB (International Auditing and Assurance Standards Board), 2004. *Exposure Draft: Proposed policy statement, 'Clarifying professional requirements in international standards issued by the IAASB; Consultation Paper, Improving the clarity and structure of IAASB standards and related considerations for Practice Statements'* ['Clarity Project'], New York: IAASB.

IAASB, 2008. *IAASB Clarity Project Update*, New York: IAASB.

IAASB, 2011. *Enhancing the Value of Auditor Reporting: Exploring Options for Change (Consultation Paper)*, New York: IAASB.

IAASB, 2012a. *Annual Report 2011*, New York: IAASB.

IAASB, 2012b. *Strategy and Work Programme*, New York: IAASB.

IAASB, 2012c. *Improving the Auditor's Report (Invitation to Comment)*, New York: IAASB.

IAIS (International Association of Insurance Supervisors), 2008a. *Standard No. 2.1.1 on the Structure of Regulatory Capital Requirements; Standard No. 2.2.6 on ERM for Capital Adequacy and Solvency Purposes; Standard No. 2.2.7 on the Use of Internal Models for Regulatory Capital Purposes*, Basel: IAIS.

IAIS, 2008b. *Principles on Group-Wide Supervision*, Basel: IAIS.

IAIS, 2008c. *Guidance Paper No. 3.5 on the Mutual Recognition of Reinsurance Supervision*, Basel: IAIS.

IFAC (International Federation of Accountants), 2003. *Reform Proposals*, New York: IFAC.

IFAC, 2012. *Annual Report 2011*, New York: IFAC.

IIF (Institute of International Finance), 2010. *Interim Report on the Cumulative Impact on the Global Economy of Proposed Changes in the Banking Regulatory Framework*, June.

Investors' Committee, 2009. *Principles and Best Practices for Hedge Fund Investors: Report to the President's Working Group on Financial Markets*, January.

IOSCO (International Organization of Securities Commissions (IOSCO), 1999. *Hedge Funds and Other Highly Leveraged Institutions*, November.

IOSCO, 2003a. *Report on the Activities of Credit Rating Agencies*, Madrid: IOSCO.

IOSCO, 2003b. *IOSCO Statement of Principles Regarding the Activities of Credit Rating Agencies. A Statement of the Technical Committee of the International Organization of Securities Commissions*, 25 September, Madrid: IOSCO.

IOSCO, 2004. *Code of Conduct Fundamentals for Credit Rating Agencies*, Madrid: IOSCO.

IOSCO, 2006. *The Regulatory Environment for Hedge Funds: A Survey and Comparison, Final Report*, November.

IOSCO, 2009. *Hedge Funds Oversight*, 22 June.

Jackson, P., et al., 1999. 'Capital Requirements and Bank Behaviour: The Impact of the Basel Accord', *BCBS Working Paper* no. 1 (April).

Jakobi, A.P. 2013. *Common Goods and Evils? The Formation of Global Crime Governance*, Oxford: Oxford University Press.

Johannesen, N., and G. Zucman, 2012. 'The End of Bank Secrecy? An Evaluation of the G20 Tax Haven Crackdown', *Paris School of Economics Working Papers*, Working Paper No. 2012–04.

Johnson, R.B., and J. Abbott, 2005. 'Placing Bankers in the Front Line', *Journal of Money Laundering Control* 8(3): 215–219.

Joint Communiqué by France, Germany, Italy, Spain, the United Kingdom, and the United States on the occasion of the publication of the 'Model Intergovernmental Agreement to Improve Tax Compliance and Implement FATCA', <http://www.treasury.gov/press-center/press-releases/Documents/joint%20communique.pdf> (accessed on 29 June 2013).

Jones, A. 2011. 'Ledger domain', *Financial Times*, June 27.

Journal of Accountancy, 2008. 'SEC Road Map for Transition to IFRS Available', *Journal of Accountancy* (November).

Jurczyk, J. 2010. 'Rating Agencies: Ver.di Downgrades Moody's: Ratings Are Only Coffee Reading' (Press Release: Ver.di—Vereinte Dienstleistungsgewerkschaft, 20 June). Berlin: Ver.di-Bundesvorstand.

JURI, 2012. 'Specific Requirements Regarding Statutory Auditing of Public Interest Entities', *JURI Report* (December), p. 3, Brussels: European Parliament, Committee on Legal Affairs.

JURI, 2013a. 'Amendment of Directive 2006/43/EC on Statutory Audits and Consolidated Accounts', *JURI Report* (January), p. 5, Brussels: European Parliament, Committee on Legal Affairs.

JURI, 2013b. 'Reforming EU Audit Services to Win Back Investors' Confidence' (Press Release, 25 April), Brussels: EC.

Kapstein, E. 1992. 'Between Power and Purpose: Central Bankers and the Politics of Regulatory Convergence', *International Organization* 46(1): 265–287.

Kapstein, E. 1994. *Governing the Global Economy: International Finance and the State*, Cambridge, MA: Harvard University Press.

Katz, J.G., E. Munoz, and C. Stephanou, 2009. 'Credit Rating Agencies: No Easy Regulatory Solutions', *The World Bank Group, Financial and Private Sector Development Vice Presidency, Crisis Response Policy Brief* 8, <http://ssrn.com/abstract=1485140> (accessed on 25 February 2013).

Kerwer, D., and R. Hülsse, 2011. 'How International Organisations Rule the World: The Case of the Financial Action Task Force on Money Laundering', *Journal of International Organization Studies* 2(1): 50–67.

Keys, B.J., T. Mukherjee, A. Seru, and V. Vikrant, 2008. *Did Securitization Lead to Lax Screening? Evidence From Subprime Loans*, Working Paper, <http://ssrn.com/abstract=1093137> (accessed on 25 February 2013).

Köhler, A., H. Merkt, and W. Böhm, 2009. *Evaluation of the Possible Adoption of International Standards on Auditing (ISAs) in the EU*. Duisburg: University of Duisburg-Essen.

Lall, R. 2011. 'From Failure to Failure: The Politics of International Banking Regulation', *Review of International Political Economy* 19(4): 609–638.

Lanois, P. 2007. 'Between a Rock and a Hard Place: The Sarbanes–Oxley Act and Its Global Impact', *Journal of International Law and Policy* 5(4): 1–19.

Latysheva, D. 2011. 'Taming the Hydra of Derivatives Regulation: Examining New Regulatory Approaches to OTC Derivatives in the United States and Europe', *Cardozo Journal of International and Comparative Law* 20: 465–500.

Leblond, P. 2005. 'The International Dimension of the Harmonization of Accounting Standards in the EU', Paper for delivery at the EUSA Ninth Biennial International Conference, 31 March–2 April, Austin, Texas.

Leblond, P. 2011. 'EU, US and International Accounting Standards: A Delicate Balancing Act in Governing Global Finance', *Journal of European Public Policy* 18(3): 443–461.

Lee, P. 1992. 'Securities Houses Face Capital Clampdown', *Euromoney* (April): 32–43.

Leslie, J., and A. Elijah, 2012. 'Does N=2? Trans-Tasman Economic Integration as a Comparator for the Single European Market', *Journal of Common Market Studies* 50: 975–993.

Levin, C. 2010. *Opening Statement of Senator Carl Levin, U. S. Senate Permanent Subcommittee on Investigations Hearing: Wall Street and the Financial Crisis: The Role of Credit Rating Agencies*, 27 April.

Lieberman, J.I. 2003. *Rating the Raters: Enron and the Credit Rating Agencies Hearing Before the Committee on Governmental Affairs, United States Senate One Hundred Seventh Congress Second Session*, Diane Publishing.

Loft, A., C. Humphrey, and S. Turley, 2006. 'In Pursuit of Global Regulation: Changing Governance and Accountability Structures at the International Federation of Accountants', *Accounting, Auditing and Accountability Journal* 19(3): 428–451.

Luettringhaus, J.D. 2012. 'Regulating Over-The-Counter Derivatives in the European Union—Transatlantic (Dis)harmony after EMIR and Dodd–Frank: The Impact on (Re)Insurance Companies and Occupational Pension Funds', *Columbia Journal of European Law Online* 18(3): 19–32.

Lutton, D. 2008. 'The European Union, Financial Crises and the Regulation of Hedge Funds: A Policy Cul-de-Sac or Policy Window?', *Journal of Contemporary European Research* 4(3): 167–178.

Lütz, S. 2002. *Der Staat und die Globalisierung von Finanzmärkten*, Frankfurt am Main: Campus.

Lynch, T. 2010. 'Deeply and Persistently Conflicted: Credit Rating Agencies in the Current Regulatory Environment', *Indiana University Maurer School of Law—Bloomington Legal Studies Research Paper* Series 133, <http://papers.ssrn.com/sol3/papers.cfm?abstract_id=1374907> (accessed on 25 February 2013).

MacKenzie, D. 2006. *An Engine, Not a Camera: How Financial Models Shape Markets*, Cambridge, MA: MIT Press.

Maes, I. 2009. 'On the Origins of the BIS Macroprudential Approach to Financial Stability', *National Bank of Belgium Working Paper Research* No. 176 (October).

Managed Funds Association, 2007. *Sound Practices for Hedge Fund Managers*, Washington.

MARC (Maastricht Accounting, Auditing and Information Management Research Centre), 2009. *Evaluation of the Differences Between International Standards on Auditing (ISA) and the Standards of the US Public Company Accounting Oversight Board (PCAOB)*, Maastricht: MARC.

Marcussen, M., 2006. 'The Fifth Age of Central Banking in the Global Economy', Paper presented at the conference '*Frontiers of Regulation*', University of Bath, 7–8 September.

Martens, K., and A. Jakobi, 2010. *The OECD's Global Role: Agenda Setting and Policy Diffusion*, Oxford: Oxford University Press.

Martinez-Diaz, L. 2005. 'Strategic Experts and Improvising Regulators: Explaining the IASC's Rise to Global Influence, 1973–2001', *Business and Politics* 7(3): Article 3.

Mattli, W., and T. Büthe, 2005. 'Accountability in Accounting? The Politics of Private Rule-Making in the Public Interest', *Governance* 18(3): 399–429.

McCahery, J. 1997. 'Market Integration and Particularistic Interests: The Dynamics of Insider Trading Regulation in the US and Europe', in *The New World Order in International Finance*, edited by G.R.D. Underhill, 50–75, Houndsmills: Macmillan.

McIntyre, M.J. 2009. 'How to End the Charade of Information Exchange', *Tax Notes International* 56(4): 255–268.

Meinzer, M. 2012. *Bank Account Registries in Selected Countries: Lessons for Registries of Trusts and Foundations and for Improving Automatic Tax Information Exchange*, London: Tax Justice Network/CCFD-Terre Solidaire, <http://www.taxjustice.net/cms/upload/pdf/BAR2012-TJN-Report.pdf> (accessed on 29 June 2013).

Miles, D., J. Yang, and G. Marcheggiano, 2011. 'Optimal Bank Capital', *External MPC Unity*, Discussion Paper No. 31, January.

Mitsilegas, V., and B. Gilmore, 2007. 'The EU Legislative Framework Against Money Laundering and Terrorist Finance: A Critical Analysis in the Light of Evolving Global Standards', *International and Comparative Law Quarterly* 56(1): 119–140.

Möllers, T.M.J. 2009. 'Regulating Credit Rating Agencies. The New US and EU Law—Important Steps or Much Ado about Nothing?', *Capital Markets Law Journal* 4(4): 477–500.

Möllers, T.M.J. 2010. 'Sources of Law in European Securities Regulation—Effective Regulation, Soft Law and Legal Taxonomy from Lamfalussy to de Larosière', *European Business Organization Law Review* 11: 379–407.

Moloney, N. 2010. 'EU Financial Market Regulation After the Global Financial Crisis: "More Europe" or More Risks?', *Common Market Law Review* 47(5): 1317–1383.

Moloney, N. 2011a. 'The European Securities and Markets Authority and Institutional Design for the EU Financial Market—A Tale of Two Competences: Part (1) Rule-Making', *European Business Organization Law Review* 12(1): 41–86.

Moloney, N. 2011b. 'The European Securities and Markets Authority and Institutional Design for EU Financial Markets—A Tale of Two Competences: Part (2) Rules in Action', *European Business Organization Law Review* 12(2): 177–225.

Moloney, N. 2012. 'The Legacy Effects of the Financial Crisis on Regulatory Design in the EU', in *The Regulatory Aftermath of the Global Financial Crisis*, edited by E. Ferran, N. Moloney, J.G. Hill, and J.C. Coffee, Cambridge: Cambridge University Press.

Moloney, N., 2013. 'Financial Market Governance and the European Supervisory Authorities: Lessons since January 2011–Evolution and Revolution?' (Draft, on file, for Amsterdam Centre for European Law and Governance Conference on 'A New

Role for the EU in Economic Governance. Lessons from Emerging and Existing Models', 9 November 2012).

Monitoring Group, 2009. 'Monitoring Group Announces Adoption of Formal Charter' (Press Release, 19 May), Madrid: Monitoring Group.

Monitoring Group, 2010. *Review of the IFAC Reforms—Final Report*, Madrid: Monitoring Group.

Monitoring Group, 2012. *Public Consultation on the Governance (With Special Focus on the Organizational Aspects, Funding, Composition and the Roles) of the Monitoring Group, the PIOB and the Standard Setting Boards and Compliance Advisory Panel Operating under the Auspices of IFAC*, Madrid: Monitoring Group.

Monitoring Group, 2013. *Monitoring Group Statement on Governance*, Madrid: Monitoring Group.

Moschella, M., and E. Tsingou, 2013. *Great Expectations, Slow Transformations: Incremental Change in Post-Crisis Regulation*, Colchester: ECPR Press.

Mosley, L. 2010. 'Regulating Globally, Implementing Locally: The Financial Standards and Codes Effort', *Review of International Political Economy* 17(4): 724–761.

Mügge, D.K. 2006. 'Private–Public Puzzles: Inter-firm Competition and Transnational Private Regulation'. *New Political Economy* 11(2): 177–200.

Mügge, D.K. 2007. 'The Transatlantic Politics of Global Accounting Standard Harmonization', Paper presented at Garnet-ESRC workshop on National and International Aspects of Financial Development, 25–26 October.

Mügge, D.K. 2010. *Widen the Market, Narrow the Competition: Banker Interests and the Making of a European Capital Market*, Colchester: ECPR.

Mügge, D.K. 2011a. 'From Pragmatism to Dogmatism: European Union Governance, Policy Paradigms and Financial Meltdown', *New Political Economy* 16(2): 185–206.

Mügge, D.K. 2011b. 'Limits of Legitimacy and the Primacy of Politics in Financial Governance', *Review of International Political Economy* 18(1): 52–74.

Mügge, D.K. 2011c. 'The European Presence in Global Financial Governance: A Principal-Agent Perspective', *Journal of European Public Policy* 18(3): 383–402.

Mügge, D.K., and B. Stellinga, 2010. 'Absent Alternatives and Insider Interests in Postcrisis Financial Reform', *Der Moderne Staat: Zeitschrift für Public Policy, Recht und Management* 3(2): 321–338.

Mügge, D.K., and B. Stellinga, 2014. 'The Unstable Core of Global Finance: Contingent Valuation and Governance of International Accounting Standards', *Regulation and Governance*, DOI: 10.1111/rego.12052.

Murray, P., and Moxon-Browne, 2013. 'The European Union as a Template for Regional Integration? The Case of ASEAN and Its Committee of Permanent Representatives', *Journal of Common Market Studies* 51: 522–537.

Nance, M.T., and P. Cottrell, 2014. 'A Turn Toward Experimentalism? Rethinking Security and Governance in the Twenty-First Century', *Review of International Studies* 40(2): 277–301.

Nicolaïdis, K. 2007. 'Trusting the Poles? Constructing Europe Through Mutual Recognition', *Journal of European Public Policy* 14: 682–698.

Nicolaïdis, K., and G. Schaffer, 2005. 'Transnational Mutual Recognition Regimes: Governance Without Global Government', *Law and Contemporary Problems* 68: 263–317.

Nielson, D., and M. Tierney, 2003. 'Delegation to International Organizations: Agency Theory and World Bank Environmental Reform', *International Organization* 57(2): 241–276.

Nobes, C. 1985. 'Harmonisation of Financial Reporting', in *Comparative International Accounting*, edited by C. Nobes and R. Parker, 331–352, New York: St. Martin's Press.

Nobes, C., and R. Parker. 2012. *Comparative International Accounting* (12th edition), Harlow: FT/Prentice Hall.

Nölke, A. 2009. 'The Politics of Accounting Regulation: Responses to the Subprime Crisis', in *Global Finance in Crisis: The Politics of International Regulatory Change*, edited by E. Helleiner, S. Pagliari, and H. Zimmermann, 37–55, London and New York: Routledge.

Nölke, A., and J. Perry, 2007. 'The Power of Transnational Private Governance: Financialization and the IASB', *Business and Politics* 9(3): 1–25.

Norton, J.J. 1995. *Devising International Bank Supervisory Standards*, The Hague: Martinus Nijhoff Publishers.

Oatley, T., and R. Nabors, 1998. 'Redistributive Cooperation: Market Failure, Wealth Transfers, and the Basel Accord'. *International Organization* 51(1): 35–54.

OECD (Organisation for Economic Cooperation and Development), 1998. *Harmful Tax Competition: An Emerging Global Issue*, Paris: OECD.

OECD, 2002. *Agreement on Exchange of Information on Tax Matters*, Paris: OECD.

OECD, 2012. *Automatic Exchange of Information: What it is, How it Works, Benefits, What Remains to be Done*, Paris: OECD.

OECD, 2013a. *Global Forum on Tax Transparency Shifts Focus to Effectiveness of Information Exchange*, <http://www.oecd.org/tax/exchange-of-tax-information/global-forum-on-tax-transparency-shifts-focus-to-effectiveness-of-information-exchange.htm> (accessed on 29 June 2013).

OECD, 2013b. *Addressing Base Erosion and Profit Shifting*, Paris: OECD.

Onagoruwa, G.A. 2012. *Cross-Border Bank Resolution: Legal and Institutional Underpinnings for Africa* (unpublished PhD thesis, on file).

Pagliari, S. 2011. 'Who Governs Finance? The Shifting Public–Private Divide in the Regulation of Derivatives, Rating Agencies, and Hedge Funds', *European Law Journal* 18(1): 44–61.

Palan, R. 2006. *The Offshore World: Sovereign Markets, Virtual Places, and Nomad Millionaires*, Ithaca: Cornell University Press.

Palan, R., R. Murphy, and C. Chavagneux, 2010. *Tax Havens: How Globalization Really Works*, Ithaca: Cornell University Press.

Pan, E.J. 2009. 'Four Challenges to Financial Regulatory Reform', *Villanova Law Review* 55: 743–772.

Partnoy, F. 1999. 'The Siskel and Ebert of Financial Markets. Two Thumbs Down for Credit Rating Agencies', *Washington University Law Quarterly* 77(3): 619–714.

Partnoy, F. 2002a. *Infectious Greed: How Deceit and Risk Corrupted the Financial Markets*, New York: Times Books.

Partnoy, F. 2002b. 'ISDA, NASD, CFMA, and SDNY: The Four Horsemen of Derivatives Regulation?', *Brookings-Wharton Papers on Financial Services*: 5213–5252.

Perez, O. 2011. 'Private Environmental Governance as Ensemble Regulation: A Critical Exploration of Sustainability Indexes and the New Ensemble Politics', *Theoretical Inquiries in Law* 12(7): 543–579.

Perry J., and A. Nölke, 2005. 'International Accounting Standard Setting: A Network Approach', *Business and Politics* 7(3): 1–32.

Perry, J., and A. Nölke, 2006. 'The Political Economy of International Accounting Standards', *Review of International Political Economy* 13(4): 559–586.

Persaud, A. 2000. 'Sending the Herd Off the Cliff Edge: The Disturbing Interaction Between Herding and Market-Sensitive Risk Management Systems', *World Economics* 1(4): 15–26.

Persaud, A. 2009. 'Macroprudential Regulation: Fixing Fundamental Market and Regulatory Failures', Crisis Response (Note number 6), The World Bank Group, Financial and Private Sector Development, July, <http://siteresources.worldbank.org/EXTFINANCIALSECTOR/Resources/282884-1303327122200/Note6.pdf> (accessed on 13 February 2014).

Persaud, A. 2010. 'The Locus of Financial Regulation: Home Versus Host', *International Affairs* 86(3): 637–646.

Pierson, P. 1996. 'The Path to European Integration: A Historical Institutionalist Analysis', *Comparative Political Studies* 29: 123–163.

Pieth, M. 2006. 'Multistakeholder Initiatives to Combat Money Laundering and Bribery', *Basel Institute on Governance, Working Paper* No. 02.

Pieth, M., and G. Aiolfi, 2003. 'The Private Sector Becomes Active: The Wolfsberg Process', *Journal of Financial Crime* 10(4): 359–365.

PIOB (Public Interest Oversight Board), 2012a. *Seventh Public Report of the PIOB*, Madrid: PIOB.

PIOB, 2012b. *PIOB Work Program 2012 and Beyond: Public Consultation Paper*, Madrid: PIOB.

PIOB, 2013. *PIOB Recommendations in Response to its Consultation on the PIOB Work Program 2102 and Beyond*, Madrid: PIOB.

Plumridge, H. 2010. 'EU Hedge Fund Compromise Looks Possible', *Wall Street Journal*, 20 May.

Porter, B., M. Simon, and D. Hatherly, 2008. *Principles of External Auditing* (3rd edition), Hoboken: John Wiley and Sons.

Porter, T. 1993. *States, Markets and Regimes in Global Finance*, New York: St. Martin's Press.

Porter, T. 2005. 'Private Authority, Technical Authority, and the Globalization of Accounting Standards', *Business and Politics* 7(3): 1–30.

Posner, E. 2009. 'Making Rules for Global Finance: Transatlantic Regulatory Co-operation at the Turn of the Millennium', *International Organization* 63(4): 665–699.

Posner, E. 2010a. 'The Lamfalussy Process: Polyarchic Origins of Networked Financial Rulemaking in the EU', in *EU Governance: Towards a New Architecture?* edited by C. Sabel and J. Zeitlin, 43–60, Oxford: Oxford University Press.

Posner, E. 2010b. 'Sequence as Explanation: The International Politics of Accounting Standards', *Review of International Political Economy* 14(4): 639–664.

Posner, E. 2014. 'An Experimentalist Turn in International Financial Regulatory Cooperation?'

Posner, E., and N. Véron, 2010. 'The EU and Financial Regulation: Power Without Purpose?', *Journal of European Public Policy* 17(3): 400–415.

President's Working Group on Financial Markets, 1999. *Hedge Funds, Leverage, and the Lessons of Long-Term Capital Management*, April.

Putnam, R. 1988. 'Diplomacy and Domestic Politics: The Logic of Two-Level Games', *International Organization* 42(3): 427–460.

Quaglia, L. 2008. 'Financial Sector Committee Governance in the European Union', *Journal of European Integration* 30(4): 563–578.

Quaglia, L. 2009. 'The Politics of Regulating Credit Rating Agencies in the European Union', *Centre for Global Political Economy Working Paper* 5.

Quaglia, L. 2010a. *Governing Financial Services in the European Union*, London: Routledge.

Quaglia, L. 2010b. 'Completing the Single Market in Financial Services: The Politics of Competing Advocacy Coalitions', *Journal of European Public Policy* 17(7): 1007–1023.

Quaglia, L. 2011a. 'The European Union in Regulating Global Finance', Paper presented at the *EUSA Conference*, 3–5 March 2011, Boston.

Quaglia, L. 2011b. 'The "Old" and "New" Political Economy of Hedge Funds Regulation in the European Union', *West European Politics* 34(4): 665–682.

Quaglia, L. 2011c. 'The Politics of Insurance Regulation Reform in the European Union', *Comparative European Politics* 9(1): 100–122.

Quaglia, L. 2012a. 'The Regulatory Response of the European Union to the Global Financial Crisis', in *Crisis and Control: Institutional Change in Financial Market Regulation*, edited by R. Maintz, 171–198, Frankfurt: Campus Verlag.

Quaglia, L. 2012b. 'The Old and New Politics of Financial Services Regulation in the European Union', *New Political Economy* 17(4): 515–535.

Quaglia, L. 2013. 'The EU, the US and International Financial Harmonisation in Regulatory Fora', *New Political Economy*.

Radaelli, C.M. 1999. 'Harmful Tax Competition in the EU: Policy Narratives and Advocacy Coalitions', *Journal of Common Market Studies* 37(4): 661–682.

Radaelli, C.M. 2003. 'The Code of Conduct Against Harmful Tax Competition: Open Method of Coordination in Disguise?', *Public Administration* 81(3): 513–531.

Radaelli, C.M., and U.S. Kraemer, 2008. 'Governance Arenas in EU Direct Tax Policy', *Journal of Common Market Studies* 46(2): 315–336.

Rahn, R. 2003. 'Follow the Money: Confusion at Treasury'. Available at: <http://www.cato.org/publications/commentary/follow-money-confusion-treasury> (accessed on 22 December 2013).

Reinicke, W.H. 1995. *Banking, Politics and Global Finance: American Commercial Banks and Regulatory Change, 1980–1990*, Cheltenham: Edward Elgar.

Romey, C., and B. Drut, 2008. *Analysis of Subprime RMBS Ratings in the USA. Risk and Trend Mapping—No. 4*, Paris: Autorité des marches financiers.

Rona-Tas, A., and S. Hiss, 2010. 'Consumer and Corporate Credit Ratings and the Subprime Crisis in the US with Some Lessons for Germany', in *Consumer Loans and the Role of the Credit Bureaus in Europe* (EUI Working Paper RSCAS 2010/44), edited by H.W. Micklitz, 5–28, Badia Fiesolana: European University Institute.

Rosamond, B. 2002. 'Imagining the European Economy: "Competitiveness" and the Social Construction of "Europe" as an Economic Space', *New Political Economy* 7(2): 157–177.

Ross, V. 2012. Keynote Address ICMA Conference—Milan 24 May 2012. ESMA/2012/328.

Sabel, C.F., and J. Zeitlin, 2008. 'Learning from Difference: The New Architecture of Experimentalist Governance in the EU', *European Law Journal* 14: 271–327.

Sabel, C.F., and J. Zeitlin, 2010. *Experimentalist Governance in the European Union: Towards a New Architecture*, Oxford: Oxford University Press.

Sabel, C.F., and J. Zeitlin, 2011. *Experimentalism in Transnational Governance. Emergent Pathways and Diffusion Mechanisms*, Warwick: GR:EEN Working Paper No. 3.

Sabel, C.F., and J. Zeitlin, 2012a. 'Experimentalism in the EU: Common Ground and Persistent Differences', *Regulation and Governance* 6: 410–426.

Sabel, C.F., and J. Zeitlin, 2012b. 'Experimentalist Governance', in *Oxford Handbook of Governance*, edited by Levi-Faur, Oxford: Oxford University Press.

Sanderson, R. 2009. 'Europe's Schism Threatens Global Accounting Rules', *Financial Times*, 16 November.

Sapir, A., M. Hellwig, and M. Pagano, 2012. *A Contribution from the Chair and Vice-Chairs of the Advisory Scientific Committee to the Discussion on the European Commission's Banking Union Proposals*. ESRB, Advisory Scientific Committee, No 2. Frankfurt.

Sarkozy, N. President of the French Republic and Merkel, A. Chancellor of Germany, 2009. *Letter to Mirek Topolanek, Prime Minister of the Czech Republic and Jose Manuel Barroso, President of the European Commission in preparation for the G-20 Summit*, 16 March.

Schammo, P. 2011. *EU Prospectus Law*, Cambridge: Cambridge University Press.

Schammo, P. 2012. 'EU Day-to-Day Supervision or Intervention-Based Supervision: Which Way Forward for the European System of Financial Supervision?', *Oxford Journal of Legal Studies* 32: 771–797.

Schmidt, V.A. 2008. 'Discursive Institutionalism: The Explanatory Power of Ideas and Discourse', *Annual Review of Political Science* 11: 303–326.

Seabrooke, L., and E. Tsingou, forthcoming 2014. 'Distinctions, Affiliations, and Professional Knowledge in Financial Reform Expert Groups', *Journal of European Public Policy*.

SEC (Securities and Exchange Commission), 2003. *Report on the Role and Function of Credit Rating Agencies in the Operation of the Securities Markets: As Required by Section 702(b) of the Sarbanes-Oxley Act of 2002*, Washington DC: SEC, January.

SEC, 2008a. *Summary Report of Issues Identified in the Commission Staff's Examinations of Select Credit Rating Agencies By the Staff of the Securities and Exchange Commission*, Washington DC: SEC.

SEC, 2008b. *Annual Report on Nationally Recognized Statistical Rating Organizations: As Required by Section 6 of the Credit Rating Agency Reform Act of 2006*, Washington DC: SEC, June.

SEC, 2010. *Dodd–Frank Wall Street Reform and Consumer Protection Act*, <http://www.sec.gov/about/laws/wallstreetreform-cpa.pdf> (accessed on 29 June 2013).

SEC, 2012. *Joint Press Statement of Leaders on Operating Principles and Areas of Exploration in the Regulation of the Cross-Border OTC Derivatives Market*. Washington, DC.

Senate Committee on Banking, Housing, and Urban Affairs, 2006. *Report to Accompany S. 3850, Credit Rating Agency Reform Act of 2006*, Report 109–326, 109th Cong., 2d Sess. (6 September).

Sharman, J.C. 2006. *Havens in a Storm—The Struggle for Global Tax Regulation*, Ithaca: Cornell University Press.

Sharman, J.C. 2008. 'Power and Discourse in Policy Diffusion: Anti-Money Laundering in Developing States', *International Studies Quarterly* 52: 635–656.

Sharman, J. 2010. 'Offshore and the New International Political Economy', *Review of International Political Economy* 17(1): 1–19.

Sharman, J.C. 2011. *The Money Laundry: Regulating Criminal Finance in the Global Economy*, Ithaca: Cornell University Press.

Sharman, J.C. 2012. 'Canaries in the Coal Mine: Tax Havens, the Decline of the West and the Rise of the Rest', *New Political Economy* 17(4): 493–513.

Sharman, J.C., M. Findley, and D. Nielson, 2013. *Global Shell Games: Experiments in Transnational Relations*, Cambridge: Cambridge University Press.

Shearman & Sterling, 2012. *OTC Derivatives Regulation and Extraterritoriality*, 5 September, London.

Shiller, R.J. 2008. *The Subprime Solution: How Today's Global Financial Crises Happened, and What to Do about It*, Princeton and Oxford: Princeton University Press.

Sikka, P. 2009. 'Financial Crisis and the Silence of the Auditors', *Accounting, Organizations and Society* 34: 868–873.

Simmons, B. 2001. 'The International Politics of Harmonization: The Case of Capital Market Regulation', *International Organization* 55(3): 589–620.

Simonova, A. 2011. 'The Risk-Based Approach to Anti-Money Laundering: Problems and Solutions', *Journal of Money Laundering Control* 14(4): 346–358.

Sinclair, T.J. 2003. 'Global Monitor: Bond Rating Agencies', *New Political Economy* 8(1): 147–161.

Sinclair, T.J. 2005. *The New Masters of Capital: American Bond Rating Agencies and the Politics of Creditworthiness*, Ithaca: Cornell University Press.

Singer, D. 2007. *Regulating Capital: Setting Standards for the International Financial System*, Ithaca: Cornell University Press.

Spendzharova, A.B. 2010. 'Multi-Level Governance of Banking Regulation in the EU: Evidence from Developing Bank Supervision in Bulgaria and Hungary', *European Integration* 32(3): 249–268.

Steil, B. 1993. *Competition, Integration and Regulation in EC Capital Markets*, London: Royal Institute of International Affairs.

Steil, B. 1999. 'Regional Financial Market Integration: Learning from the European Experience', *Tokyo Club Papers* 12: 99–126.

Stemper, M-M. 2010. *Rechtliche Rahmenbedingungen des Ratings*, Baden-Baden: Nomos.

Stockhammer, E. 2007. *Some Stylized Facts on the Finance-Dominated Accumulation Regime*, Amherst, MA: Political Economy Research Institute WP 142, University of Massachusetts Amherst.

Stone, D. 2012. 'Transfer and Translation of Policy', *Policy Studies* 33(6): 483–499.

Story, J., and I. Walter, 1997. *Political Economy of Financial Integration in Europe: The Battle of the System*, Manchester: Manchester University Press.

Strier, F. 2008. 'Rating the Raters: Conflicts of Interest in the Credit Rating Firms', *Business and Society Review* 113(4): 533–553.

Tabb, W. 2012. *The Restructuring of Capitalism in Our Time*, New York: Columbia University Press.

Tafara, E., and R.J. Peterson, 2007. 'A Blueprint for Cross-Border Access to U.S. Investors: A New International Framework', *Harvard International Law Journal* 48: 31–68.

Tarullo, D.K. 2008. *Banking on Basel: The Future of International Financial Regulation*, Washington: Peterson Institute for International Economics.

Tarullo, D.K. 2012. 'Regulation of Foreign Banking Institutions', Speech at *Yale School of Management Leaders Forum*, New Haven, Connecticut, <http://www.federalreserve.gov/newsevents/speech/tarullo20121128a.htm> (accessed on 22 March 2014).

Telo, M. 2005. *Europe: A Civilian Power? European Union, Global Governance, World Order*, London: Palgrave.

Tsingou, E. 2003. *Transnational Policy Communities and Financial Governance: The Role of Private Actors in Derivatives Regulation*, Warwick: Centre for the Study of Globalisation and Regionalisation.

Tsingou, E. 2008. 'Transnational Private Governance and the Basel Process', in *Transnational Private Governance and its Limits*, edited by J.C. Graz, and A. Nölke, 58–68, London: Routledge.

Tsingou, E. 2010. 'Global Financial Governance and the Developing Anti-Money Laundering Regime: What Lessons for International Political Economy?', *International Politics* 47(6): 617–637.

Tsingou, E. 2012. *Club Model Politics and Global Financial Governance—The Case of the Group of Thirty*, PhD thesis, University of Amsterdam, <http://dare.uva.nl/record/418085> (accessed on 22 March 2014).

Tucker, P. 2011. 'Reforming Finance: Are We Being Radical Enough?', *Clare Distinguished Lecture in Economics*, Cambridge, 18 February.

Turner, A. 2011. 'Reforming Finance: Are We Being Radical Enough?', Clare Distinguished Lecture in Economics and Public Policy, Cambridge, 18 February, <http://www.fsa.gov.uk/pubs/speeches/0218_at_clare_college.pdf> (accessed on 22 March 2014).

Turner, A. 2012. 'Macroprudential Policy in Deflationary Times', Speech, delivered at Financial Policy Committee, Regional Visit, Manchester, 20 July, <http://www.fsa.gov.uk/library/communication/speeches/2012/0720-at.shtml> (accessed on 13 February 2014).

Underhill, G.R.D. 1995. 'Keeping Governments Out of Politics: Transnational Securities Markets, Regulatory Cooperation and Political Legitimacy', *Review of International Studies* 21: 251–278.

Underhill, G.R.D. 1997a. 'The Making of the European Financial Area: Global Market Integration and the EU Single Market for Financial Services', in *The New World Order in International Finance*, edited by G.R.D. Underhill, 101–123, Basingstoke: Macmillan.

Underhill, G.R.D. 1997b. 'Private Markets and Public Responsibility in a Global System: Conflict and Co-Operation in Transnational Banking and Securities Regulation', in *The New World Order in International Finance*, edited by G.R.D. Underhill, 17–49, Basingstoke: St. Martin's Press.

Underhill, G.R.D., and J. Blom, 2012. 'The International Financial Architecture: Plus ça change. . . . ?', in *Crisis and Control: Institutional Change in Financial Market Regulation*, edited by R. Maintz, 279–294, Frankfurt: Campus Verlag.

United Nations Commission of Experts on Reforms of the International Monetary and Financial Systems, 2009. *Recommendations*, New York: United Nations.

US Office on Drugs and Crime, 2011. *Estimating Illicit Financial Flows Stemming Resulting from Drug Trafficking and Other Transnational Organised Crimes*, Research Report, Vienna: UNODC.

United States Congress, 2006. *Credit Rating Agency Reform Act of 2006, 109th Congress*, Washington, DC.

van Hulle, K. 2004. 'From Accounting Directives to International Accounting Standards', in *The Economics and Politics of Accounting: International Perspectives on Research Trends, Policy, and Practice*, edited by C. Leuz, D. Pfaff, and A. Hopwood, 349–375, Oxford: Oxford University Press.

Verdier, P.H. 2011. 'Mutual Recognition in International Finance', *Harvard International Law Journal* 52: 55–108.

Verdun, A. 2012. 'Experimentalist Governance in the European Union: A Commentary', *Regulation and Governance* 6: 410–426.

Verhage, A. 2009. 'Between the Hammer and the Anvil? The Anti-Money Laundering Complex and its Interactions with the Compliance Industry', *Crime, Law and Social Change* 52(1): 9–32.

Véron, N. 2011. 'Keeping the Promise of Global Accounting Standards', *Peterson Institute for International Economics Policy Brief* No. 11-11.

Véron, N., M. Autret, and A. Galichon, 2006. 'Smoke and Mirrors Inc.: Accounting for Capitalism', in *Accounting for Capitalism*, Ithaca: Cornell University Press.

Vogel, D. 2013. *The Politics of Precaution: Regulating Health, Safety and Environmental Risks in Europe and the United States*, Princeton: Princeton University Press.

Wagner, H. 2012. 'Is Harmonization of Legal Rules an Appropriate Target? Lessons from the Global Financial Crisis', *European Journal of Law and Economics* 33(3): 541–564.

Walter, A. 2008. *Governing Finance: East Asia's Adoption of International Standards*, Ithaca: Cornell University Press.

Walter, I., and R. Smith, 2000. *High Finance in the Euro-Zone: Competing in the New European Capital Market*, Harlow: Pearson Education.

Warwick Commission, 2009. *The Warwick Commission on International Financial Reform: In Praise of Unlevel Playing Fields*, December, Coventry: University of Warwick.

Waters, R. 1993. 'IOSCO Drops Common Capital Rules Plan', *Financial Times*, 11 February.

Waters, R., and L. Kellaway, 1990. 'Europe's Investors Seek a Cad with Sense of Fair Play', *Financial Times*, 9 February.

Wei, T.B. 2007. 'The Equivalence Approach to Securities Regulation', *Northwestern Journal of International Law and Business* 27: 255–299.

White, L.J. 2009. 'The Credit Rating Agencies: Understanding Their Central Role in the Subprime Debacle of 2007–2008', *SSRN Working Paper*, <http://ssrn.com/abstract=1434483> (accessed on 25 February 2013).

White, L.J. 2010. 'Markets. The Credit Rating Agencies', *Journal of Economic Perspectives* 24(2): 211–226.

White, W. 2006. 'Procyclicality in the Financial System: Do We Need a New Macrofinancial Stabilisation Framework?', *BIS Working Paper* 193 (January).

Willey, S., and C. Reynolds. 2011. *The Review of The Market in Financial Instruments Directive: The European Commission Publishes Legislative Proposals*, London: White & Case LLP.

Woll, C. 2012. 'The Defense of Economic Interests in the European Union: A Strategic Analysis of Hedge Fund Regulation', in *Crisis and Control: Institutional Change in Financial Market Regulation*, edited by R. Mayntz, 195–209, Frankfurt am Main: Campus.

Woll, C. forthcoming 2014. 'Financial Reform Between Business Influence and Geopolitics: A Strategic Analysis of Hedge Fund Regulation in Europe', *Journal of Common Market Studies* 51 (2).

Wood, D. 2005. *Governing Global Banking. The Basel Committee and the Politics of Financial Globalisation*, Aldershot: Ashgate.

Young, K. 2012. 'Transnational Regulatory Capture? An Empirical Examination of the Transnational Lobbying of the Basel Committee on Banking Supervision', *Review of International Political Economy* 19(4): 663–688.

Young, K., and S.H. Park, 2013. 'Regulatory Opportunism? Cross National Responses in National Banking Regulatory Responses After the Global Financial Crisis', *Public Administration* 91(3): 561–581.

Youngs, R. 2010. *Europe's Decline and Fall: The Struggle against Global Irrelevance*, London: Profile Books.

Zeff, S.A. 2012. 'The Evolution of the IASC into the IASB, and the Challenges it Faces', *Accounting Review* 87(3): 807–837.

Zimmermann, H. 2010. 'Varieties of Global Financial Governance? British and German Approaches to Financial Market Regulation', in *Global Finance in Crisis*, edited by E. Helleiner, S. Pagliari, and H. Zimmermann, Abingdon: Routledge.

Index